"In *The Catholic Epistles, Hebrews, and Revelation*, Daniel J. Scholz masterfully integrates the later New Testament writings into the broader theological, ecclesial, literary, and social contexts in which they were composed. Solidly rooted in the best modern scholarship, his approach is both profoundly Catholic and thoroughly historical, revealing to students the connections between the biblical writings and the postbiblical Christian tradition to which they gave rise. As an accessible and reliable text for undergraduates beginning their Scripture studies, the book stands apart from a crowded field. Both students and teachers are indebted to Dr. Scholz for his clear and concise presentation of the scholarly debates and theological issues that make these writings especially important. Highly recommended!"

—Lance Richey
University of Saint Francis

"In *The Catholic Epistles*, Daniel J. Scholz offers careful scholarship in a readable style and accessible format. In each chapter, he pairs books of the New Testament with early extracanonical literature (e.g., James with the *Didache*). This approach encourages readers to compare the books in question and to consider the breadth of early Christian literature. It is a pleasure to recommend this volume."

—Jeannine K. Brown
Bethel Seminary, San Diego

AUTHOR ACKNOWLEDGMENTS

I offer my sincere thanks and appreciation to Dr. James A. Kelhoffer of Uppsala University and to Kathleen Walsh and Maura Hagarty of Anselm Academic, who have become an invaluable editorial team.

Publisher Acknowledgments

The publisher owes a special debt of gratitude to James A. Kelhoffer, PhD, who advised throughout this project. Dr. Kelhoffer's expertise and passion both as teacher and scholar contributed immeasurably to this work. Dr. Kelhoffer holds a PhD in New Testament and Early Christian Literature from the University of Chicago and is professor of Old and New Testament Exegesis at Uppsala University in Sweden.

The publisher also wishes to thank the following individual who reviewed this work in progress:

Jeffrey S. Siker
Loyola Marymount University, Los Angeles, California

The Catholic Epistles, Hebrews, and Revelation

Introducing the New Testament

Daniel J. Scholz

James A. Kelhoffer, Academic Editor

Created by the publishing team of Anselm Academic.

The scriptural quotations in this book are from the *New American Bible, revised edition* © 2010, 1991, 1986, and 1970 by the Confraternity of Christian Doctrine, Inc., Washington, DC. Used by permission of the copyright owner. All rights reserved. No part of this work may be reproduced in any form without permission in writing from the copyright owner.

Cover image: © The British Library

Copyright © 2016 by Daniel J. Scholz. All rights reserved. No part of this book may be reproduced by any means without the written permission of the publisher, Anselm Academic, Christian Brothers Publications, 702 Terrace Heights, Winona, Minnesota 55987-1320, *www.anselmacademic.org*.

Printed in the United States of America

7076

ISBN 978-1-59982-709-4

Dedication

This book is dedicated to my parents, Ed and Betty Scholz, who planted in me a love and passion for the study of Scripture.

CONTENTS

Introduction: Studying the Later New Testament Writings   9

1. **James and Early Christian Wisdom Literature**   17

    Introduction / 17
    Part 1: The Letter of James / 19
    Part 2: The *Didache* / 38

2. **First Peter and Early Christian Writings on Relations to Outsiders**   55

    Introduction / 55
    Part 1: The First Letter of Peter / 57
    Part 2: The Seven Letters of Ignatius, the *Martyrdom of Polycarp*, the *Apology of Quadratus*, and the *Epistle to Diognetus* / 76

3. **Second Peter, Jude, 1, 2, and 3 John, and Early Christian Letters**   93

    Introduction / 93
    Part 1: The Letter of Jude and the Second Letter of Peter / 95
    Part 2: The First, Second, and Third Letters of John / 109
    Part 3: *First Clement* and Polycarp's *Epistle to the Philippians* / 123

4. **Hebrews and Early Christian Exhortations** 135
   Introduction / 135
   Part 1: Hebrews / 137
   Part 2: The *Epistle of Barnabas* and *2 Clement* / 153

5. **Revelation and Early Christian Apocalypses** 171
   Introduction / 171
   Part 1: The Revelation of John / 174
   Part 2: The *Shepherd of Hermas* and the *Apocalypse of Peter* / 195

Index 215

INTRODUCTION

Studying the Later New Testament Writings

In addition to the four Gospels, the Acts of the Apostles, and the thirteen letters attributed to Paul, the New Testament includes nine other writings: Hebrews, James, 1–2 Peter, 1–3 John, Jude, and the Revelation of John. This book primarily focuses on these nine texts, which are usually referred to as the later New Testament writings. The term "later" does not allude to their date of composition, as these books were composed within the same general time period as the four Gospels and the deutero-Pauline letters, roughly 70–140 CE. Rather, it refers to their placement within the list of the twenty-seven books in the New Testament; these are the last nine books in the New Testament canon.[1]

Seven of these writings—James, 1–2 Peter, 1–3 John, and Jude—are commonly grouped together under the label "Catholic" or "General" Epistles. Eusebius of Caesarea (a church historian and bishop of Caesarea who died around 340) was apparently the first to use the term "Catholic Letters" to designate this group of writings. Eusebius refers to both James and Jude as Catholic Epistles but, interestingly, denies the epistles of James and Jude a place in the New Testament

---

1. Not all of the earliest manuscripts of the New Testament contain the exact same writings or the same order of writings. Some early manuscripts, for example, list the *Didache* among the New Testament writings. The list of the last nine books found in the canonical New Testament is found in manuscripts such as the fourth-century codex known as Codex Sinaiticus. For a good resource on this topic, see Bruce M. Metzger, *The Canon of the New Testament: Its Origin, Development, and Significance* (Oxford: Clarendon, 1987).

canon because few ancient authorities had quoted those two writings, despite their use in most churches:

> Such is the story about James, whose is said to be the first of the Epistles called Catholic. It is to be observed that its authenticity is denied, since few of the ancients quote it, as is also the case with the epistle called Jude's, which is itself one of the seven called Catholic; nevertheless we know that these letters have been used publicly with the rest in most churches.[2]

Although the debate about James and Jude continued into the fourth century, these writings, too, were eventually included in the New Testament canon.

Nowadays, when scholars refer to these writings, the terms *letter* and *epistle* may be used interchangeably. Previously New Testament scholarship argued for a distinction between a specific "letter" (for example, Paul's letters addressed to particular congregations) and a catholic, or more general, "epistle" that addressed the church as a whole. Today scholars recognize that these seven writings, just like those attributed to Paul, are occasional documents written to address a specific audience or situation.

As early as the third century, these seven New Testament writings were grouped together as a collection.[3] This was not the case with the book of Hebrews or the Revelation of John. The book of Hebrews circulated in the early church with the thirteen letters of Paul, even though Paul himself did not write it. The Revelation of John was thought to have been written by the same author that produced the Gospel and letters of John, especially given the writer's self-identification as "John" (Rev 1:1, 4, 9, 22:8). In addition, some second- and third-century Church Fathers seemed to support that claim.

---

2. Eusebius, *Church History* 2.23.24–25.

3. Darian Lockett, *An Introduction to the Catholic Epistles* (New York: T&T Clark, 2012), 3, identifies early-third century priest and author Origen of Alexandria as the first to cite these seven letters as the "Catholic Epistles."

Apostolic and Familial Claim of Authorship

Over time each of these nine later New Testament writings became identified with figures from the period of the original apostles. Association with the apostles or, in some cases, Jesus' relatives contributed to the authority of these writings and confirmed their status in the eyes of their intended recipients.

Apostle/Relative	New Testament Text
Peter	First and Second Peter
John	First, Second, and Third John and the Revelation of John
James	Letter of James
Jude	Letter of Jude
Paul	Book of Hebrews

Some of these writings appear to be pseudonymous. Derived from the Greek *pseudos*, "false," and *onoma*, "name," the term *pseudonymity* refers to the act of writing in another person's name. Many scholars are convinced, for example, that 1 and 2 Peter are from different authors who wrote in the late-first or early-second centuries. The Apostle Peter is thought to have been martyred in the mid-sixties, which would mean he could not have written either of them. Other writings, such as Hebrews and 1 John, are anonymous, making no claim of authorship, although tradition has associated Hebrews with the Apostle Paul because of its attachment in Greek manuscripts to the Pauline collection of letters. In the case of the letters of James and Jude, the Gospels of Mark and Matthew (Matt 13:55; Mark 6:3) identify a "James" and a "Judas" (Jude) as "brothers" (Greek: *adelphoi*) of Jesus.

In volumes 1 and 2 of this series, *Introducing the New Testament*, extracanonical gospels and extracanonical apocryphal writings associated with Paul were included as a final chapter in *Jesus in the Gospels and Acts* and *The Pauline Letters*. For this third volume, a somewhat different approach is employed. While *The Later New Testament Writings* focuses on the last nine books of the canon, it also presents eleven writings from the "Apostolic Fathers." These extracanonical writings include *1 Clement*, *2 Clement*, the *Didache*, the seven letters of Ignatius, Polycarp's *Letter to the Philippians*, the *Shepherd of Hermas*, the *Apocalypse of Peter*, Quadratus's *Apology*, the *Epistle of Barnabas*, *Martyrdom of Polycarp*, and the *Epistle to Diognetus*. Rather than devoting a final chapter to these extracanonical writings, introductions to these extracanonical writings are integrated into each chapter with the canonical writings since early Christian works of the first, second, and third centuries were not distinguishable as canonical and extracanonical writings. The original addressees, for example, of the Letter of James and the *Didache*, would have likely heard both writings as early Christian wisdom literature. Thus, for example, while chapter 1 covers mainly the Letter of James, it also includes the *Didache*.[4]

These eleven writings are discussed alongside the nine New Testament texts for four additional reasons. First, these twenty canonical and extracanonical texts stem from roughly the same time period: the late-first century to mid-second century. While these nine New Testament writings date to as early as 90 (1 Peter) and as late as 140 (2 Peter), the writings of the Apostolic Fathers begin with *1 Clement* (about 95) and extend to about 155 with the *Epistle to Diognetus*. Second, believers in this period read some of these extracanonical texts alongside the canonical writings, considering them as instructive in the faith and as authoritative as the latter. The fourth-century text the *Apostolic Canons*, for example, even lists *1–2 Clement* as part of an early New Testament canon. In fact, some of the earliest New Testament manuscripts, for example Codex Alexandrinus, included *1–2 Clement*, while Codex Sinaiticus apparently even counted *Barnabas* and the *Shepherd of Hermas* among the New Testament writings. Third, like the later New Testament writings, these texts—and the genres in which they were written (wisdom, apologies, letters, exhortations, and apocalypses)—reflect the struggles and development

---

4. It should be noted that the title of "Apostolic Fathers" is a modern construct (originating from the sixteenth century) and that the exact content of the writings of the Apostolic Fathers varies somewhat in different scholarly editions. Moreover, the *Apocalypse of Peter*, which is discussed in chapter 5, is not included among the Apostolic Fathers.

of the emerging Christian community. And fourth, it is pedagogically helpful to introduce similar types of early Christian literature together. Inclusion of these canonical and extracanonical texts in each chapter offers a more holistic view of this complex period of early Christianity. It is important to remember that the New Testament as known today did not exist in the beginning stages of Christianity. One of the main goals of this third volume is to introduce the readers to the later New Testament writings, and in doing so, employ a methodology common among biblical scholars—studying extracanonical texts alongside canonical ones.

> **From the Apostolic Age to the Apostolic Fathers**
>
> The period in which the original twelve apostles lived is traditionally known as the "apostolic age." It covers approximately seventy years, from the death of Christ (around 30) to the presumed date for the death of the last apostle, John. Certain writings from the next generation of Christian leaders, who lived from the late-first to the mid-second century, are called the "Apostolic Fathers." This term refers not only to early church bishops, such as Papias of Hierapolis, Ignatius of Antioch, and Polycarp of Smyrna, but also to the unknown authors of significant writings from this time period, such as the *Didache*, the *Shepherd of Hermas*, the *Apocalypse of Peter*, *Barnabas*, *1–2 Clement*, and the *Epistle to Diognetus*.

Most of the writings studied in this book are commonly referred to as letters. Letters were the most common form of communication in the ancient world and certainly within the New Testament itself. Indeed, twenty-one of the twenty-seven New Testament writings are letters. However, the letter framework often served as the vehicle to accomplish other purposes, such as defense of the faith (apology) or education and formation in the faith (exhortation). For that reason, the five chapters in this volume are arranged according to ancient literary forms: wisdom literature, apologies, letters, exhortations, and apocalypses. While most of these writings present themselves as letters in the broadest sense of the word (with such standard elements as sender, receiver, greeting, body, and farewell), the style and content very often point to a more dominant genre or genres. For example, while the Epistle of James clearly takes the form of a letter, much of the content contains marked similarities to earlier Jewish "wisdom literature."

Each chapter in the book contains two parts. The first part addresses the canonical texts (those writings that came to be included in the New Testament). The second part treats a number of similar extracanonical writings (those works belonging to the category of the Apostolic Fathers). For each chapter, twice as much space is given to the New Testament writings. Outlines of the canonical and extracanonical books are provided along with an overview of the historical settings (author, audience, date, and place of composition) and the occasion of the texts. Major themes, including the theology and ethics of these canonical and extracanonical writings, are also discussed.

The Subject Matter and Organization of This Book

The Catholic Epistles, Hebrews, and Revelation contains five chapters arranged according to the predominant theme and structure of these writings. Listed below is a general definition of each genre and the New Testament writings and the writings of the Apostolic Fathers assigned to each chapter:

	Theme or Genre	New Testament Books	Noncanonical Books
Chapter 1	Wisdom: Literature characterized by instructions, admonitions, and moral sayings that emphasize the right way of living.	Letter of James	The *Didache*

Continued

The Subject Matter *Continued*

	Theme or Genre	New Testament Books	Noncanonical Books
Chapter 2	Apologies: Rooted in the Greek word *apologia*, meaning "speaking in defense," works of this type are not apologetic in the modern sense, but typically defend an idea or tradition to outsiders.	The First Letter of Peter	The seven letters of Ignatius The *Martyrdom of Polycarp* The *Apology of Quadratus* The *Epistle to Diognetus*
Chapter 3	Letters: Private or public written communication characterized by an opening, a body, and a farewell.	The First Letter of John The Second Letter of John The Third Letter of John The Second Letter of Peter The Letter of Jude	*First Clement* Polycarp's *Epistle to the Philippians*
Chapter 4	Exhortations: Written or oral communication intended to persuade, educate, and form its recipients.	The Book of Hebrews	The *Epistle of Barnabas* *Second Clement*

Continued

The Subject Matter *Continued*

	Theme or Genre	New Testament Books	Noncanonical Books
Chapter 5	Apocalypses: Derived from the Greek word *apocalypsis*, meaning "revelation," these works often focus on end time (end of the world) scenarios.	The Revelation of John	The *Shepherd of Hermas* The *Apocalypse of Peter*

Studying the last nine books of the New Testament alongside the writings of the Apostolic Fathers highlights a historical and comparative approach to texts that shaped Christianity in the late-first century through the mid-second century.

CHAPTER 1

James and Early Christian Wisdom Literature

INTRODUCTION

The Letter of James and the *Didache* fit within the broad category of wisdom literature because they contain instructional material that strongly parallels the wisdom traditions found in the Old Testament.[1] While James barely takes the form of a letter and the *Didache* functions more as an instructional guide, they both focus on proper ethical conduct (paraenesis) as the source of true wisdom. Given their content, the Letter of James and the *Didache* serve as some of the earliest examples of Christian wisdom literature. Studying the Letter of James with the *Didache* allows modern readers to see more broadly how the early Christians used the genre of wisdom to educate and form their respective communities.

Part 1 of this chapter provides an overview of the historical context of James (author, audience, date, and place of composition) and addresses such topics as the relationship between this letter and the letters of Paul and the reception of the Letter of James in church history. It highlights major theological and ethical themes, including faith and good works, the importance of upright moral and ethical conduct, and the power of prayer. Part 2 examines the *Didache*, the first of the texts from the Apostolic Fathers. The discussion of the *Didache* begins with a look at the historical context of this work and

---

1. The exact parameters of wisdom literature are difficult to define since its form and content varies greatly. See John Kampen, *Wisdom Literature* (Grand Rapids: Eerdmans, 2011), 12–15, who offers a good introduction to the literary form and genre of wisdom. Kampen defines wisdom literature as "instructional material that can be identified with the biblical tradition of wisdom," 14.

examines its literary integrity, in particular, whether this text was ever given authoritative status as a part of Scripture. Part 2 also explores the *Didache*'s theology (Christology and eschatology) and ethics (the "two ways"; instructions on baptism, fasting, prayer, and the Eucharist; and directives on how to treat, select, and discern leadership). Part 2 examines the historical setting of the *Didache* and summarizes its content in terms of its theology and ethics.

James as a Thoroughly Jewish Text

The Letter of James is thoroughly Jewish in its tone and content with very little reflecting the Christian environment evident in the other writings of the New Testament.[2] It consistently speaks to the importance of proper ethical conduct within the community of believers. Its concerns about the rich taking care of the poor, performing good works as outward evidence of faith in God, controlling one's tongue, seeking wisdom though humility, avoiding worldly desires, and praying for sinners bear striking resemblance to some of Israel's most cherished wisdom traditions found in Old Testament texts such as Proverbs, Sirach, and Tobit. Unlike most of the other New Testament texts, for example the Letters of Paul and the Gospels, which are fundamentally Christocentric, James has a predominantly theocentric and ethical focus. In fact, Jesus' name appears only twice in James (1:1, 2:1: "Lord Jesus Christ") and common Christian themes, such as Jesus' cross and Resurrection from the dead and the inclusion of the Gentiles, are altogether absent.

The Earliest Instructions for Baptism

The *Didache* serves as the earliest existing version of instruction for Christians preparing to be baptized. It is a composite text, offering instructions for Christian ethical conduct, rituals, and church order. It begins with the "two paths" (*Did.* 1–6)—the way of life and the

---

2. Many modern commentators have noted the Jewish character of the Letter of James. See, for example, Patrick J. Hartin, *James*, SP 14 (Collegeville, MN: Liturgical Press, 2003), 1; Helmut Koester, *History and Literature of Early Christianity*, 2nd ed. (New York and Berlin: Walter de Gruyter, 1982, 2000), 162; Darian Lockett, *An Introduction to the Catholic Epistles* (New York: T&T Clark, 2012), 9.

The *Didache* (7.1–3) calls for baptism to be performed in "living" (i.e., running) water, as in this early Christian painting from the catacombs of San Callisto (after 150), but accepted as valid the pouring of water over the head.

way of death—wisdom instruction to be taught to persons preparing for baptism. Next it provides directives for ceremonial practices associated with baptism, fasting, prayer, and the Eucharist (*Did.* 7–10). It concludes with advice for welcoming teachers and prophets (including ways to discern the false ones) and directions on how to appoint bishops and deacons (*Did.* 11–15) as well as a brief exhortation to remain faithful until the end times (*Did.* 16).

PART 1: THE LETTER OF JAMES
Historical Context

Attempts to establish the historical setting for the books of the New Testament—that is, to determine the authorship, date, place of composition, and intended audience—are based on internal and external evidence. Internal evidence comes from an analysis of the text itself, while external evidence is found in source material outside the original text. The Letter of James provides very little internal evidence.

As a result, scholars must rely more heavily on external evidence—for example, from other New Testament books and the writings of early Church Fathers—when attempting to determine the letter's historical setting. At times, scholars can only point out probabilities or possibilities in regard to when and where James was written, and to whom.

Outline of the Letter of James

1:1–1	**Greeting** The letter opens with a greeting from someone named James, the sender of the letter, to "the twelve tribes in the dispersion," the intended recipients.
1:2–4	**On Being "Perfect and Complete"** In his opening remarks, James challenges his readers to allow their faith to be tested, which will help them be "perfect and complete, lacking in nothing."
1:5–27	**Overview of Epistolary Themes** James then introduces the major themes of his letter: wisdom overcoming the doubt of "two minds" (vv. 5–8); wealth and poverty (vv. 9–11); temptations strengthening faith (vv. 12–18); faith in action (vv. 19–25); controlling the tongue (v. 26); and separating from the world (v. 27).
2:1–13	**Avoiding Partiality toward the Rich** The text warns against showing preferential treatment toward those with wealth or status over those who are poor. James appeals to the "royal law" (another term for the Mosaic Law), which states, "You shall love your neighbor as yourself." James concludes with an emphasis on showing "mercy" over judgment.

Continued

Outline of the Letter of James *Continued*

2:14–26 — **The Uselessness of Faith without Deeds**
From Genesis and Joshua, James cites two Old Testament examples—one man and one woman—whose faith was "completed" by their good deeds: Abraham, by his willingness to sacrifice Isaac, and Rahab, by rescuing two Hebrew spies. James is insistent: "Faith of itself, if it does not have works, is dead."

3:1–12 — **Master the Tongue**
James cautions his readers about the dangers of the tongue, warning, "No human being can tame the tongue," and, "From the same mouth come blessings and cursing." If one can control the tongue, one becomes "perfect."

3:13–4:12 — **Humility as Key to Wisdom from Above**
James implores his readers to be humble, merciful, and sincere, in order to obtain true wisdom from God. He contrasts such behavior with jealousy and ambition, which have their roots in worldly desires and demonic intent: "A lover of the world makes himself an enemy of God." Humility is shown by neither judging nor speaking evil of others.

4:13–17 — **Dangers of Presumption**
James advocates seeking to do God's will and not making plans based solely on one's own desires.

5:1–6 — **Warning to the Rich**
Once again, the letter warns that love of money will be the ruin of the rich who cling to earthly possessions and exploit the poor.

Continued

Outline of the Letter of James *Continued*	
5:7–12	**The Coming of the Lord** James advises his readers to wait patiently and avoid swearing any oaths in anticipation of the second coming of Christ.
5:13–20	**Final Instructions: Pray** The letter concludes with a set of directives: pray for and anoint the sick, confess your sins, pray for one another, and convert the sinner.

Author and Audience

Outside of the letter's initial greeting, where the author identifies himself as "James, a slave of God and of the Lord Jesus Christ," the text gives no information about the author's identity. Most scholars today believe that the "James" identified as the author in 1:1 is intended to refer to James of Jerusalem, the "brother of the Lord," but that the actual author is an unknown Hellenized Christian Jew.

The New Testament mentions five people named "James," although only two are considered possible authors of this letter: James, the apostle and son of Zebedee, and James, the "brother of the Lord" and the "pillar" of the church in Jerusalem.[3] According to the Acts of the Apostles, the Apostle James was martyred ("killed by the sword," Acts 12:2) by Herod Agrippa I, who ruled over Judea in the years 41–44. Most scholars date the Letter of James to sometime later than the 40s, which rules him out as a possible author. This leaves James, the

---

3. The five people in the NT named "James" are James, the son of Zebedee (one of the apostles and brother to the Apostle John: Matt 4:21; Mark 1:19; Luke 5:10; Acts 12:2); James, the son of Alphaeus, also an apostle (Mark 3:18; Luke 6:15); James the younger (Mark 15:40); James, the father of the Apostle Judas (not Judas Iscariot: Luke 6:16; Acts 1:13); and James, the "brother of Jesus" and the so-called "pillar" of the church in Jerusalem (Mark 6:3; Acts 12:17, 15:13, 21:18; 1 Cor 15:7; Gal 1:19, 2:9, 12; Jude 1).

"brother of the Lord,"[4] as the most viable candidate. James was one of the main church leaders in Jerusalem (Acts 12:17, 15:13, 21:18), and therefore the "James" most likely referred to at the opening of this letter. It cannot be answered with certainty whether the historical James of Jerusalem actually wrote this letter or if someone else wrote it in his name. Although anonymous works written in the name of notable historical figures (pseudepigrapha) were very common in antiquity, including in Jewish literature,[5] some scholars argue that James himself wrote this letter.[6] If so, the letter would have been written quite early—perhaps in the late 50s or early 60s. The first-century Jewish historian Josephus notes that James, "the brother of Jesus," was stoned to death by the high priest, Ananias the Younger, around 62.[7] Those who favor the authorship of the historical James of Jerusalem point out that the letter makes no reference to the destruction of the Jerusalem Temple in 70, that it includes variations to some of Jesus' sayings (for example, Jas 2:5, 4:10) that appear to predate the written Gospels' words of Jesus, and that the debate about faith and works (Jas 2:14–26), with its strong emphasis on the Law, reflects the likely view of a strict Jewish Christian like James.

Other scholars propose that the Letter of James was redacted, or edited, in a two-stage process. They argue that the letter was composed and sent in the name of James shortly after his death based on traditions or sermons associated with James of Jerusalem (stage 1) and then adapted to new circumstances for the next generation of believers (stage 2).[8]

---

4. In support of James of Jerusalem as author, see Udo Schnelle, *The History and Theology of the New Testament Writings*, trans. M. Eugene Boring (London: SCM, 1998), 384–85; Hartin, 16; Koester, 161; Lockett, 10–11.

5. For example, wisdom writings of the Old Testament (Proverbs, the book of Ecclesiastes) attribute sections of these books to King Solomon. Greek texts composed centuries after the Old Testament were attributed to great figures of Israel's past (for instance, Adam and Eve in *The Life of Adam and Eve* and Moses in the *Assumption of Moses*). See *The Old Testament Pseudepigrapha*, ed. James H. Charlesworth, 2 vols. (New York: Doubleday, 1983, 1985) for a comprehensive resource for the pseudepigraphic writings of the Old Testament.

6. See, for example, Luke Timothy Johnson, *The Letter of James: A New Translation with Introduction and Commentary*, AB 37A (New York: Doubleday, 1995), 92–107; Richard J. Bauckham, *James: Wisdom of James, Disciple of Jesus the Sage* (New York: Routledge, 1999), 25.

7. *Antiquities* 20.199–203.

8. Hartin, 24–25, 27.

Most scholars, however, view the Letter of James as a pseudepigraphic writing, similar to other New Testament texts written in the name of a variety of figures from the apostolic period, such as Paul (1 Timothy, 2 Timothy, and Titus), Peter (1 Peter and 2 Peter), and Jude (the Letter of Jude).[9] Numerous factors support this position. First, internal clues, such as the description in the address ("the twelve tribes in the dispersion"), suggest a Hellenistic Jewish Christianity (that is, outside of Palestine) rather than a Palestinian Jewish Christianity, where James the Lord's brother was active as a leader. Second, the author's references to himself as "slave of God and of the Lord Jesus Christ" (1:1) and as a "teacher" (3:1) indicate a position of less authority than the more weighty title of "the brother" of the Lord

---

"James the Just"

Within the New Testament, the James who is identified as Jesus' *adelphos* (Greek for "brother": Matt 13:55; Mark 6:3) receives considerable attention. In Acts, he is presented as a main leader of the church in Jerusalem (12:17, 15:13–21, 21:17–26), and in the Letters of Paul he is called "the brother of the Lord" (Gal 1:19) and a "pillar" in the Jerusalem church (Gal 2:9), and is listed among those to whom the resurrected Jesus appeared (1 Cor 15:7, in a private encounter between Jesus and James).

Despite these many mentions of James, nowhere in the New Testament is he called "James the Just." That designation is first found more than a century after James died. In writing about James's death, the fourth-century church historian Eusebius of Caesarea reports a tradition associated with James that he received from Hegesippus, a church historian from the late second century. Eusebius quotes Hegesippus, who speaks of James's "unsurpassable righteousness" and how that led to the honorary title of "the Just" (*Church History* 2.23). According to Hegesippus, James prayed so often and so hard for his people that his knees developed calluses like a camel's.

---

9. Schnelle, 388; Koester, 162. In fact, most scholars consider nearly half of the New Testament writings (12 of 27) to be pseudepigraphic.

and may, in fact, better reflect the real author's actual role within his community as a leader but not as a "pillar." Finally, second-century Church Fathers themselves questioned the authenticity of the Letter of James, expressing doubt that James, the Lord's brother, wrote it.[10]

The opening address of this letter—"to the twelve tribes of Israel"—provides only minimal clues about the depicted audience. This reference would imply that the addressees were Christian Jews living outside of the Jewish homeland of Palestine but not a specific individual community (such as, for example, the community that Paul addressed in Philippi). It seems likely that the letter was written with a larger network of churches in mind and that individual churches would then circulate the letter after having read it. The letter reveals tensions faced by these various communities: frequent trials, temptations, and tests of faith (1:2–18); preferential treatment for the rich (2:1–13); jealousy and quarreling among community members (3:1–12); believers drawn to worldly desires and possessions (4:1–12); and landowners exploiting their workers (5:1–6).

Furthermore, references to Old Testament characters (for instance, Abraham, Isaac, and Rahab, 2:20–25), quotes from the Old Testament (for example, Lev 19:18 in Jas 2:8–9 and Prov 3:34 in Jas 4:6), and the use of Old Testament metaphors ("the perfect law of freedom," 1:25; "the royal law," 2:8) pervade this letter, implying that the readers and hearers were thoroughly familiar with the Old Testament. This new application of Israel's traditions has led most scholars to conclude that the Letter of James was most likely intended to be circulated to a number of Greek-speaking Jewish Christian communities.[11]

Date and Place of Composition

This chapter assumes the Letter of James was composed by an unknown Jewish Christian author at or near the end of the first century. Assigning a date for the writing of the Letter of James directly depends on its authorship. If James of Jerusalem was the

---

10. See for example, Eusebius, *Church History* 2.23–25. For a good translation and introduction of this ancient text, see Paul L. Maier, *Eusebius: The Church History* (Grand Rapids: Kregel, 2007).

11. Lockett, 14; Hartin, 27; Bauckham, 14; Schnelle, 389; Koester, 162.

author, then composition had to predate his martyrdom around 62. If the letter was composed shortly after James's death, and was based in part on source material from James himself, a date of mid to late 60s (prior to the destruction of the Temple in 70) is plausible. However, the majority of scholars consider the Letter of James pseudepigraphic and commonly date the letter to around 80–110. The ongoing interpretation of the relationship between faith and works that began with Paul (for example, compare Jas 2:14–26 with Rom 4:5–16), the conflict between rich and poor versus Jew and Gentile, and the letter's exhortation to "be patient" (Jas 5:7) while awaiting the return of Christ suggest a date closer to the end of the first century.

Jesus' "Brother" James

The earliest reference to James in the New Testament comes from the author of the earliest surviving Christian literature, the Apostle Paul. In his Letter to the Galatians (mid-fifties), Paul uses the phrase, "James the brother of the Lord" (1:19). Two Gospel writers (Mark and Matthew) as well as the Jewish historian Josephus, all writing a few decades after Paul, likewise speak of someone named James who was known as "the brother of Jesus." These writers likely believed that Jesus had a "brother" named James. The question of Jesus' family did not present a theological point of interest until the second and third centuries.

The place of composition remains uncertain. The letter provides only a few clues. Frequent references to water or the sea (1:6: "a wave of the sea that is driven and tossed about by the wind"; 3:7: "sea creature"; 3:12: "Neither can salt water yield fresh"), ships (3:4: "It is the same with ships . . . steered by a very small rudder"), and business trades (4:13: "spend a year there doing business, and make a profit") suggest a familiarity with communities close to harbor cities, which makes a city such as Alexandria a strong possibility. Jerusalem could also be considered a possible place of composition given the fact that the anonymous writer associates himself with James of Jerusalem.

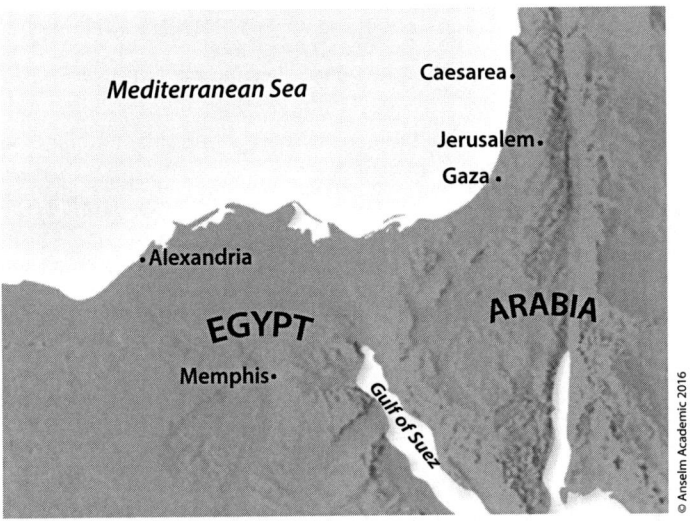

This map shows the locations of both Jerusalem and Alexandria. Internal references in James pointing to a community close to a harbor city (sea, ships, and business trades) favor Alexandria as the letter's place of composition.

However, Jerusalem as the place of composition would not fit the real author's identity as a Hellenistic Jewish Christian argued above. At present, scholars have not reached consensus on where the Letter of James was written.

Summary of Historical Setting for James

Author	unknown Hellenistic Jewish Christian
Audience	Christian Jews in the "dispersion" (Jewish believers scattered outside Palestine)
Date of Composition	unknown; probably toward the end of the first century CE
Place of Composition	unknown; possibly Jerusalem or Alexandria

The Letter of James and the Pauline Letters

Historically, scholarly interpretation of this letter has centered on how it relates to the Pauline Letters because, like Paul, the author discusses the relationship between faith and works at length and both in relation to the figure of Abraham (2:14–26). At the heart of the debate lies the question of the necessity of works for *justification*—that is, what does God require of believers? Traditionally, scholars have concluded that James and Paul give two different answers to the question of justification. Paul insists on justification by faith alone and not by works of the Mosaic Law:

> Rom 3:28 "For we consider that a person is justified by faith apart from works of the law."
>
> Gal 2:16 "Yet [we] who know that a person is not justified by works of the law but through faith in Christ Jesus, even we have believed in Christ Jesus that we may be justified by faith in Christ and not by works of the law, because by works of the law no one will be justified."

According to James, however, justification involves both faith and action:

> Jas 2:24, 26 "See how a person is justified by works and not by faith alone. . . . For just as a body without a spirit is dead, so also faith without works is dead."

Numerous variables come into play when attempting to explain the reason for this apparent contradiction about justification before God: Did Paul write before or after James? Is James directly responding to Paul, and if so, does he do so positively or negatively? Did James and Paul write completely independently of each other? How scholars treat the relationship between James and Paul often relates directly to how they answer these questions.

Much of Paul's insistence on the need for faith alone for salvation and not the works of the Law had its roots in the Jewish-Christian debate over whether or not Gentile Christians had to observe the Jewish Law in order to be Christians. Paul strongly advocated for Gentile inclusion in God's covenantal promises to Israel through their belief in the death and Resurrection of Christ, citing Abraham as the model of faith in God *before* the Mosaic Law was even given to Israel (see, for example, Gal 3:1–14). Although James, too, cites Abraham as a model of faith in God, his larger point to his fellow Christian Jews is that Abraham's justification lay in his willingness to sacrifice Isaac, thus demonstrating—through action—his faith in God (Jas 2:18–22). Notably, both Paul and James quote Genesis 15:6 ("Abra[ha]m put his faith in the Lord, who attributed it to him as an act of righteousness"), but use that text to make widely different points about faith in relation to works.

A definitive answer cannot be given to the above questions, but plausible explanations are possible. The author of James could be reacting to an extreme form of Paulinist theology[12] that viewed (in a very un-Pauline way) a Christian's behavior as completely unrelated to faith. Already in Galatians 5:13, Paul found it necessary to implore, "For you were called for freedom, brothers. But do not use this freedom as an opportunity for the flesh; rather, serve one another through love." The severe warnings given by the author of James could well have applied to any Paulinist Christians who ignored the advice of Galatians 5:13. An important difference between Paul and James is that, whereas Paul argued that Gentile Christians should not be obligated to undergo circumcision or follow the whole Mosaic Law, James never even mentions the acceptance of Gentile believers, which was an issue central to Paul's theology and worldview. Thus James may be reacting not directly to Paul's theology, but to a particular development within part of the later Pauline tradition that used the figure of Abraham in Genesis 15 as an excuse to ignore living according to the Gospel's moral demands.

What Kind of Ancient "Letter" Is James?

Twenty-one of the twenty-seven writings in the New Testament fall into the category of letters. Most of them are easily identifiable as such because they follow the typical basic structure of an ancient Greek letter: a salutation that included the name of the sender and

Continued

---

12. That is, a stance adopted by later Pauline communities or the interpretation of Paul made in later communities.

> **What Kind of Ancient "Letter" Is James?** *Continued*
>
> receiver as well as a brief greeting; an expression of thanksgiving (often a prayer); the body of the letter; a command signaling the close of the body; a conclusion that included a peace wish, sending greetings to others, and a benediction.
>
> The Letter of James clearly begins like a typical ancient letter and certainly contains a body, but other elements, such as an initial thanksgiving and a conclusion, are missing. The body provides important clues as to the type of ancient letter it is. It contains many moral sayings (2:13, 3:12), numerous short essays (2:1–13, 14–26, 3:1–12) and is held together by catchwords, the most common being "brothers" (*adelphoi*, used fifteen times) and "my brothers" (*adelphoi mou*, 2:1, 14, 3:1). The body of the letter focuses on moral instructions and admonitions—all the hallmarks of Jewish wisdom literature. It may be most appropriate to think of James as an ancient Jewish Christian wisdom writing that loosely follows the letter format. It should be noted that the inclusion of so much wisdom material within a letter was a true innovation.

The Reception of James in Church History

The history of how the Letter of James was received by the church divides into two periods: its reception in the early church until the end of the fourth century and its reception during the sixteenth-century Reformation. In terms of the early church, the Letter of James is not among the New Testament books listed in the ancient fragment known as the Muratorian Canon, which some scholars date as early as 200. There is no solid evidence to support the Letter of James being accepted as a canonical writing in the Eastern Church until Origen of Alexandria around 250. In 367 Bishop Athanasius of Alexandria wrote an Easter letter in which he listed the canonical books of the New Testament, including James among them. In the churches of the West, fourth-century Church Fathers, including Rufinus and Jerome, treated James as a canonical book. Under the influence of Augustine, the Third Synod of Carthage (397) officially listed James among the canonical writings, and by the end of the fourth century, the Letter of James was accepted in the canon by both the Eastern and Western Churches.

No one challenged the canonical status of James until the Reformation in the sixteenth-century. Two leading reformers, Martin Luther and Erasmus, doubted that James himself wrote this letter. Luther went so far as to criticize the theology of James, especially on the issue of justification by faith alone (Jas 2:14–26), seeing it as a direct challenge to Paul's teaching on justification. In 1522 Luther famously dismissed the Letter of James as no more than "an epistle of straw" and placed it, along with the Revelation of John, at the end of his German translation of the New Testament.

The other Reformers did not share Luther's doubts about James. John Calvin, for example, wrote a commentary on James in 1551, in which he supported the canonical status of James, seeing the moral and ethical advice in James as applicable to daily Christian life. In the end, despite Luther's personal misgivings, all Protestant denominations accepted James as canonical, including the Lutheran Church. Reacting to Luther, the Roman Catholic Church defended and affirmed the Letter of James as having apostolic authority and as being part of the New Testament canon in the Council of Trent (1546–1563). Since the Council of Trent declared the canon of the New Testament officially closed, the Letter of James has remained unchallenged in subsequent Catholic theological discourse.

Summary: Historical Context of James

CORE CONCEPTS

- The unknown author of the Letter of James was a Hellenized Christian Jew writing toward the end of the first century.
- How James and Paul viewed justification (faith alone saves versus faith and action saves) connects directly to their different cultural and theological contexts.
- The acceptance of the Letter of James into the Christian canon was challenged by some in the early church as well as during the sixteenth-century Protestant Reformation.

Continued

> **Summary: Historical Context of James** *Continued*
>
> **SUPPLEMENTAL INFORMATION**
> - The Letter of James is a thoroughly Jewish New Testament text.
> - Most scholars think an anonymous author wrote in the name of James of Jerusalem, the "brother of the Lord."
> - The Letter of James was likely intended to be shared by the Jewish believers scattered outside of Palestine.
> - The earliest lists of New Testament books do not include the Letter of James.
> - Martin Luther had a low opinion of the Letter of James, but Protestants accepted its canonicity nonetheless.
> - The Council of Trent (1546–1563) reaffirmed the canonicity of James for Roman Catholics.

Theology and Ethics

The opening verses of James set the tone of the letter and provide its overriding theme: "Be perfect and complete, lacking in nothing" (1:4). For James, being "perfect" (that is, putting one's faith into action) represents the essence of true wisdom. Consequently, the Letter of James sets out to teach its intended readers how to live out one's faith in such a manner that reflects this "wisdom from above" (3:17) in daily life. Embedded within this ethical framework is the letter's theology, which touches on the themes of God, the "perfect human," and the Parousia, the return of Christ.

God

The Letter of James fundamentally portrays God as one who shows a clear preference for the poor, giving them faith and making them "heirs of the kingdom" (2:5).[13] God desires all believers to remain "unstained by the world" (1:27). In fact, for James, "to be a lover of the

---

13. References to God pervade the Letter of James, with the word "God" (sixteen times) and the term "Lord" (eleven times) appearing most frequently. The letter uses the designation God "the Father" three times (1:17, 27, 3:9) and includes a single reference to God as "lawgiver and judge" (4:12).

world means enmity with God" (4:4). Those who become "rich" in this world by exploiting others receive God's condemnation. James warns them, "Weep and wail over your impending miseries" (5:1). James's position on the rich is counter-cultural in that the ancient world associated wealth with honor. James anticipates a great reversal and calls the wealthy to be prepared with deeds of benevolence now.

At the outset of the letter, James presents God as eager to assist believers in their journey toward wisdom: "If any of you lacks wisdom, he should ask God who gives to all generously and ungrudgingly" (1:5). Although believers are tested and experience temptation, God is not the cause of "temptation to evil" (1:13). Temptation and sin are rooted in selfish desires (1:14–15). For James, God is "the Father of lights" (1:17), who "from above" sends "all good giving and every perfect gift" so that believers "may be a kind of first fruits of his creatures" (1:17–18).

"Perfect Human"

James calls his readers to become "perfect and complete" (1:4). The perfect person, that is, one whose faith is put into action, learns to master doubt. The believer who doubts lives with "two minds" and, like waves on a windy sea, is "unstable" (1:6–8), but the person of faith is "lacking in nothing." He "perseveres in temptation" and ultimately wins "the crown of life" promised to those who love God (1:12. Above all, the "perfect human" has full control of "his whole body" through his ability to control his tongue (3:2).

As the letter unfolds, James outlines how a person of faith achieves spiritual perfection: by seeking wisdom, putting faith into action, separating from worldly desires, treating the poor with dignity, and focusing on prayer. Those grounded in faith, who remain in control and seek perfection and completion, overcome doubt, temptation, and the trappings of wealth.

Parousia

The Letter of James says surprisingly little about Jesus. Indeed, it mentions him only twice by name, "Lord Jesus Christ" (1:1, 2:1), although it includes a few indirect references using such terms as "the noble name" (2:7) and "Lord" (5:14–15).

The most sustained discussion of Jesus occurs toward the end of the letter when James writes about preparing for "the coming of the

Lord" (5:7–12). It gives two specific instructions in anticipation of the second coming of Christ. First, it counsels believers to "be patient" (5:7). Here the letter highlights the farmer as a model of patience (5:7b–8) and also refers to the perseverance of Job (5:10–11). Second, the letter advises readers to avoid swearing any oaths, since this can result in "condemnation" (5:12). Patience and the integrity of one's word serve as the best preparation for the eschaton, the "end time."

> ## The Wisdom Sayings in "Q"[14]
>
> In order to account for written material shared by Matthew and Luke—about 235 verses—that does not derive from the Gospel of Mark, biblical scholars have posited the existence of a now-lost source used by both authors, which they refer to as the "Sayings Source" or "Q," from the German word *Quelle*, meaning "source." It basically consisted of sayings of Jesus and, like James and the *Didache*, contained much wisdom material.
>
> | A good person out of the store of goodness in his heart produces good, but an evil person out of a store of evil produces evil; for from the fullness of the heart the mouth speaks.

("Q": LUKE 6:45) | For where jealousy and selfish ambition exist, there is disorder and every foul practice.

(JAMES 3:16) | Search out the presence of the holy ones each day, so that you may find comfort in their words.

(DID. 4.2) |
> |---|---|---|
>
> All three—the Sayings Source (Q), the Letter of James, and the *Didache*—serve as examples of early Christian wisdom literature.

The Letter of James emphasizes the need to think and behave wisely. In fact, the letter states early on that God offers assistance to

---

14. See Patrick Hartin, *James and the "Q" Sayings of Jesus* (Sheffield, UK: Sheffield Academic Press, 1991) for a good background study on the Letter of James and Q as wisdom documents.

those who lack wisdom (1:5). The wise person knows first and foremost how to "tame the tongue" (3:8). One part of the letter refers to mastering the power of the tongue (controlling one's speech) as the key to wisdom (3:1–12). James uses various metaphors, such as horses and bits, ships and rudders, flames and a forest ablaze, to emphasize how the tongue controls the whole body: "From the same mouth comes come blessing and cursing" (3:10). What comes out of the mouth of the believer reflects what is in the heart and mind of the believer (3:11–12). The truly wise person lives a life marked by humility, peacefulness, and gentleness. Such a life is "full of mercy and good fruits," draws on wisdom "from above," and avoids the "jealousy and selfish ambition" rooted in the desires of this world (3:13–18).

For James, the wise person draws near to God in humility; such a person avoids speaking evil of others or judging his or her neighbor. The sins of pride and arrogance cause division within the mind and division among community members (4:13–17). Thus the believer is not a "lover of the world" who succumbs to passions and is divided by "two minds" (4:1–12). Nor does the wise person make provisions for the future or presume to know God's will.

Faith in Action

The Letter of James uses the word "faith" nineteen times, most often as a simple noun and usually to refer to the faith of the community of believers. One of the strongest moral imperatives issued in the Letter of James is the call to put one's faith into action: "Be doers of the word and not hearers only, deluding yourselves" (1:22). Action constitutes the heart of the Law ("the perfect law of freedom") and serves as the cause from which the believer "shall be blessed" (1:25). For James, "pure and undefiled" religion calls for a two-fold action: caring for the orphans and widows and abstaining from the world (1:27). The concern for widows and orphans has close ties to the requirements of the Israelites stated by the Mosaic Law (see, for example, Exod 22:21–23).

One of the most well-known and controversial parts in the Letter of James is the section on faith and works (2:14–26). This text has received more attention than most parts of the letter because of its perceived conflict with Paul's insistence that faith *without* works "saves" (see, for example, Rom 3:21–31; Gal 2:15–21). When read independently of Paul's letter, this section's point is clear and consistent with the ethics in the rest of the letter: "Faith of itself, if it does not have works, is dead" (2:17). James goes on to cite Abraham and Rahab as Old Testament examples of people who put their faith into action and were therefore "justified" by God.

> ### Rahab
>
> The story of Rahab the harlot is found in Joshua 2:1–24. The author of the Letter of James hails Rahab (along with Abraham) as an exemplar of faith in action. Rahab, who lived in Jericho, disobeyed the order of the king to turn over the two Israelite men sent by Joshua to spy on the city. Rahab not only protected the spies in defiance of the king, but also devised a plan to save them, acknowledging, "The LORD, your God, is God in heaven above and on earth below" (Josh 2:11b). In return, she pleaded for the safety of her family after the Israelites captured the town.
>
> Two New Testament texts, the Letter to the Hebrews (11:31) and the Letter of James (2:25), cite Rahab as a woman who acted out of faith and serves as a model of faith in action. The story of Rahab is an example of arguing "from the greater to the lesser"—that is, although she was a non-Israelite and a prostitute, her faith in action matters.

Wealth and Poverty

Wisdom includes having the proper attitude toward wealth and poverty. Riches, after all, "fade away" over time and it is the poor (the "lowly") who have "high standing" before God (1:9–11). Therefore James gives considerable attention to the sin of "partiality" toward the rich (2:1–13). Dishonoring the poor by showing preference for the rich violates God's commandment to assist the poor. The rich should see what God does for the poor: God makes the poor "rich in faith and heirs of the kingdom" (2:5). Showing partiality for the rich implies judgment of the poor, and "the law of freedom" (2:12) requires the believer to show mercy, for "mercy triumphs over judgment" (2:13).

Toward the end of the letter, James issues a final caution to the rich, especially those who have exploited the poor to achieve wealth. He warns that the "cries" of the poor ("the harvesters") have "reached the ears of the Lord of hosts" (5:4). "Impending miseries" await the rich who live now in "luxury and pleasure."

Importance of Prayer

The Letter of James ends with a brief section on prayer. It consists of two parts, dealing respectively with who to pray for and how to pray. Believers are instructed to pray for (and anoint) the sick and suffering (5:13–16), and for the conversion of sinners (5:19–20). The "prayer of faith" will "save the sick person" on the last day, and the believer who converts a sinner "will save his soul from death and will cover a multitude of sins" (5:20b).

The best method of prayer, according to the letter, involves both a confession of one's sins to others as well as a willingness to pray for each other. Citing the example of the prophet Elijah, who prayed "earnestly" for a drought and then rainfall (see 1 Kings 18:1–46 for the complete story), James highlights the power of "fervent prayer" from the "righteous person" of faith.[15] This powerful image concludes the letter. James has clearly delineated the characteristics of the "righteous person," the one who seeks wisdom, defeats temptations, shows mercy rather than judgment, puts faith into action, controls the tongue, acts with humility, prays for others, and converts sinners.

Anointing of the Sick

Like James 2:14–26, which discusses faith and works, 5:13–15 has received much scholarly attention. Since the Council of Trent (1545–1563), this biblical text has been cited in support of the Anointing of the Sick, one of the seven Roman Catholic sacraments. Central to James's instructions, the "presbyter [elder] of the church" is to pray and anoint with oil the sick person "in the name of the Lord." For James, this prayer and anointing both forgives sins and prepares the person for the end time. James himself, however, never refers to this directive as a "sacrament." In 1551, the Roman Catholic Church declared this anointing of the sick as a sacrament "instituted by Christ and promulgated by blessed James the apostle and brother of the Lord."

---

15. In the eighth-century BCE, the prophet Elijah is said to have fervently and successfully defended the God of Israel against Ahab (king of the southern kingdom of Judea) and his wife, Jezebel, and the four hundred and fifty prophets of Baal.

> ## Summary: Theology and Ethics in James
>
> **CORE CONCEPTS**
>
> - The main theme of the Letter of James is found in the opening verses: "Be perfect and complete, lacking in nothing."
> - The Letter of James is more theocentric than Christocentric, referring to God thirty-one times but to Jesus only twice.
> - The ethical imperative in James consists of putting faith into action.
>
> **SUPPLEMENTAL INFORMATION**
>
> - According to James, God desires believers to be "unstained by the world."
> - The "perfect human" does not succumb to doubt, divided by "two minds."
> - Patience and integrity of one's word prepares one for the "end time."
> - The wise believer has control over his tongue.
> - Wisdom begins with the proper disposition toward wealth and poverty.
> - The Letter of James ends with a discussion of who to pray for and how to pray.

PART 2: THE *DIDACHE*

Part 2 examines the *Didache*, the first of the texts from the Apostolic Fathers. The title that scholars assign this writing derives from the Greek word *didachē*, meaning "teaching," and is an abbreviation of the longer title of this work: *The Teaching of the Twelve Apostles*. The discussion of the *Didache* begins with a look at the historical context of this work and examines its literary integrity, in particular, whether this text was ever given authoritative status as a part of Scripture. Part 2 also explores the *Didache*'s theology (Christology and eschatology) and ethics (the "two ways"; instructions on baptism, fasting, prayer, and the Eucharist; and directives on how to treat, select, and discern leadership).

Historical Context

As with the books of the New Testament, attempts to determine the historical setting of any of the writings of the Apostolic Fathers (95–155)—authorship, date, place of composition, and intended audience—derive from the internal and external evidence. Internal evidence from the *Didache* provides some insight into these historical questions. External evidence from the New Testament and the writings of the early Church Fathers also offer some information about the *Didache*'s historical setting.

Outline of the *Didache*[16]

1.1–6.2	**The Two Ways** The *Didache* opens with a discussion of the "two paths, one of life and one of death," and contains the text's Wisdom material. Most of the letter centers on the way of life (moral and ethical imperatives for proper living), with only a few concluding remarks on behavior that exemplifies the way of death. This section closes with a warning not to be led astray.
6.3–10.7	**Christian Rituals** The next section moves immediately into instructions on how believers should conduct themselves in terms of what food to eat, how to baptize, how and when to fast, and how to pray. An extended discussion on the Eucharist concludes this section.

Continued

---

16. English translations of the *Didache* are taken from *The Apostolic Fathers*, ed. and trans. Bart D. Ehrman, 2 vols., LCL (Cambridge, MA: Harvard University Press, 2003), 1:416–43.

> **Outline of the *Didache*** Continued
>
> | | |
> |---|---|
> | 11.1–15.3 | **Church Organization**
 This section deals with issues of leadership and authority within the congregation, with particular attention given to teachers, apostles, and traveling prophets. Of special interest are itinerant visitors, with strict guidelines to determine their authenticity. The section ends with instructions for "the Lord's own day," directives for appointing bishops and deacons within the community of believers, and a call to reprove each other as needed. |
> | 16.1–8 | **Eschatological Warnings**
 The *Didache* ends with a brief warning to be properly prepared for the coming of the Lord, which will be accompanied by signs such as the arrival of false prophets, the spread of anarchy, and the appearance of the "world-deceiver." The end time will then be ushered in with the sky opening, trumpets sounding, the dead rising, and the Lord coming from the heavens. |

Author and Audience

The author who compiled the instructional guide known as the *Didache* is unknown. Given the *Didache*'s heavily Jewish tone and outlook, the Didachist is likely a Christian Jew. His attribution of the work to the "twelve apostles" is a probably an attempt to gain authoritative status for his work. In compiling the *Didache*, the author had access to the Torah, many of the prophetic writings of the Hebrew Scriptures, numerous Jewish intertestamental writings (such as the wisdom text of Sirach), and early Christian sayings and traditions that may well predate the written New Testament Gospels. Additionally, sayings and traditions included in the *Didache* (or at least those that serve as source material for the *Didache*) have close parallels to the Gospel of Matthew.

The intended audience of the *Didache* likewise remains unknown. The directives in chapter 7 of the *Didache*, however, leave the impression that the *Didache* could have been used as an instructional guide for the newly baptized. The likely recipients of the *Didache*—possibly a cluster of communities—seem to fit the same broad profile as the Gospel of Matthew's community, which is traditionally associated with the city of Antioch in Syria: an assembly of Jewish believers in Jesus as the Messiah (see reference to Jesus as the "Christ," 9:4), with ties to synagogue worship (for instance, the prayers on the Eucharist in chapters 9 and 10 compared to Jewish blessings), informed and shaped by the Torah (for example, chapter 2 on the "way of life" relies heavily on the Torah, especially the Decalogue), and open to Gentile inclusion ("Everyone who comes in the name of the Lord should be welcomed," 12.1). While this community profile could apply to numerous regions in the Roman Empire with a heavily Jewish population, Christian congregations of Jewish believers in Syria certainly qualify as a possible intended audience.

The Rediscovery of the *Didache*

The early Church Fathers knew of the *Didache*. For example, in his work, *Church History*,[17] the fourth-century church historian Eusebius refers to the text using its longer title, the *Teachings of the Apostles*. However, the *Didache* was thought to be lost until its rediscovery in 1873 in Constantinople by Philotheos Bryennois, a professor of church history and the Orthodox Bishop of Serrae. He found a Greek manuscript of the *Didache* quite by accident while working on the tenth-century Codex Hierosolymitanus. Bryennois did not make his rediscovery of the *Didache* known for another ten years as he worked with and translated the Greek text into a publishable edition, which appeared in 1883.

Continued

---

17. See 3.25.

> **The Rediscovery of the *Didache*** Continued
>
> Study of the *Didache* since its rediscovery has allowed New Testament scholars to see the Letter of James in a new light. Both texts, for example, speak about the end times: James 5:7–12 and *Didache* 16:1–8. The eschatology in the *Didache* resembles that found in the Synoptic Gospels, thus underscoring the unique eschatology in James with its almost singular focus on waiting patiently for the return of Christ.

Date and Place of Composition

With some exceptions,[18] most scholars date the *Didache* to somewhere near the end of the first century or the beginning of the second century.[19] It should be noted, however, that since the *Didache* exists as a composite text, one or more parts[20] may date to an earlier period. Scholarly debates on the literary relationship between the *Didache* and the Gospel of Matthew have affected the dating of this text. If the *Didache* depends on the written Gospel of Matthew, then a later date is preferred. If the *Didache* is independent of Matthew, then an earlier date is plausible.

In terms of the place of composition, many scholars favor the general area of Syria, and possibly even Antioch, the city associated with the Gospel of Matthew.[21] Antioch had a large population of Jewish Christians, and while there may be no literary dependency between Matthew and the *Didache*, their numerous parallels indicate some connection between these documents, as seen, for example, in the comparisons of warnings against false teachers (Matt 5:19//*Did.*

---

18. See Aaron Milavec, *The Didache: Text, Translation, Analysis, and Commentary* (Collegeville, MN: Liturgical Press, 2004), xiii–xiv, who dates the *Didache* to the mid-first century.

19. Jonathan A. Draper, "The *Didache*," in *The Writings of the Apostolic Fathers*, ed. Paul Foster (New York: T&T Clark, 2007), 13–20, at 15; Koester, 163; Jefford, 5; Ehrman, 411. Schnelle, 355, dates the *Didache* to 110.

20. Especially the wisdom and eschatological sections, *Did.* 1–6 and 16, respectively.

21. Koester, 163–64. Ehrman, 411–12, sees Syria or even Egypt as possible places of composition.

11.1–2), the Lord's Prayer (Matt 6:9–13//*Did.* 8.2) and the Trinitarian formula (Matt 28:19//*Did.* 7.1).

Summary of Historical Setting for the *Didache*

Author	anonymous compiler, probably by a Christian Jew
Audience	unknown, possibly Christian congregations of Syria
Date of Composition	late first or early second century
Place of Composition	plausibly the region of Syria, possibly city of Antioch

The Literary Integrity of the *Didache*

When addressing the historical context of any ancient text, questions often arise about whether the current form of a text is the same as its original form, or if its current form is the result of bringing together independent writings. In the case of the *Didache*, scholars have questioned whether some parts of it may have circulated independently before the text was preserved in its final form sometime in the early second century.

Various clues have led some scholars to conclude that chapters 1–6 of the *Didache*, the discussion of "the two paths," may have circulated on its own sometime in the late first century CE. *Didache* 1–6 is preserved independently in a Latin translation,[22] and significant parts of its contents appear in the *Epistle of Barnabas* 18–20. Additionally, *Didache* 6.2 appears to be a transitional verse created by the Didachist to connect the sections of the "two paths" (1.1) with the instructions on Christian rituals (6.3). This verse, furthermore, does

---

22. For some history and context of this Latin tradition, see Jefford, 7–9.

not appear in the Latin form of the *Didache*, known as the *Doctrina apostolorum*. Many scholars also view chapter 16 (eschatology) as a separate tradition.²³

> ### The Dangers of the Tongue in the Letter of James and the *Didache*
>
> One demonstration of how the Letter of James and the *Didache* exemplify early Christian wisdom literature is their similar focus on right ethical behavior, the texts' moral exhortations. Compare, for example, the stress on connecting faith with actions (Jas 2:14–26; *Did.* 2.5, 4.8) or avoiding the sin of partiality to the rich (Jas 2:1–4; *Did.* 4.3). Warnings about the dangers of the tongue also present an interesting parallel:
>
> | | |
> |---|---|
> | "No human being can tame the tongue. It is a restless evil, full of deadly poison. With it we bless the Lord and Father, and with it we curse human beings who are made in the likeness of God. From the same mouth come blessing and cursing. This need not be so, my brothers." (Jas 3:8–10) | "Do not be of two minds or double-tongued because a double-tongue is a lethal snare." (*Did.* 2.4) |
>
> Seeing the mutual concern in James and the *Didache* over mastering one's tongue suggests this moral exhortation may have been part of the "rule of faith" among the earliest Christians.

Was the *Didache* Considered Scripture?

The process of canonization of the books of the New Testament emerged over many centuries, beginning in the second. For several

---

23. See Ehrman, 407–11, for an extended discussion on the literary integrity of the *Didache*.

centuries, writings were often granted authority by the individual churches that possessed them. Only after a long period of time did criteria for admittance into the New Testament include whether a particular text had apostolic origin, supported the "rule of faith," and was used and acknowledged in all the churches.[24] Interestingly, none of the writings that now make up the canon of the New Testament fit all of these criteria.

The longer title of the *Didache* (*Teaching of the Twelve Apostles*) suggests an attempt to establish its apostolic origin. Its pervasive moral exhortations resemble those found in many of the books that eventually came to be accepted as canonical, thus supporting the "rule of faith." In addition, many early church leaders, including Irenaeus, Clement of Alexandria (who speaks of the *Didache* as "scripture"), and Origen of Alexandria, knew of it. Eusebius, in fact, refers to the *Didache* directly, acknowledging that some place it "in the canon."[25] Although the *Didache* was not ultimately accepted into the New Testament canon, a number of church leaders, along with their communities, appear to have embraced it among the writings in their emerging canon of scripture.

Summary: Historical Context of the *Didache*

CORE CONCEPTS

- The *Didache* is an instructional guide compiled by an anonymous author.
- It was likely intended to be read and followed by the churches in the region of Syria, in particular, prior to the baptism of a new believer.
- Although compiled in the early second century, the *Didache* probably contains earlier wisdom, liturgical, and eschatological material.

Continued

---

24. Schnelle, 358.

25. Eusebius, *Church History* 3.25. The *Didache* fell into Eusebius's third category of disputed writings used by some but not all.

> **Summary: Historical Context of the *Didache* Continued**
>
> **SUPPLEMENTAL INFORMATION**
> - The author of the *Didache* was likely a Jewish believer in Christ.
> - Similar to the Letter of James, the *Didache* exemplifies the genre of wisdom literature.
> - The Didachist had access to the Hebrew Scriptures, Jewish intertestamental writings, and very early Christian sayings and traditions predating the written Gospels.
> - The basic criteria for canonization were apostolic origin, support of the "rule of faith," and use or acknowledgment by all the churches.
> - The *Didache* was viewed and used as a part of Scripture by some early Church Fathers.

The Theology and Ethics of the *Didache*

Christology

The *Didache* offers few Christological statements. Christ's cross and Resurrection, themes central to the "gospel" that Paul preached in the mid-first century, do not appear in the *Didache*, although parts of the book may stem from the same time period (for example, the "two paths" chapters). This text does, however, parallel the Q-source, which likewise fashioned a Christology independent of the Passion and Resurrection narrative. The *Didache* includes sayings of Jesus (for example, 1.3–4), but presents them without any setting or context, similar to the presentation in Matthew's Sermon on the Mount discourse (Matt 5–7).

Although the *Didache* does not provide a theology of the death and Resurrection of Jesus, the titles it uses for Jesus shed light on its Christology. The Eucharistic prayers of chapters 9 and 10, for example, frequently refer to Jesus as "child" (Greek, *pais*), a direct reference to Jesus as the child of "our Father." This idea of Jesus as the child of God is reinforced by the Trinitarian formula used in the *Didache*: "baptize in the name of the Father and of the Son and of the Holy

Spirit" (7.1, 3). The text also refers to Jesus as "the Lord" (8.2, 9.5, 15.3, 16.1) and "Christ" (9.4).

> ### The Eucharist in the *Didache*
>
> Scholars have compared the words of the Eucharistic liturgy in the *Didache* (9–10) with the earliest attestation of the Lord's Supper in the New Testament, 1 Corinthians 11:23–26. They often highlight three points of comparison. First, the *Didache* makes no connection between the bread and wine and Jesus' impending death, Resurrection, and return. In other words, there is no "institution of the Eucharist" as in Paul and later in the Gospel narratives. Second, the meal blessing begins with the wine and then the bread (the opposite of the Pauline tradition), with the cup as a symbol linking Jesus to the Davidic covenant and the bread as a symbol of the unity of the community. And third, the *Didache* associates the Eucharist with a purity ritual: only the "holy" may participate, while the unbaptized are excluded. Given these differences, scholars have raised the question whether the rite described in the *Didache* was a Eucharist, or what kind of Eucharist it was.

Eschatology

The final chapter of the *Didache* begins with a brief warning: "Be watchful for your life. . . . For you do not know the hour when our Lord is coming" (16:1). This eschatological ("end time") outlook also appears in the Gospel narratives, as seen in, for example, Matthew 24; Luke 12:35–40, 21:5–36; and James 5:7–12.

According to the *Didache*, the end of time, the "final moment" (16.2) will be characterized by various catastrophic events: the arrival of "false prophets and corruptors," "lawlessness" within the community, and the appearance of the "world-deceiver," creating unparalleled havoc ("He will perform lawless deeds, unlike anything done from eternity"16.4b). The end time will then be ushered in with the "signs of truth": the sky opening, trumpets sounding, and the dead rising. With these culminating events, "the world will see the Lord coming on the clouds of the sky" (16.8). The text of the *Didache* literally ends in mid-sentence.[26] The Gospel narratives also record terrible events associated with the end time, although they describe them somewhat differently than the *Didache*, for example, the destruction of the Temple, famines, and earthquakes (Matt 24:1–7; Luke 21:5–11). These apocalyptic events, however, are altogether absent from the eschatology of the Letter of James.

The Path of Life and the Path of Death

The *Didache* begins with a discussion of the "two paths—one of life and one of death," which, as discussed above, is a hallmark of wisdom literature. Chapters 1–6 focus mostly on the path of life, with only a few concluding remarks on the path of death. The discussion of the baptism ritual that immediately follows[27] suggest that this instruction on the path of life and the path of death comprised part of the instruction for newly baptized.

The section on the two paths opens by commenting on the essence of the path of life: the double command to love God and love neighbor (see Deut 6:5 and Lev 19:18) followed by the Golden Rule: "[Love] your neighbor as yourself. And whatever you do not want to happen to you, do not do to another" (*Did.* 1.2). The remaining discussion on the path of life begins with a collection of Jesus-tradition sayings (1.3–6), which parallel the Q-source material found in Matthew's Sermon on the Mount (Matt 5–7) and Luke's Sermon on the Plain (Luke 6). The bulk of the "path of life" material follows the structure of the Ten Commandments (2.1–7), a catalogue of virtues and vices (3.1–10), rules for the community (4.1–4, 12–14), rules about giving and receiving (1.5–6, 4.5–8), and household guidelines (4.9–11). Indeed, much of the material in chapters 2–4 strongly parallels the legal codes of the Torah, thus showing how the wisdom material in the *Didache* reinterprets the non-wisdom material in the Torah.

The discussion of the "path of death," in sharp contrast, is limited to a list of vices (5.1–2), some of which clearly reflect Gentile

---

26. A similar type of abrupt ending is also found in the Gospel of Mark (see Mark 16:8), leading scholars to conclude in both cases that the original ending of these texts may be lost.

27. "But with respect to baptism, baptize as follows" (7.1).

practices that the Didachist found particularly offensive. These include magic ("feats of magic"), astrology ("sorceries"), and abortion ("murders of children"). The two paths section concludes with a warning ("Take care that no one lead you astray from the path of this teaching," 6.1) and an interesting caveat about following the two paths: "But if you cannot, do as much as you can" (6.2). The "path of death," too, can be connected to what follows about baptism. The pursuit of moral excellence is expected of new believers, but perfection is not a requirement to be baptized.

> ### The "Two Paths" in Jewish and Christian Tradition
>
> The *Didache* begins abruptly: "There are two paths, one of life and one of death." The idea of the "two paths" was a common motif found throughout Jewish and Christian literature from antiquity. It appears in a range of Old Testament texts (Deut 30:15; Prov 12:28; Jer 21:8), OT Apocrypha (Sir 15:17), and OT Pseudepigrapha (*2 Enoch*) as well as in the New Testament (Matt 7:13–14; Gal 5:17–18), NT Apocrypha (*Ps.–Clem.* 5.7), and writings of other Apostolic Fathers (*Barn.* 18.1; Herm. *Mand.* 6.2.1).
>
> The exact language of the "two paths" is not always used, but the general motif is present. For example:
>
> | "See, I have today set before you life and good, death and evil."

(Deut 30:15) | "In the path of justice is life, but the way of abomination leads to death."

(Prov 12:28) | "For the flesh has desires against the Spirit, and the Spirit against the flesh; these are opposed to each other, so that you may not do what you want. But if you are guided by the Spirit, you are not under the law."

(Gal 5:17–18) |
> |---|---|---|

Baptism, Fasting, Prayer, and the Eucharist

Immediately following the section on the "two paths," the Didachist offers instructions on various Christian practices community members were expected to follow. This set of instructions reveals a prescriptive approach different from that found in the New Testament writings, especially in regard to baptism and the Eucharist. For example, the Gospel narratives and Letters of Paul associate baptism with repentance and forgiveness of sins (Matt 3:1–6; Mark 1:2–8) and the believer's experience of dying with Christ (Rom 6:4). In the *Didache*, baptism focuses on ritual purity (proper preparation) associated with the baptizing water and fasting, with no mention of repentance, forgiveness of sins, or even the cross (7.1–4). The tradition regarding the Eucharist in the *Didache* is clearly independent from the earliest tradition preserved within the New Testament (1 Cor 11:23–26) and places an emphasis, instead, on ritual purity that serves to exclude from participation those who are deemed unworthy (9.1–10.7).

The *Didache* lays out strict guidelines about when to fast (Wednesdays and Fridays) and when not to fast (Mondays and Thursdays) as a means of differentiating believers from "the hypocrites" (8.1), a likely reference to the non-Christ-believing Pharisaic Jews. This arbitrary distinction shows both the proximity of the Didachist's community to synagogue practices and to possible competition, or even conflict, with the synagogue. Finally, regarding prayer, the version of the Lord's Prayer found in *Didache* 8.2 closely parallels the version found in the Q-source (especially Matt 6:9–13; compare Luke 11:2–4) and concludes with the directive, "Pray like this three times a day" (8.3). Many scholars view this as evidence that Matthew's Gospel, but perhaps not the other three New Testament Gospels, was accepted as Scripture in the Didachist's community.

Directives Regarding Leadership

The *Didache* allots considerable space to the topic of differentiating a legitimate teacher, apostle, and prophet from a false one, who ought to be dismissed as "a Christmonger" (12.5). The Didachist's concern about how long teachers, apostles, and prophets stay and what they eat points to likely problems with wandering, charismatic figures present at times within the community of believers. The problem was not that they wandered but that, for the Didachist, they did not wander enough. This picture of a highly fluid church leadership bears a certain resemblance to Paul, who was an itinerant missionary, but differs from the one presented in the Pastoral Epistles and the letters of Ignatius, where a more fixed structure of recognized elders/bishops in each congregation existed. In the early church, there was not just one model of leadership. In addition to a hierarchy of leadership, spirit-filled prophets appear to have been common and were to be handled very carefully by the congregation (11.7–12), since a sin against the Spirit "will not be forgiven" (11.7).

Prophets like Agabus (Acts 21:10–12), depicted in this eighteenth-century illustration, circulated among the early Christian communities. The *Didache* provides guidelines for distinguishing true prophets from charlatans.

The communities reading and applying the instructions and directives of the *Didache* were not only concerned about itinerant Christian apostles, teachers, and prophets, but were also anxious to appoint appropriate and more permanent leaders within their communities. According to the Didachist, these church leaders should be "gentle men who are not fond of money, who are true and approved" (15.1) since they, too, function as prophets and teachers.

> ## Summary: The Theology and Ethics of the *Didache*
>
> **CORE CONCEPTS**
> - The Didache employs a variety of titles for Jesus.
> - The "two paths" section of the *Didache* presents some of the earliest instructions for Christians preparing for baptism.
> - In the congregations reading the *Didache*, itinerant and charismatic leaders existed alongside teachers, prophets, bishops, and deacons.
>
> **SUPPLEMENTAL INFORMATION**
> - The *Didache* makes no mention of the cross and Resurrection of Jesus. It is an open question how these prominent parts of Pauline theology may have played a role in the Didachist's theology.
> - The "two paths" teachings combine Jesus-tradition sayings and Torah legal codes with the wisdom genre.
> - The version of the Lord's Prayer in the *Didache* closely parallels the version in the Gospel of Matthew.
> - Community members were expected to pray the Lord's Prayer three times a day.
> - The New Testament and the *Didache* offer various teachings and instructions about baptism and Eucharist.
> - The Didachist expresses considerable concern over discerning between true and false teachers, apostles, and prophets.

Questions for Review

1. Which of the "Jameses" mentioned in the New Testament do scholars consider a possible author of this letter?
2. Do James and Paul view justification differently? If so, how?
3. When in the history of the church was the canonical status and apostolic authority of the Letter of James recognized?
4. In what ways does the Letter of James place high priority on thinking and behaving wisely?

5. What does the Letter of James mean by the sin of "partiality"? How does the letter challenge the norms of the Greco-Roman society that privileged the wealthy?
6. What makes dating the time of composition of the *Didache* somewhat complicated?
7. What do the Letter of James and the *Didache* say about the end times and the return of Christ? What can be learned from these two wisdom writings about the early Christian belief in the Parousia?
8. In the *Didache*, what is a "Christmonger"?
9. According to the *Didache*, what are some good practices to use in selecting and discerning leaders?
10. How does the role of itinerant leaders in *Didache* 15 compare with the Pastoral Epistles and Ignatius?

Questions for Reflection

1. Which instructions or directives in the Letter of James do you find most challenging?
2. How do the Letter of James and the *Didache* connect faith and action. What do you see as the relationship between faith and action?
3. Considering the "two paths" teaching on the requirement for baptism (*Did.* 1–6), what is your reaction to "who is in" and "who is out" according to the Didachist?
4. What details about early Christian beliefs and practices does the *Didache* mention that are not attested in New Testament writings?

Recommendations for Further Reading

The Letter of James

Batten, Alicia. *What Are They Saying about the Letter of James?* New York: Paulist, 2009.

    Batten provides a survey of scholarly research on the Letter of James, especially of the last thirty years. She begins with questions of the letter's genre, structure, and rhetoric, then addresses issues of authorship and audience. Thematic concerns such as the relationship between James and Paul and between poverty and wealth in James are also explored. Batten concludes with a discussion on James and the sayings of Jesus.

Hartin, Patrick. *James of Jerusalem: Heir to Jesus of Nazareth*. Collegeville, MN: Liturgical Press, 2004.

Hartin offers information about a variety of topics: James as part of the family of Jesus in the Gospels, James in Acts and the Letters of Paul, James outside of the New Testament, and the Letter of James as wisdom literature. Hartin focuses on the role of James of Jerusalem within early Christianity.

Johnson, Luke Timothy. *Brother of Jesus, Friend of God: Studies in the Letter of James*. Grand Rapids: Eerdmans, 2004.

Johnson holds that the historical James of Jerusalem wrote this letter and presents the history of interpretation of James by scholars and the reception of the Letter of James in the early church. Johnson takes up various topics related to James, such as the sayings of Jesus in the Letter of James, its use of Leviticus 19, and gender issues. He argues that the letter reveals the voice of the historical James.

The *Didache*

Jefford, Clayton N. *Didache: The Teaching of the Twelve Apostles*. Salem, OR: Polebridge, 2013.

Jefford provides an English translation of the *Didache*. He offers thorough notes and commentary, providing alternative translations based on manuscripts other than the main Greek text. Jefford includes a brief but helpful introduction organized around the four primary divisions of the *Didache*. A discussion about the various manuscripts of the *Didache* is also included.

O'Loughlin, Thomas. *The Didache: A Window on the Earliest Christians*. Grand Rapids: Baker Academic, 2010.

In this commentary, O'Loughlin provides many insights into the *Didache* and the community of believers who would have been its recipients. He sets the text within its Jewish roots and New Testament parallels, which allows the reader to see the issues and challenges facing the earliest believers in Jesus as the Jewish Messiah. O'Loughlin provides an English translation of the *Didache* at the end of the book.

CHAPTER 2

First Peter and Early Christian Writings on Relations to Outsiders

INTRODUCTION

Chapter 2 discusses the First Letter of Peter and several writings of the Apostolic Fathers: the seven letters of Ignatius, the *Martyrdom of Polycarp*, the *Apology of Quadratus*, and the *Epistle to Diognetus*. These works are grouped together under the general category of "relations to outsiders" because each offers an example of the challenges early Christians faced from non-believers (outsiders) who were hostile or suspicious toward their Christian faith. First Peter, the letters of Ignatius, and the *Martyrdom of Polycarp* were written during a time of varying levels of duress and mostly deal with persecution. The *Apology of Quadratus* and the *Epistle to Diognetus* present arguments for the legitimacy of Christian beliefs. The *Apology of Quadratus* is a fragment of an apology reacting to the Roman state, while the *Epistle to Diognetus* is a letter written in response to ancient philosophy. Studying First Peter alongside these numerous extracanonical writings offers a wider view of the sometimes unfriendly environment surrounding the early Christians.

Part 1 of this chapter provides an overview of the historical context of 1 Peter (author, audience, date, and place of composition) and addresses such topics as the scope of suffering and persecution within the community and connections between this letter and the letters and theology of Paul. It also explores major themes, such as baptism, Christology, ecclesiology, and eschatology. The letter's ethical admonitions, which include the imperative to love one's fellow believers and to conform to social and hierarchical norms, are also examined. Part 2 examines the historical settings of the seven letters of Ignatius, the *Martyrdom of Polycarp*, the *Apology of Quadratus*, and the *Epistle to Diognetus* along with a brief overview of the contents of these writings.

Metaphor and Early Christian Identity

The opening verse of 1 Peter offers some insights into the symbolic language employed by the early Christian communities:

> Peter, an apostle of Jesus Christ, to the chosen sojourners of the dispersion in Pontus, Galatia, Cappadocia, Asia, and Bithynia.

The phrase "chosen sojourners of the dispersion" appropriates two terms used to describe Israel in the Old Testament: the "chosen" people of God and the "dispersion," a reference to the scattering of the Jewish people from Palestine after they were conquered by the Babylonians. Embedded in the words "chosen" and "dispersion" is the author's invitation to the predominantly Gentile believers in Christ to embrace Israel's history as their own and to view their experience as socially marginalized people as an extension of Israelite history. The word "sojourners" is also metaphorical language.[1] The term *sojourner* (or "alien") implies people living temporarily in a strange land, who do not enjoy the same rights, social connections, and privileges as citizens of that land. For reasons not entirely clear to a modern reader, the Gentile believers in Christ do not find themselves at home in the Roman provinces of Asia Minor. Their faith in Christ makes them aliens in their own land. First Peter reassures the Gentile believers that their alien status (and the accompanying suffering) is only temporary and will end with the imminent return of Christ (1:5, 7, 13, 20, 2:12, 4:5, 7, 13, 5:1, 4).

---

1. See James A, Kelhoffer, *Persecution, Persuasion and Power: Readiness to Withstand Hardship as a Corroboration of Legitimacy in the New Testament*, WUNT 270 (Tübingen: Mohr Siebeck, 2010), 98.

Early Defenders of Christianity

As Christianity grew and spread throughout the Roman Empire in the first and second centuries, it met with increasing criticism from non-believers. Some Christians began to formally defend the faith in writing. Christian apologists (defenders of the faith) were very active in the second and third centuries. Two of the most well-known second-century apologists were the philosopher Justin Martyr (ca. 100–165) and Irenaeus of Lyons, a bishop in Gaul (ca. 135–202). Justin argued for the philosophical superiority of Christianity over other competing philosophies, and Irenaeus fought against rising heretical movements. Most scholars consider the *Apology of Quadratus* and the *Epistle to Diognetus* to be second-century Christian apologies; others believe these works predate Justin and Irenaeus.

PART 1: THE FIRST LETTER OF PETER

Historical Context

The First Letter of Peter offers some internal evidence about its authorship, date and place of composition, and intended audience. Additional external evidence, found in other New Testament books and the writings of the early Church Fathers, helps establish its historical context.

Outline of the First Letter of Peter

1:1–2	**Greeting** The letter opens with a greeting from "Peter," who is described as "an apostle of Jesus Christ," and the sender of the letter, to its intended recipients, the "chosen sojourners" in five provinces of Asia Minor: Pontus, Galatia, Cappadocia, Asia, and Bithynia.

Continued

Outline of the First Letter of Peter *Continued*

1:3–2:10	**Christian Identity** Peter begins by highlighting believers' "new birth" (1:3; that is, baptism) as the foundation of their Christian identity. Through baptism, believers are saved by Jesus' death and Resurrection and are called to a life of obedience, reverence, and mutual love. Peter concludes this section with the image of Christ as the cornerstone of faith, the "living stone" who unites all believers as "God's people."
2:11–3:12	**Christian Conduct in a Hostile World** Peter next offers advice on proper social relationships between believers and non-believers. He implores that they be good examples to Gentiles, respecting human authorities (the emperor and local provincial governors), showing obedience and endurance in "unjust suffering" (with Christ as the model), and treating spouses with dignity and fellow believers with love, compassion, and humility.
3:13–4:11	**Defense of the Faith in a Hostile World** Peter then acknowledges that believers are "maligned" and that non-believers "vilify them." He advises believers to explain to outsiders the reason for their hope in Christ, and he reminds them that "Christ also suffered in the flesh" and that they should adopt "the same attitude" as Christ in their suffering. With the end time soon, Peter urges believers to focus on showing hospitality and love to each other.
4:12–5:11	**Counsel to Those Suffering and Persecuted** Peter next speaks of a "trial by fire" for believers. He asserts, "Rejoice to the extent that you share in the sufferings of Christ . . . (and) are insulted for the name of Christ," since you are "blessed"

Continued

	Outline of the First Letter of Peter *Continued*
4:12–5:11	with the "Spirit of glory and of God." He concludes by encouraging the community leaders (presbyters and younger members) to serve God's "flock" willingly, with humility, sobriety, and vigilance amid their suffering.
5:12–14	**Conclusion** Peter concludes by exhorting believers to "remain firm" in their faith. He sends greetings from "the chosen one at Babylon" (probably the Christian community in Rome) and from someone named Mark, and identifies Silvanus as the bearer of the letter.

Author and Audience

The letter opens with the words, "Peter, an apostle of Jesus Christ" (1:1), indicating Peter as the author. Unlike the Letter of James, where numerous people named "James" mentioned in the New Testament could have qualified as the attributed author, this letter holds out only one possible "Peter," clearly intending its audience to identify the author as one of the original twelve apostles of Jesus (see, for example, Mark 3:13–19). Indeed, the traditional view, dating back to second-century Church Fathers (see Papias, Polycarp, and Irenaeus)[2] and including one of the later New Testament writings (see 2 Pet 3:1), held that the Apostle Peter wrote 1 Peter. Even some modern scholars argue for the possibility that the Apostle Peter was the author of 1 Peter.[3]

---

2. Irenaeus, in *Against Heresies* (dated around 180), is the first to explicitly mention Peter as the author of 1 Peter by citing a passage from 1 Peter as the words of Peter (see, for example 4.9.2, 5.7.2). Earlier second-century Church Fathers use quotes from 1 Peter, presupposing Peter as the author (see Polycarp, *Epistle to the Philippians* 8.1; Papias, according to Eusebius, *Church History* 3.39.19).

3. See, for example, Luke Timothy Johnson, *Living Jesus: Learning the Heart of the Gospel* (San Francisco: HarperCollins, 1998), 91: "There is no compelling reason to deny the possibility that Peter the disciple of Jesus was that author [of First Peter], even as there is no decisive way to demonstrate that he was." See also Norman Hillyer,

The far more common view held by scholars today is that 1 Peter is a pseudonymous writing, meaning that someone wrote this letter in Peter's name so as to draw upon Peter's authority. Scholars cite numerous compelling reasons to support this claim: The sophisticated Greek and the rhetorical style of the letter does not seem to correspond to Peter, a Galilean fisherman whose mother tongue was Aramaic and who would have lacked a formal education; the author of 1 Peter cites Old Testament texts primarily from the Greek translation and not from the original Hebrew, as would be expected from a Palestinian Jew; the letter contains no direct references to Peter's extended interactions with the historical Jesus, a strange omission from one of Jesus' closest apostles; and the growth and spread of Christianity into Asia Minor, with its established structures and leadership in the five Roman provinces, likely did not occur within Peter's lifetime.[4]

If Peter himself did not write this letter, then who might have written it? Two theories have been offered in recent decades. One argument holds that 1 Peter was composed by Silvanus, either during Peter's lifetime or sometime soon after his death. First Peter 5:12 offers the clue: "I [Peter] write you this briefly through Silvanus, whom I consider a faithful brother."[5] Silvanus, it is argued, may have functioned as a secretary for Peter in the writing of the letter. Those who view this letter as a pseudonymous writing but who argue against Silvanus as its composer interpret the phrase "through Silvanus" as simply signaling that Silvanus is the bearer of the letter, the letter-carrier.[6] This chapter assumes the latter position that Silvanus was the letter-bearer of 1 Peter and not the actual author.

---

1 and 2 Peter, Jude (Grand Rapids: Baker Books, 1992), 1: "Although doubts have been expressed about Simon Peter's being the author of the two letters bearing his name, there are no irrefutable reasons for rejecting the claims of the letters themselves to have been written by the apostle."

4. See Udo Schnelle, *The History and Theology of the New Testament Writings*, trans. M. Eugene Boring (London: SCM, 1998), 400–401; Donald P. Senior, *1 Peter, Jude and 2 Peter*, SP 15 (Collegeville, MN: Liturgical, 2003), 4; Helmut Koester, *History and Literature of Early Christianity*, 2nd ed. (New York and Berlin: Walter De Gruyter, 1982, 2000), 162; Darian Lockett, *An Introduction to the Catholic Epistles* (New York: T&T Clark, 2012), 43–44; Bart D. Ehrman, *The New Testament: A Historical Introduction to the Early Christian Writings*, 6th ed. (New York and Oxford: Oxford University Press, 2016), 502.

5. See, for example, Peter H. Davids, *The First Epistle of Peter*, NICNT (Grand Rapids: Eerdmans, 1990), 3–7.

6. Ehrman, 502; Senior, 5; Lockett, 43.

A second theory about the possible authorship of 1 Peter posits the existence of a "Petrine group" in the city of Rome.[7] These scholars argue that Peter carried on his missionary work in his final years in Rome, establishing a community and a group of followers there. After Peter's death in the 60s, Petrine followers invoked Peter's name and authority to address and encourage believers in new situations in the outlying communities of the Roman Empire, such as Asia Minor. Thus, some argue, leaders from the Petrine group in Rome wrote 1 Peter in order to encourage believers in Asia Minor to continue to bear witness to the faith despite their sufferings and hardships.

Still other scholars admit there is much that remains unknown about the letter's authorship, location, and date. In any case, some pseudonymous author viewed the enduring legacy of Peter as a source of inspiration for encouraging Christ-believers in Asia Minor, a Greek-speaking region far from the horizons of the uneducated Palestinian fisherman who had followed Jesus.

Silvanus

First Peter concludes with a reference to Silvanus, the bearer of this letter to five Roman provinces:

> I [Peter] write you this briefly through Silvanus, whom I consider a faithful brother, exhorting you and testifying that this is the true grace of God. Remain firm in it. (1 Pet 5:12)

Within the New Testament, the name Silvanus (also known as Silas) is closely associated with Paul. He is identified as a co-sender of the two letters to the Thessalonians (1 Thess 1:1; 2 Thess 1:1), a preacher with Paul and Timothy to the church in Corinth (2 Cor 1:19), and a coworker with Paul on his missionary trips (Acts 15–18). Identifying Silvanus as the letter bearer of 1 Peter may have been an attempt on the part of the pseudonymous writer to add credibility to his writing by tying the letter not only to the Apostle Peter but also to Pauline Christianity.

---

7. John H. Elliott, *First Peter: A New Translation with Introduction and Commentary*, AB (New York: Doubleday, 2000), 118–30. In support of the "Petrine group" authorship, see Senior, 5–7.

Despite this uncertainty about the identity of the author, the letter offers some internal clues as to the makeup of the intended audience. The letter is addressed "to the chosen sojourners of the dispersion in Pontus, Galatia, Cappadocia, Asia, and Bithynia." Assuming the pseudonymous author has not provided a fictive audience, he intends the letter to reach a wide geographic area. These five Roman provinces cover nearly 130,000 square miles and extend east-west across central Asia Minor, modern-day Turkey.[8] Frequent references to their former way of life as ignorant and futile (1 Pet 1:14, 18, 2:25, 4:3), along with the invitation to be part of the people of God set within Israel's Torah and prophetic traditions (2:10, 3:6), suggest a mainly Gentile readership. The two references to the audience as "sojourners" (1:1b) and "aliens" (2:11) most likely serve as metaphors for the sufferings the Gentile believers in Christ experience at the hands of their own people: the faithfuls' true home awaits them in heaven after the return of Christ (1:13, 17, 3:21–22).[9]

The letter offers two additional insights about its intended audience. These Gentile congregations had both preaching and serving ministries within their communities (4:10–11), as well as some type of a leadership structure, with presbyters overseeing the daily functions and "younger members" assigned to additional duties (5:1–7). Furthermore, the congregations faced various types of conflicts and suffering ranging from unjust sanctions from authorities (3:17) to local harassment (4:12–19). The intended audience clearly faced some degree of persecution from outsiders.[10]

Date and Place of Composition

Building on the inference that the letter is pseudonymous, most scholars date 1 Peter to a generation or so after the Apostle Peter's death, toward the end of the first century, around 80–110.[11] Several factors support this dating. First, it would have taken some time for Christianity to spread beyond its Palestinian roots and take firm root

---

8. Senior, 8; Lockett, 45.

9. Ehrman, 499–501; Senior, 10.

10. See David G. Horrell, *1 Peter* (New York: T&T Clark, 2008), 45–60, for a good discussion on the intended audience of 1 Peter in relation to their situation, identity, and suffering.

11. Kelhoffer, 103; Koester, 296; Schnelle, 403; Senior, 7–8.

in the Roman provinces across Asia Minor. Second, in this letter believers in Christ no longer defined themselves relative to Judaism, but more in terms of their pagan environment. Third, the use of the term "Babylon" in reference to Rome (1 Pet 5:13) is a post-70 development. Fourth, 2 Peter, written as late as 140, seems to assume the existence of 1 Peter (see 2 Pet 3:1). And finally, around 140, Polycarp, bishop of Smyrna, apparently quotes 1 Peter 2:21–22, 24 in his *Epistle to the Philippians* (8.1–2).

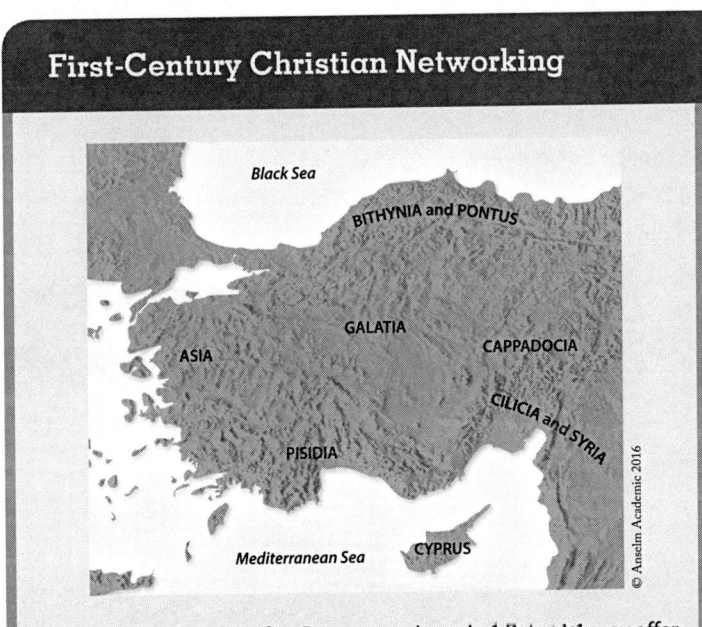

First-Century Christian Networking

The identification of the five Roman provinces in 1 Peter 1:1 may offer some clues about communication networks in early Christianity. Scholars suspect that the order in which 1 Peter lists the five provinces may be the order in which the letter bearer (Silvanus) would have traveled to deliver it: beginning with Pontus, proceeding south through Galatia and Cappadocia, then west to Asia and then turning east and north back through Bithynia to Pontus. The personal delivery of 1 Peter to these Gentile Christ-believing congregations would assure its safe arrival as well as offer the opportunity for clarifications and further discussions. Unfortunately, 1 Peter offers no clues as to how those churches had a communications network with each other.

Although the place of composition for 1 Peter is uncertain, the letter's concluding remarks imply that it was sent from the city of Rome: "The chosen one at Babylon sends you greeting, as does Mark, my son." The word "Babylon" is used here as a code word for Rome (see, for example, Rev 17:1–6). This brief reference serves as the letter's sole internal evidence for place of composition, and since no solid evidence exists to the contrary, most scholars conclude that 1 Peter was probably written from Rome.[12] However, others argue for Asia Minor as a possible place of composition, given that the letter targets Christian congregations in Asia Minor.[13] But these churches in Asia Minor were a long way from Rome, nearly nine hundred miles east, making communication less likely. Further complicating this matter is the fact that in pseudepigraphical writings, including 1 Peter, both the author and the location can be fictive.[14] Nevertheless, this chapter assumes the city of Rome as 1 Peter's place of composition.

Summary of Historical Setting for 1 Peter

Author	unknown; pseudonymous writing
Audience	predominantly Gentile Christians living in five Roman provinces covering much of Asia Minor
Date of Composition	80–110
Place of Composition	possibly Rome

---

12. See, for example, Lockett, 44–45; Senior, 6; Koester, 297.

13. See Schnelle, 401–2, who sees Asia Minor as a possible place of composition: "While a firm decision is not possible, it seems to me that the list of addressees speaks more for Asia Minor than for Rome as the place of origin," 402.

14. See Bart D. Ehrman, *Forgery and Counterforgery: The Use of Literary Deceit in Early Christian Polemics* (New York: Oxford University Press, 2013). Ehrman discusses 1 Peter in chapter 9, "Forgeries in Support of Paul and His Authority."

Suffering and Persecution

The idea of believers suffering for their faith pervades this letter. Scholars commonly point out that the Greek term *paschō* ("suffer") appears a total of forty-two times in the New Testament, with twelve of them occurring in 1 Peter. The author clearly aims to offer advice on how to cope with suffering and wishes to put the persecution in a context that both defends the faith from outsiders and offers relief to insiders. The extent of the suffering and persecution discussed in 1 Peter has been a point of debate. Does the letter reflect a systematic attempt by Roman officials to persecute believers, or is this more of a local harassment by non-believers?

The majority of scholars conclude that the suffering referred to in 1 Peter probably takes the form of discrimination, verbal and physical abuse, and false accusation by local authorities and hostile non-believers rather than statewide persecution sanctioned by the Roman Empire.[15] Systematic and widespread persecution of Christians is thought to have officially begun with Emperor Decius, 249–251. Persecution of Christians by Roman officials did occur prior to the mid-third century, but took place more on a local level; Emperor Nero (54–68), for example, persecuted Christians in Rome but not elsewhere in the empire. Moreover, there is no evidence that Christians suffered persecution during the reigns of some other Roman emperors, such as Vespasian (69–79) and Titus (79–81).

The suffering discussed in 1 Peter likely reflects a spontaneous, local opposition to some Christ-believers in these five Romans provinces, most likely on a sporadic and informal basis. Just for being "Christians," believers were subject to slander and false accusations (2:12, 15, 3:9, 16, 4:4), endured physical assault (2:19–20), and were even brought before courts, where they were treated similarly to murderers and thieves (4:15–16). First Peter's reference to "a trial by fire" (4:12) aptly describes how intense these persecutions appeared to the addressees. One of 1 Peter's concluding remarks—"your fellow

---

15. See Schnelle, 404–5; Senior, 7; Ehrman, 501–2. Koester: "A more widespread hostility against Christians in a large geographical area (*130,000 square miles*, emphasis added) is hardly possible much before the end of the 1st century," 297. See also Candida Moss, *The Myth of Persecution: How the Early Christians Invented a Story of Martyrdom* (New York: HarperCollins, 2013), who calls into question the extent of persecutions of Christians.

believers throughout the world undergo the same sufferings" (5:9)—is historically implausible and may simply reflect the author's belief that suffering is part of the life of a Christian in general.[16]

> ### Early Christian Writings Connected to Peter[17]
>
> Early Christians found Peter a very attractive figure. Some appear to have taken advantage of the name and authority of Peter to further advance their causes and positions.
>
> As mentioned above, the New Testament contains two documents written in Peter's name (1 and 2 Peter) that appear to have begun this tradition in the late first and early second centuries. Add to this numerous extracanonical texts that spanned the second through fourth centuries that were either attributed to or written about Peter:
>
> - *Gospel of Peter*: discovered in 1887, the surviving fragment focuses mainly on the Passion of Christ.
> - Two "Apocalypses" of Peter
>   - *Greek Apocalypse of Peter*: discovered in 1887, presents the risen Christ revealing to Peter visions of heaven and hell.
>   - *Coptic Apocalypse of Peter*: discovered in 1945, contains an account of Jesus' crucifixion.
> - Four "Acts" of Peter
>   - *Acts of Peter* (two versions): stories from the life of Peter, including a description of a miracle contest between Peter and Simon Magnus, and the earliest account of Peter's martyrdom, being crucified head-down.
>   - *Acts of Peter and Andrew*: stories consisting of a series of miracles connected to Andrew and Peter.
>
> *Continued*

---

16. Karen H. Jobes, *1 Peter* (Grand Rapids: Baker Academic, 2005), 9.

17. For a good resource on these early Christian writings associated with Peter, see Wilhelm Schneemelcher, ed. *New Testament Apocrypha*, trans. R. M. Wilson, 2 vols., rev. ed. (Louisville: Westminster John Knox, 1991).

> **Early Christian Writings Connected to Peter** *Continued*
>
> - *Acts of Peter and Paul*: stories presenting adventures in the life of Peter and Paul, including Paul's journey from the island of Gaudomeleta to Rome, the death of Paul by beheading, the assignment of Peter as Paul's brother.
> - *Acts of Peter and the Twelve Apostles*: an allegory tale similar to the parable of the pearl (Matt 13:45–46).
>
> - *Preaching of Peter*: survives today only in fragments as quotations from Clement and Origen, two church leaders from Alexandria.
> - *Letter of Peter to Philip*: discovered in 1945, the surviving fragment contains a brief letter purporting to be from Peter to Philip, followed by a narrative and discourse upon the nature of Christ.
>
> Many early Christians believed some of these writings were actually authored by Peter.

First Peter and the Letters of Paul

One of the many remarkable features of 1 Peter is its apparent connections to the letters and theology of Paul. There is some evidence to suggest a direct connection between 1 Peter and some Pauline letters. First, strong parallels exist between 1 Peter and Romans, with the author of 1 Peter likely modifying parts of Romans to fit his current situation (1 Pet 2:13–17 and Rom 13:1–7, on submission to the Roman state, and 1 Pet 3:8–12 and Rom 12:14–21, a general exhortation to the community to allow the Lord alone to judge). Second, the author of 1 Peter appears to depend upon the Pauline letter format (for example, sender, receiver, body, final greeting, and blessing), even using an opening blessing formula (1 Pet 1:3: "Blessed be the God and Father of our Lord Jesus Christ") identical to the one found in 2 Corinthians 1:3 and Ephesians 1:3. Third, 1 Peter concludes by mentioning Silvanus and Mark, both of whom are identified as Paul's co-workers in his letters as well as in Acts. Fourth, terms Paul uses to structure the framework of his theology (for example, *grace, call, freedom, election,* and *righteousness*) are also used extensively throughout 1 Peter. The only appearance outside of Paul's letters of the Pauline phrase *en Christō* ("in Christ") appears, notably, in 1 Peter (3:16, 5:10, 14).

Most scholars are convinced that the author of 1 Peter was at least influenced by the Pauline theology already present in the general Christian tradition by the end of the first century.[18] It is also very possible that the author of 1 Peter had a direct connection to Paul, especially to the letters of Romans and Ephesians.[19]

> ## Summary: Historical Context of First Peter
>
> **CORE CONCEPTS**
>
> - First Peter is a pseudonymous writing composed around 80–110.
> - The scope of suffering and persecution in 1 Peter includes discrimination, verbal and physical abuse, and false accusation by some local authorities and hostile non-believers.
> - First Peter was likely influenced by, and possibly had a direct connection to, Pauline theology already present in the general Christian tradition by the end of the first century.
>
> **SUPPLEMENTAL INFORMATION**
>
> - The recipients of 1 Peter were predominantly Gentile believers.
> - Most scholars identify the city of Rome as the likely place of composition of 1 Peter.
> - The verb "to suffer" appears more in 1 Peter than in any other New Testament writing.
> - Systematic and widespread persecution of Christians officially began with Emperor Decius (249–251), more than a century after the sufferings discussed in 1 Peter.
> - The suffering discussed in 1 Peter likely occurred on a sporadic and informal basis.
> - Parts of 1 Peter agree extensively with sections from Paul's Letter to the Romans, especially the emphasis on the need to submit to the authorities whom God has approved.

---

18. Koester, 296; Schnelle, 410–11; Senior, 12–13.

19. See Kelhoffer, 94–96, who argues for a direct connection between 1 Peter and Paul.

Theology and Ethics

The author of 1 Peter applies his theological ideas to the letter's overriding pastoral concern: to assist Gentile believers in dealing with the suffering they experience as "sojourners" and "aliens." In doing so, the letter presents a theology of baptism, a Christology focused on the suffering Christ, a discipleship connected to suffering, an ecclesiology grounded in the believing community as "Israel," and a renewed hope for the end time. The ethics of 1 Peter requires mutual love and restraint along with conformity to social norms.

Baptism

First Peter equates baptism of adults (children were not baptized) with a new life, employing various terms to describe the new identity they receive thereby: "new birth" (1:3), "born anew" (1:23), "newborn infants" (2:2). The author uses it as the letter's opening theological motif because baptism was central to their community identity.

First Peter 3:20–21 asserts that "the ark, in which a few . . . persons were saved through water," prefigures baptism—an analogy unique to this author. In this fresco (ca. 1100), Noah and family safely ride out the flood.

First Peter describes baptism as fundamentally rooted in God's "great mercy" (1:3a). It "saves" because it serves as "an appeal to God for a clear conscience" (3:21). By participating in this "new birth," Gentile believers can connect to "a living hope through the resurrection of Jesus Christ from the dead" and can anticipate "an inheritance . . . kept in heaven for them" (1:3–4), where Jesus now waits "at the right hand of God" (3:22). Heaven offered a welcome destiny for those who, because of their faith, suddenly found themselves "aliens" in their own land.

Through baptism, believers are "born anew" with an "imperishable seed" rooted in God's "living and abiding word" (1:23). Initiation into the Christian congregation through baptism gave entry into God's family, a new reality grounded in "the word of the Lord [that] remains forever" (1:25). The newly initiated baptized faithful are like "newborn infants" who "long for pure spiritual milk" that provides the substance necessary to "grow into salvation" (2:2). Baptism into the community of faith offered believers a new and eternal home in heaven, a familial affiliation through God's seed, and the nutrition needed for salvation.

Christology

Since one of the primary aims of this pastoral letter consists of helping Christians who experienced persecution from outsiders, much of the Christology centers on Jesus' suffering. First Peter focuses on the saving effects of Jesus' suffering, death, and Resurrection, and emphasizes the idea that suffering is a fundamental aspect of Christian life.

Jesus' suffering and death on the cross not only "ransomed" believers from their "futile conduct" (1:18) but also "healed" (2:24) their wounds and "saved" (4:18) them. Jesus was rejected by his own people; therefore he understands the plight of his followers when they are rejected. Jesus became the "cornerstone" (2:6–7), a "living stone, rejected by human beings but chosen and precious in the sight of God" (2:4). Even so, Jesus' suffering and death had a larger purpose: "Christ . . . suffered . . . that he might lead you to God" (3:18). Just as Jesus suffered through his trials, so too, believers should prepare "to suffer through various trials" (1:6). First Peter encourages its readers to understand Christ through his suffering and to fully embrace their own suffering.

Discipleship

Discipleship in 1 Peter is closely connected to Christology. Persecution from outsiders was a lived reality for many believers. In fact, readiness to suffer was an integral part of discipleship. First Peter warns believers: "For to this [suffering] you have been called, because Christ also suffered for you, leaving you an example that you should follow in his footsteps" (2:21). For Christians, suffering tests one's faith (1:7) and ultimately leads to glory (1:11, 5:1): "Rejoice to the extent that you share in the sufferings of Christ, so that when his glory is revealed you may also rejoice exultantly" (4:13). First Peter invites believers to recognize that true discipleship requires a total embrace of the life, death, and Resurrection of Christ.

Ecclesiology

The ecclesiology of 1 Peter (that is, how the author envisions the church) is grounded in the image of Israel, and even defines the church as "Israel."[20] In its opening verses, 1 Peter uses Israel as a metaphor by connecting the community of believers to Israel's prophets. Israel's prophets foresaw the coming salvation offered through Christ (1:10), were possessed by "the Spirit of Christ" (1:11), and prophesied on behalf of those current believers (Jewish and Gentile) who now profess faith in Christ (1:12). Scattered throughout the letter are quotations from Israel's sacred scriptures that establish the church's legitimacy (for example, 4:18–19) and set the church's normative behavior (2:17, 21–25, 3:6, 10–12). In addition, the image of Jesus Christ as the "living stone," the "cornerstone" upon which the church is now built and through whom "spiritual sacrifices acceptable to God" (2:4–6) are offered, solidifies the image of the church in light of the history and theology of Israel. Through faith in Christ, the rejected cornerstone, Gentile members of the church are to understand themselves as God's "chosen race," "a people of his own," who now are rightly called "God's people" (2:9–10).

---

20. See, for example, Koester, 298; Senior, 14–15.

> ### Jewish Scriptures in 1 Peter
>
> The author of 1 Peter drew upon a rich tradition of Jewish materials in the composition of his letter. Much of this material is drawn from stories connected to the Jewish Law and Prophets, such as the story of Noah and the ark (3:19–22) and the words of the prophet Isaiah (for example, 1:24–25, 2:22–25). But the author of 1 Peter also uses material from so-called extracanonical Jewish literature (for example, the *Testament of Abraham* in 3:5–6 and *1* and *2 Enoch* in 2:16 and 3:19–20), leaving some scholars to speculate that he might have regarded these works as canonical.

Eschatology

First Peter is replete with references to the end time (eschaton) that would be ushered in at the return of Christ (1:5, 7, 13, 20, 2:12, 4:5, 7, 13, 5:1, 4). The letter's consistent focus on the Parousia (the second coming of Christ) both offers believers hope for an imminent future of unimaginable joy and puts their suffering and persecution into a new perspective, as a time of temporary hardship to be followed by eternal joy (4:13).

First Peter understands the church as the eschatological people of God. As such, they wait in hope for the second coming and even "rejoice" in their suffering, since their persecution serves as a prelude to the return of Christ (1:6–7) and promises a share in Christ's glory (5:4). First Peter presents the idea that believers are living in the "final time" (1:5, 20, 4:7); believers must maintain "good conduct" in anticipation of the imminent arrival of Christ (2:12), who will judge both the living and the dead (4:5). Although a generation or two had passed since Paul, the hope of an imminent end remained strong, at least for this pseudonymous author.

Mutual Love and Restraint

As the people of God, baptized in the faith, Christians are called to maintain a high code of conduct, rooted in holiness. This obligation applies to how Christians act not only to fellow believers but also to the wider society in which non-believers may well persecute those who profess the faith. First Peter expresses the moral imperative early on in the letter: "Be holy because I am holy" (1:16).

First Peter calls members of the Christianity community to live a life of obedience and reverence in anticipation of the return of Christ (1:13–21) and to love one another "from a pure heart" (1:22). Love for each other is essential to the community's survival. Of equal importance is the idea that believers must set a good example in the public sphere by resisting worldly desires and maintaining "good conduct" (2:11–12). The letter urges slaves to act with reverence to their masters, good or bad (2:18–22), and calls upon Christians to treat their spouses with kindness and humility, whether the spouse is a believer or not (3:1–7). Christians are challenged to resist the "swamp of profligacy [decadence]" that surrounds them in the larger society (4:4) and encouraged to take the higher ground by returning blessings for insults and good for evil (3:9).

The Exhortations of 1 Peter

First Peter contains many exhortations that challenge believers to uphold high moral standards despite enduring trials of suffering and persecution by non-believers:

1:13–15	Be holy in your conduct.
1:22	Love one another.
2:1–2	Rid yourselves of malice, deceit, envy, and slander.
2:11–12	Keep away from worldly desires.
2:13–17	Be subject to every human institution.
3:8–9	Be of one mind; do not return evil for evil.

Continued

> **The Exhortations of 1 Peter** *Continued*
>
> | | |
> |---|---|
> | 3:15–16 | Always be ready to explain the reason for your hope. |
> | 4:1–2 | Arm yourselves with the same attitude of Christ. |
> | 4:7–9 | Be hospitable to one another without complaining. |
> | 4:12–13 | Rejoice to the extent you share in the sufferings of Christ. |
> | 5:1–9 | Be humble in tending the flock of God. |
>
> Living an upright, moral life was one of the best ways to avoid attracting unnecessary attention and resistance from outsiders who might otherwise be hostile to members of the Christian community.

Conformity to Social Norms

In addition to expressing concerns about moral and ethical behavior within the community and the larger society, 1 Peter also urges believers to live in accordance with the expected cultural norms. This may well stem from the desire that believers avoid provoking any trouble and harassment from non-believers or even the appearance of doing so.

First Peter makes a bold demand in this regard: "Be subject to every human institution for the Lord's sake" (2:13a). These "human institutions" range from the political establishment run by kings and governors (2:13b–14) to the institutions of slavery and marriage (2:18–3:7). The letter presents a very favorable view of the emperor and local government leaders who "are sent by him [God] for the punishment of evildoers and the approval of those who do good" (2:14). First Peter offers a summary position on this idea of obedience to human institutions: "Give honor to all, love the community, fear God, honor the king" (2:17).

Household Codes of Conduct

The household codes of 1 Peter contain exhortations addressed to the whole community, to slaves, and to wives. The advice is similar to those codes present in the Pauline letters for slaves (see 1 Cor 7:21–24; Eph 6:5–8; Col 3:22–25; 1 Tim 6:1–2) and spouses (see Eph 5:21–33; Col 3:18–19). Christian slaves and wives could be especially vulnerable to hardships and even abuse. In 1 Peter, the household codes offer comfort and support to slaves "unjustly suffering" and to wives trying to convert their husbands.

These codes in the Petrine and Pauline traditions appear, in part, to recast traditional social structures in light of the freedom experienced through one's faith in Christ.

Summary: Theology and Ethics in First Peter

CORE CONCEPTS

- First Peter presents the church using Israel as a defining metaphor.
- The ethical imperative in 1 Peter is summed up in 1:16: "Be holy because I am holy."
- Believers must submit to human authorities that have been set up by God. This mandate applies in particular to slaves, who may serve harsh masters, and to wives, who may face difficult circumstances at home with an unbelieving husband.

SUPPLEMENTAL INFORMATION

- Christian baptism is rooted in God's "mercy."
- The Christology of 1 Peter is grounded in the sufferings of Jesus.
- Fundamental to the identity of the church is its designation as the eschatological people of God.
- According to 1 Peter, believers are already living in the final times. Therefore, their current period of suffering should be brief.
- Believers are called to love one another and restrain from worldly desires.
- Believers are also expected to conform to the larger social norms.

PART 2: THE SEVEN LETTERS OF IGNATIUS, THE *MARTYRDOM OF POLYCARP*, THE *APOLOGY OF QUADRATUS*, AND THE *EPISTLE TO DIOGNETUS*

Historical Contexts[21]

The same method for establishing the historical context (author, audience, date, and place of composition) for the New Testament writings applies to other early Christian writings, including the Apostolic Fathers: analysis of both internal and external evidence. The texts to be introduced on the following pages do provide some evidence about their historical contexts; however, the use of external sources, such as the writings of the Church Fathers and other early Christian apologists, is also needed.

Letters of Ignatius

The internal evidence of the seven letters of Ignatius provides much of the data needed to determine the historical context for these letters. The author is Ignatius, the second bishop of Syria, a province north of Palestine whose capital city was Antioch.[22] Beyond what can be gleaned about Ignatius from his letters, little else is known about him. He was obviously a leading figure in the Christian congregation in Antioch and was apparently known by other congregations in Asia Minor. Community members from at least five churches in Asia Minor met him in the cities of Smyrna and Troas while he made his journey toward martyrdom in Rome. From these encounters, Ignatius wrote to the churches in Ephesus, Magnesia, Tralles, Smyrna, and Philadelphia. He also wrote a letter to the church in Rome, and a letter to Polycarp, the bishop of Smyrna. Ignatius may not have been an uncontested leader, however. His warnings about false teachers and his repeated encouragements to submit to the (proto-orthodox) elders and bishops seem to indicate a church hierarchy still in the initial stages of development.

---

21. All English translations of the letters of Ignatius, the *Martyrdom of Polycarp*, the *Apology of Quadratus*, and the *Epistle to Diognetus* are taken from *The Apostolic Fathers*, ed. and trans. Bart D. Ehrman, 2 vols., LCL (Cambridge, MA: Harvard University Press, 2003).

22. Eusebius, *Church History* 3.22.

First Peter and Early Christian Writings on Relations to Outsiders 77

Most scholars date the letters of Ignatius to around 110, during the later years of the reign of Trajan (98–117).[23] They base this date

> ### The Order and Place of Composition of Ignatius's Letters
>
> Ignatius, Bishop of Antioch, wrote all seven of his letters in Greek, the same language used by the New Testament authors.
> The order and places of composition are as follows:
>
> - From the city of Smyrna, Ignatius wrote letters to four different Christian churches: *To the Ephesians, To the Magnesians, To the Trallians,* and *To the Romans.*
> - From the city of Troas, Ignatius wrote letters to two additional churches, *To the Smyrnaeans* and *To the Philadelphians,* and *To Polycarp,* addressed to his disciple, a bishop in Smyrna.
>
>
>
> Delegates from the churches in Asia Minor were sent to Smyrna and Troas to connect with and offer support to Ignatius as he faced his impending martyrdom in Rome. These delegates likely carried Ignatius's letters back to their congregations.

---

23. See, for example, Koester, 284; Ehrman, 445. See also Paul Foster in "The Epistles of Ignatius of Antioch," in *The Writings of the Apostolic Fathers* (New York: T&T Clark, 2007), 84–89, who argues for a plausibly later date of 125–150 based on the "theological character" of Ignatius's letters.

on the work of fourth-century church historian, Eusebius, bishop of Caesarea, who wrote about Ignatius's martyrdom. Unfortunately, Eusebius gives no direct time reference to this event.[24] The place of composition is explicitly mentioned in the letters; Ignatius concludes each of his missives by indicating where he wrote it, either the city of Smyrna or the city of Troas.

Martyrdom of Polycarp

The *Martyrdom of Polycarp* is actually a letter sent from the church of Smyrna in Asia to the church in the city of Philomelium (*Mart. Pol.* 1.1) in Phrygia, about one hundred miles east of Smyrna (see map on page 77). The letter, which narrates the martyrdom of Polycarp, identifies "Marcion" as the author: "You had asked for a lengthier explanation of what took place, but for the present we have mentioned only the principle points through our brother Marcion" (*Mart. Pol.* 20.1).

Most scholars date the composition of *Martyrdom of Polycarp* to 156, shortly after Polycarp's death in 154–155 based on internal evidence (*Mart. Pol.* 21.1) and on Eusebius's *Church History* 4.15.1.[25] The most likely place of composition is Smyrna, Asia, the city where Polycarp served as bishop and from which the letter claims to be sent.

The *Apology of Quadratus*

The *Apology of Quadratus* exists only as a fragment cited in Eusebius's *Church History* (4.3.2). The complete text of the *Apology* has not been discovered to date, nor does any fragment exist independently of Eusebius's citation. What little is known about Quadratus, the author of this apology, or about the text's target audience and its approximate date of composition, comes from this single reference. According to Eusebius, it was around 120 that Quadratus directed his apology to Hadrian, who was the Roman emperor from 117–138.[26] Its place of composition is unknown.

---

24. See Eusebius, *Church History* 3.36.3.

25. Koester, 308; Ehrman, 508; Sara Parvis, "The Martyrdom of Polycarp," in *The Writings of the Apostolic Fathers*, 131, sets the date of Polycarp's martyrdom at 156.

26. However, Eusebius offers different dates in two different works for Quadratus's apology to Hadrian: 117–120 in his *Church History* and 124–125 in his *Chronicle*.

Epistle to Diognetus

The author of the *Epistle to Diognetus* remains unknown, and this writing gives no internal clues about the author's identity. Given its content and focus, however, most scholars count this unknown author among the second-century apologists because this writing offers a defense of the Christian faith. External sources offer no help either, since, oddly enough, the early Church Fathers, including Eusebius and Jerome, never mention it. Likewise, the identity of the writing's intended recipient, "most excellent Diognetus," is not mentioned in any other ancient sources, although the title "most excellent" implies a person of rank, perhaps even a Roman official.

> **The Burned Manuscript of the *Epistle to Diognetus***
>
> The original manuscript of the *Epistle to Diognetus* was discovered in Constantinople around 1436 by a young priest named Thomas d'Arezzo. Tragically, in 1870, this single medieval copy of the manuscript, held in the municipal library of Strasburg, was destroyed by fire when the German forces attacked the city during the Franco-Prussian War. Fortunately, the text of the *Epistle to Diognetus* has been preserved, thanks to three transcripts dated to the sixteenth century.

Further complicating efforts to establish the historical setting for the *Epistle to Diognetus* is the fact that it is a composite text comprised of two different types of material: chapters 1–10 (the apologetic section) and chapters 11–12 (a homily) appear to be two separate works likely composed at different times, perhaps even by different authors. While most scholars date the *Epistle to Diognetus*

See Foster, 54–57, for a discussion about these two competing dates. Foster sees either date as plausible. In support of the later date, Eusebius states in the *Chronicle* that when Hadrian was in Athens in 124 or 125, Quadratus delivered an apology to him. The earlier date is plausible given the pattern of chronical ordering of events reported in Eusebius's *Church History*, which places the apology of Quadratus to Hadrian shortly after his accession (117) and before the death of Alexander, the bishop of Rome, in 120 (see *Church History* 4.4).

to sometime after 150, when other Christian apologists were active (for example, Justin Martyr and Irenaeus), the writing in its current form seems to date from an even later point in time. The writing's place of composition is also unknown.[27]

Summary of Historical Settings

	Author	Audience	Date of Composition	Place of Composition
Letters of Ignatius	Ignatius, Bishop of Syria	five churches in Asia Minor, the church in Rome, and fellow bishop Polycarp	110–117	Smyrna and Troas, in Asia Minor
Martyrdom of Polycarp	members in the church in Smyrna (Marcion)	members in the church in Philomelium	155–156	Smyrna
Apology of Quadratus	Quadratus	unknown; addressed to Emperor Hadrian	around 120	unknown
Epistle to Diognetus	unknown	"Most excellent-Diognetus" (otherwise unknown)	uncertain, likely 150–200	unknown, perhaps Asia Minor

---

27. Some scholars favor Asia Minor, an area associated with other Christian apologists.

Overview of These Writings
Letters of Ignatius

While each of the seven letters of Ignatius has its own integrity and focus, the letters generally revolve around three main themes: preparation for martyrdom, the unity of the church, and confronting false teachers. These themes shape Ignatius's thinking in the areas of ecclesiology and Christology.

Ignatius was concerned about his impending martyrdom. While he touches on this theme in most of his letters (for example, *Smyrn.* 4.2; *Pol.* 2.3), the letter *To the Romans* deals with it explicitly and even opens with a plea that Christians there not interfere with his martyrdom (*Rom.* 1.2). Understandably, some Christians may have become concerned that a bishop was to be executed and wanted to "help" by trying to prevent his death. Ignatius's eagerness to die for his faith is a theme repeated elsewhere in that letter: "I am writing all the churches and giving instructions to all, that I am willingly dying for God, unless you hinder me" (*Rom.* 4.1). Ignatius actually seems to relish the idea of his impending, torturous death:

Ignatius's death by wild beasts is depicted in this engraving. The early Christians greatly revered those who had died for their faith; some, like Ignatius, eagerly embraced the opportunity to share their fate.

> I am the wheat of God and am ground by the teeth of the wild beasts, that I may be found to be the pure bread of Christ. (*Rom.* 4.1)

> May I have the full pleasure of the wild beasts prepared for me; I pray they will be found ready for me. (*Rom.* 5.2)

While discussing his upcoming martyrdom, Ignatius focused on Christ and Christ's suffering death:

> Allow me to be an imitation of the suffering of my God (*Rom.* 6.3)

Ignatius seems convinced that by his martyrdom he would show to the world that he was a true disciple.

Church order and unity was also important to Ignatius. He considered it the most effective means for fighting the heresies (such as the docetists and Judaizers, discussed below), who, in his view, threatened to cause schisms within the Christian congregations. According to Ignatius, unity resulted from proper church order, which centered on the leadership structure of bishop, presbyters (elders), and deacons. Ignatius believed that this ecclesial structure reflected divine realities:

> I urge you to hasten to do all things in the harmony of God, with the bishop presiding in the place of God and the presbyters in the place of the council of the apostles, and the deacons, who are especially dear to me, entrusted with the ministry of Jesus Christ, who was with the Father before the ages and has been manifested at the end. (*Magn.* 6.1)

Given this view of ecclesial structure, it is not surprising that Ignatius saw the office of the bishop as the final authority on church matters:

> For when you are subject to the bishop as to Jesus Christ, you appear to me to live not in a human way but according to Jesus Christ. (*Trall.* 2.1)

Ignatius demanded that the congregation undertake nothing without the consent of the bishop and the presbyters (*Magn.* 7.1). He held that such submission to recognized church leaders would ensure that the church would remain in fellowship and unity with God and Jesus Christ (*Phld.* 3.2).

Ignatius's insistence on episcopal control, which he considered divinely ordained, stemmed from his desire to confront and challenge wrong beliefs and practices. One group he opposed consisted of Christ-believers who denied Jesus' earthly (human) existence: the docetists (from the Greek *dokein*, "to seem"), who held that Jesus only "seemed" to be human.[28] Others, the "Judaizers," maintained the necessity of Jewish customs, such as continuing to observe the Sabbath.

Against those who denied Jesus' humanity, Ignatius insisted on the reality of Jesus as both human and Son of God:

> For there is one physician, both fleshly and spiritual, born and unborn, God come in the flesh, true life in death, from both Mary and God, first subject to suffering and then beyond suffering, Jesus Christ our Lord. (*Eph.* 7.2)

> And so, be deaf when someone speaks to you apart from Jesus Christ, who was from the race of David and Mary, who was truly born, both ate and drank, was truly persecuted at the time of Pontius Pilate, was truly crucified and died, while those in heaven, on earth and under the earth looked on. He was also truly raised from the dead, his Father having raised him. In the same way his Father will also raise us in Jesus Christ, we who believe in him, apart from whom we do not have true life. (*Trall.* 9.1–2)

Much of Ignatius's theology of Mary revolves around the affirmation of Jesus' humanity. Mary, as the mother of Jesus, was instrumental in establishing Jesus' humanity. Additionally, while Ignatius affirms Mary's virginal conception of Jesus (*Eph.* 19.1),[29] his letters offer no hints about later theological developments, such as the perpetual virginity of Mary.

To dissuade those in the church who wanted to maintain Jewish ties, Ignatius implored,

> It is outlandish to proclaim Jesus Christ and practice Judaism. For Christianity did not believe in Judaism, but Judaism in Christianity—in which every tongue that believes in God has been gathered together. (*Magn.* 10.3)

---

28. Docetism could mean a denial of humanity, or a denial that Jesus really suffered and died, or both.

29. The virginal conception was not important to Paul, who simply described Jesus as "born of a woman" (Gal 4:4) without any need to defend Jesus' humanity.

Clearly, some Christ-believers saw no problem with retaining some Jewish practices; Ignatius, however, did. In directly and aggressively confronting his opponents, Ignatius maintained what he saw as the purity of the church.

> ### The Ecclesiologies of 1 Peter and Ignatius
>
> The author of First Peter and Ignatius, Bishop of Syria, understood the church differently in relation to Judaism. Whereas Ignatius argued for a complete break from the church's Jewish ties and roots, First Peter rooted his understanding of the church in the image of Israel. In fact, the author sought ways to maintain continuity with the church's Jewish heritage; for example, by connecting Jesus to Israel's prophetic tradition and citing the Hebrew Scriptures to establish the church's legitimacy and normative behavior. First Peter's inclusive approach to understanding the church becomes more evident after reading the letters of Ignatius.

Martyrdom of Polycarp

A letter sent from the congregation of Smyrna to that in Philomelium details the martyrdom of their beloved bishop, the eighty-six year-old "blessed" Polycarp (*Mart. Pol.* 1.1, 9.3, 21.1). The story of Polycarp's death claims to be based on the testimony of eye-witnesses, although many details are also clearly modeled on the Passion of Christ. Like the Passion and death of Jesus, the Christians in Smyrna viewed "all the martyrdoms" and the death of Polycarp in particular as "the will of God," since God "has ultimate authority" (*Mart. Pol.* 2.1).

The *Martyrdom of Polycarp* is actually quite an adventurous story, detailing the search for Polycarp (*Mart. Pol.* 5–6) and his arrest. It bears remarkable similarities to the New Testament Gospel accounts of Jesus' arrest and seizure: for example, the soldiers' search for Polycarp is described like "as if running down a thief" (*Mart. Pol.* 7.1; cf. Matt 26:55); Polycarp's prayer at his arrest that "God's will be done" (*Mart. Pol.* 7.1; cf. Luke 22:42); his entry into the city of Smyrna to face martyrdom "seated . . . on a donkey" ready to face

"Herod, along with his father, Nicetas" (*Mart. Pol.* 8.2; cf. Matt 21:5); and even "a voice from heaven" strengthening Polycarp as he faced death (*Mart. Pol.* 9.1; cf. John 12:28). Those similarities suggest that Jesus' suffering and death came to be interpreted as a model for those Christians who, like Jesus, would be killed for their faith.

During the trial and interrogation before the proconsul (*Mart. Pol.* 10–12), Polycarp remained steadfast, refusing to deny his faith or to "revile Christ": "How can I blaspheme my king who saved me?" (*Mart. Pol.* 9.3; cf. Mark 14:64). As a result, "the entire multitude of both Gentiles and Jews" shouted for Polycarp's execution (*Mart. Pol.* 12.2; cf. Matt 27:23); the order was given by the Roman official Philip to "burn Polycarp alive" (*Mart. Pol.* 12.3; cf. Luke 23:24). Polycarp offered a prayer as he endured his death (*Mart. Pol.* 14.1–3; cf. Luke 23:46). Miraculously, Polycarp's body "could not be consumed by the fire," and so a soldier finally had to kill Polycarp by stabbing him "with a dagger" (*Mart. Pol.* 16.1; cf. John 19:34).[30] Fearful of the heroic martyrdom witnessed by all, the Romans and the Jewish leaders who put Polycarp to death refused to give up his "body" to Polycarp's friends, worried lest "they desert the one who was crucified and begin to worship this one" (*Mart. Pol.* 17.2; cf. John 19:38–42).

Polycarp's martyrdom is depicted in this sixteenth-century fresco from Rome. The *Martyrdom of Polycarp* compares Polycarp in the fire to "gold and silver being refined in a furnace" (15.2)—a possible allusion to 1 Peter 1:7.

---

30. The account of Polycarp's death offers more fanciful details, and Jesus was already dead when stabbed.

The letter draws to a close with a eulogy for the beloved Polycarp: "For he was not only an exceptional teacher but also a superb martyr. Everyone longs to imitate his martyrdom, since it occurred in conformity with the gospel of Christ" (*Mart. Pol.* 19.2). Whereas Jesus' death was the model for Polycarp's martyrdom, Polycarp's death became a model for others. The letter concludes with multiple endings and farewells (*Mart. Pol.* 21–22; cf. John 20:30–31, 21:24–25).

Apology of Quadratus

Eusebius comments that he and others had a copy of the *Apology* that Quadratus, two centuries earlier, had sent to Emperor Hadrian (*Church History* 4.3.1). Unfortunately, the snippet quoted by Eusebius is all that remains. Yet even this small excerpt offers some insights into how Quadratus argued for the legitimacy of the Christian faith.

> ## The Apology of Quadratus
>
> Here is a translation of the whole surviving fragment of the *Apology of Quadratus*, as preserved in Eusebius:
>
> > But the works of our savior were always present, for they were true. Those who were healed and raised from the dead were not only seen when healed and raised, but they were always present—and not just while the savior was here, but even when he had gone they remained for a long time, so that some of them survived even to our own time.

Apparently some critics of the faith challenged the legitimacy of Jesus' miracles ("the works of our savior"), in particular his healing the sick and raising the dead. Quadratus countered that Jesus' powers were real and lasting, for some of those healed and raised by Jesus were still alive in Quadratus's day, as witnessed to and testified by others. The use of the lasting effects of miracles as a "proof" for a defense of the faith continued with second- and third-century

Christian apologists. Justin Martyr, for example, connected Jesus' miracles with contemporary healers and exorcists.[31]

Epistle to Diognetus

The *Epistle to Diognetus* offers a good example of how late second-century apologists defended the faith. In its present form, the writing is a composite work: chapters 1–10 comprise an apology for the faith, which addresses the futility of paganism and Judaism while claiming the superiority of Christianity; chapters 11–12 function more like a homily, offering an interpretation of the Christian faith.

Reminiscent of the prolog to Luke's Gospel (1:1–4), the letter begins with a prolog addressed to "most excellent Diognetus," which could also have served as an invitation to anyone curious about the Christian faith:

> Since I see, most excellent Diognetus, that you are extremely eager to learn about the religion of the Christians and are making such an exacting and careful inquiry about them, wishing to discover which God they obey and how they worship him. (*Diogn.* 1.1)

In explaining the Christian faith, the letter quickly launches into a description of the "misguided habit of thought" of pagan idolatry (*Diogn.* 2.1–10). It makes the case that Christians "do not serve such gods" (*Diogn.* 2.10). Although the letter is less critical of Jews than it is of polytheists,[32] it does disparage the "foolishness" of Judaism, in particular "when they regard him [God] as needing anything" (*Diogn.* 3.3). The author also criticizes Jewish maintaining purity laws, circumcision, and the Sabbath observance, which he views as little more than "vulgar silliness" (*Diogn.* 4.6).

---

31. See James A, Kelhoffer, *Miracle and Mission: The Authentication of Missionaries and Their Message in the Longer Ending of Mark*, WUNT 270 (Tübingen: Mohr Siebeck, 2000), 311–39, for many often overlooked examples from second- and third-century apologists, such as Justin Martyr, Theophilus of Antioch, Irenaeus, Tertullian, and Origen, who spoke about miracles performed by believers and not apostles or other recognized leaders.

32. "Now by abstaining from the kind of divine worship just mentioned, the Jews rightly claim to worship the one God who is over all and to consider him Master" (*Diogn.* 3.1).

After dismissing the folly of paganism and the cultic practices of Judaism, the letter presents the logic and superiority of Christianity (*Diogn.* 5–10). Christians and the church, the author claims, blend well into the larger society, live peacefully among all citizens (*Diogn.* 5.1–10), and respond with blessings when they are reviled for their beliefs (*Diogn.* 5.11–17). The letter underscores the irony that the Christians "love all people, and by all people are persecuted" (*Diogn.* 5.11).

> ### Defending the Faith to Outsiders through Social Conformity
>
> Both the authors of 1 Peter and the *Epistle to Diognetus* employed similar strategies in surviving within the larger world of the Roman Empire. Both argue that believers should conform to the norms of the social and political institutions of the day, and not retaliate against hostile actions from outsiders. In doing so, it was believed, Christians could demonstrate that they were not a threat to the Roman Empire. In effect, the author of the *Epistle to Diognetus* urged the same course of action advocated by 1 Peter some fifty years earlier, suggesting that this technique had a longstanding record of success in helping Christians to survive in a world sometimes hostile to their beliefs and practices.

The letter presents the Christian faith as reflecting an orderliness in the creation that God established from the beginning:

> But the truly all-powerful God himself, creator of all and invisible, set up and established in their hearts the truth and the holy word from heaven, which cannot be comprehended by humans. (*Diogn.* 7.2)

This understanding—that Christianity reflects God's created order—provides the letter with an opening to present its Christology: God "sent him [Jesus]" to humans (*Diogn.* 7.2), God sent Jesus "as [a] God" (*Diogn.* 7.4), and as a matter of fact, before Jesus came, no person "had any idea what God was like" (*Diogn.* 8.1). Referring to Jesus as God's "beloved child" (*Diogn.* 8.8, 11, 9.1) and "Son of God"

(*Diogn.* 9.2, 4, 10.2), the letter affirms that God's message came solely in and through Christ: God "communicated it to his child alone" (*Diogn.* 8.9).

Chapters 1–10 end abruptly in the middle of remarks about heaven and hell. Chapters 11–12 are completely different in tone and topic and read like a homily. The text speaks in the first person singular ("I") throughout, but most scholars suspect separate authors for chapters 1–10 and 11–12.[33] In chapters 11–12, Jesus is "the word" who has revealed "the mysteries of the Father" (*Diogn.* 11.3); as a result, the church is "enriched" and filled with "grace" (*Diogn.* 11.5, 7). The *Epistle to Diognetus* concludes with a brief meditation on Genesis 2–3 and the tree of the knowledge of good and evil (with which Adam and Eve disobeyed God), with God's good work better understood with the knowledge of Christ (*Diogn.* 12.1–9).

> ## Summary: Overview of Ignatius's Letters, the *Martyrdom of Polycarp*, *Quadratus*, and *Diognetus*
>
> ### CORE CONCEPTS
> - The letters of Ignatius are concerned with his impending martyrdom, church unity, and the need to obey the church's approved leaders rather than false teachers.
> - The *Martyrdom of Polycarp* is modeled after the Gospel Passion narratives.
> - The *Epistle to Diognetus* defends the faith both by attacking opponents and by claiming the superiority of Christianity.
>
> ### SUPPLEMENTAL INFORMATION
> - Ignatius criticized the belief of some Christians who denied the humanity of Jesus.
>
> *Continued*

---

33. See Foster, 156. See also Clayton A. Jefford, *The Epistle to Diognetus (with the Fragment of Quadratus): Introduction, Text, and Commentary* (Oxford: Oxford University Press, 2013), 15–29, for a good discussion of date, location, and authorship of the *Epistle of Diognetus*.

> **Summary: Overview** *Continued*
>
> - Ignatius's *Letter to the Romans* deals primarily with his upcoming martyrdom.
> - Polycarp was eighty-six years old when he was martyred.
> - Only a small fragment from Quadratus's apology survives.
> - The fragment from Quadratus defends the faith by arguing that some of those healed and raised by Jesus were still alive when Quadratus wrote.
> - The *Epistle to Diognetus* in its present form consists of two separate documents: chapters 1–10 (an apology) and chapters 11–12 (a homily).

Questions for Review

1. Why do most scholars consider 1 Peter a pseudonymous writing?
2. What kinds of suffering and persecution did the recipients of 1 Peter experience?
3. What are the main similarities between 1 Peter and the letters and theology of Paul? Would you regard 1 Peter as an updating of Paul, due to a situation of persecution that Paul himself had not anticipated for Gentile Christians?
4. How does 1 Peter speak about the eschaton (end time) in relation to believers' current situation?
5. What situations or problems does 1 Peter and these writings of the Apostolic Fathers address?
6. What are some similarities and differences between the ecclesiologies of 1 Peter and Ignatius?
7. What was Ignatius's view on the roles of the bishop, the presbyters, and the deacons?
8. List five similarities between the suffering of Jesus, as presented in the Gospels, and Polycarp's suffering, in the *Martyrdom of Polycarp*. How is Christ a model for Polycarp, and how does Polycarp become a model for other believers who suffer?

9. How does Quadratus refer to miracles in defending the legitimacy of Christianity?
10. According to the *Epistle to Diognetus*, how is Christianity superior to both polytheistic religions and Judaism?

Questions for Reflection

1. What is your reaction to 1 Peter's ethical imperative, "Be holy because I [am] holy"?
2. Is the message of 1 Peter still applicable to Christians suffering persecution today? What sufferings should religious people be willing to undergo today for God or the common good?
3. In your view, is Ignatius of Antioch's eagerness to die for his faith a model for the faith? Why or why not?
4. What do you find most compelling in the story of the *Martyrdom of Polycarp*?

Recommendations for Further Reading
The First Letter of Peter

Elliott, John H. *Conflict, Community and Honor: 1 Peter in Social-Scientific Perspective*. Eugene, OR: Cascade Books, 2007.

> This short, two-essay book ("Estrangement and Community" and "Disgraced Yet Graced") is a follow-up to Elliott's groundbreaking analysis of 1 Peter in *Home for the Homeless: A Sociological Exegesis of 1 Peter, Its Situation, and Strategy* (Philadelphia: Fortress, 1981). Elliott applies social-scientific analysis to the specifically moral discourse and the cultural values of honor and shame to show how 1 Peter is a pastoral letter addressed to early Christian communities alienated from their surroundings.

Green, Joel B. *1 Peter*. THNTC. Grand Rapids: Eerdmans, 2007.

> Green begins with a brief introduction ("Orientation") that sets 1 Peter within its historical and theological context. He then provides a readable line-by-line commentary. Green concludes with a section called "Theological Horizons" that focuses on various aspects of this text, ranging from Peter's perspective on suffering to his understanding of anthropology and salvation.

Horrell, David G. *1 Peter.* New York: T&T Clark, 2008.

> Horrell offers a brief but helpful historical and theological introduction to 1 Peter. He places the letter within its social and cultural context, addressing such topics as the letter's literary form and intended audience as well as the role of suffering in the formation of Christian identity. The volume concludes with some reflections on how contemporary readings can relate to the theology and ethics of 1 Peter.

Four Writings of the Apostolic Fathers

Castelli, Elizabeth A. *Martyrdom and Memory: Early Christian Culture Making.* New York: Columbia University Press, 2004.

> Castelli's study focuses on the early Christian martyrs (with an extended discussion of Ignatius and Polycarp) and the role they played in the development of Christian ideas. She offers the intriguing thesis that martyrs are "produced" less by the actual historical events associated with their persecution and more by the stories told later about them by the tradition.

Jefford, Clayton N. *The Epistle to Diognetus (with the Fragment of Quadratus): Introduction, Text, and Commentary.* Oxford: Oxford University Press, 2013.

> As the subtitle indicates, Jefford offers an extended introduction to the historical setting of these two texts, including a discussion of their theology and themes as well as how these texts relate to Scripture. He argues that the *Epistle to Diognetus* is one of the earliest examples of Christian apologetic literature.

CHAPTER 3

Second Peter, Jude, 1, 2, and 3 John, and Early Christian Letters

INTRODUCTION

Chapter 3 examines seven different early Christian letters. Second Peter, 1–3 John, and Jude were eventually included in the New Testament. *First Clement* and Polycarp's *Epistle to the Philippians* were not; they are today grouped with the writings of the Apostolic Fathers. Together, these seven texts provide a good sampling of early Christian letters, a popular form of communication between early Christian leaders and their congregations. Their purposes range from persuasion and support to instruction and admonition.

These letters fall easily into three groups, which correspond to this chapter's three sections. Part one examines 2 Peter and Jude, both of which focus on dealing with trouble-makers in their communities and have a clear literary interdependency. Part two investigates the three letters of John, which, along with the Gospel of John, are commonly associated with the Johannine community. Part three explores *1 Clement* and Polycarp's *Epistle to the Philippians*, two letters that reflect some of the tensions in leadership of the early Christian communities. As in previous chapters, each part presents an overview of the historical context of these writings (author, intended audience, date, and place of composition) and a summary of its contents. In addition, the theology and ethics of each will also be discussed.

Multiple Forms and Functions

These seven early Christian "letters" exhibit a significant amount of flexibility in form and function. On the one hand, each is traditionally referred to as a "letter" because it has certain epistolary elements, such as an identified sender and receiver and a body. On the other hand, the way these letters function varies considerably. For example, in some cases an identified individual is writing to a specific Christian congregation (2 John, 3 John, and the *Epistle to the Philippians*), while in others the author is pseudonymous or anonymous (Jude, 2 Peter, 1 John, and *1 Clement*) and writes either to specifically identified communities (*1 Clement*) or to unspecified communities (Jude, 2 Peter, and 1 John). While the length of each varies, 2 and 3 John are unusually short compared with other New Testament letters, closer to the typical length of an ancient letter.[1]

Dissenters and False Teachers

These letters mention a number of recurring issues, one of which is the problem of dissenters within the congregation. The author of 1 John castigates such dissenters, calling them "antichrists" (1 John 2:18–19). *First Clement* reprimands the "one or two persons" within the church in Corinth who create a "faction against" its elders and considers the existence of factions and divisions within the community "exceedingly shameful" (47.2–6). Jude speaks of "intruders" (v. 4) "who cause divisions; they live . . . devoid of the Spirit" (v. 19). The author of 3 John names one dissenter by name, Diotrephes, accusing him of "spreading evil nonsense about us" (vv.9–10). Jude and 2 Peter even refer to those who dissent as "irrational animals" (Jude 10; 2 Pet 2:12) and "accursed children" (2 Pet 2:14). Interestingly, each of these letters presumes that its version of Christianity is normative and that the false teachers are corrupting the pure faith. To what extent the so-called "heretics" may actually have based their beliefs on older Christian traditions is a matter of considerable debate in New Testament scholarship today.

---

1. See Judith Lieu, *The Second and Third Epistles of John: History and Background*, Studies of the New Testament and Its World (Edinburgh: T&T Clark, 1986), 38: "2 and 3 John alone in the New Testament conform to these standards of brevity; each would probably just fill a papyrus sheet."

In addition to dissenters, these letters also reflect considerable worry about Christian leaders who spread false teachings and who are perceived as negatively impacting the community. Many of these "false teachings" are Christological in nature and appear to be early forms of Docetism (from the Greek *dokein*, "to seem"), teachings that denied Jesus' humanity, or denied that Jesus really suffered and died, or both.[2] The false teachings addressed in these books range from the rejection of belief in Jesus as the Christ (1 John 2:22; Jude 4) to a denial that Jesus came "in the flesh" (1 John 4:2; 2 John 7; Pol. *Phil.* 7.1) or that he would one day return (2 Pet 3:4). References to and warnings against destructive factions (2 Pet 2:1) and those who consider themselves as "progressive" (2 John 9) may also reflect concerns over an undue influence from the pagan environment in general.

PART 1: THE LETTER OF JUDE AND THE SECOND LETTER OF PETER
Historical Context

The internal evidence available from Jude and 2 Peter offers only minimal information about their historical context, such as the identity of the author, the audience, and the date and place of composition. Information gleaned from external sources, such as other New Testament books and the writings of the early Church Fathers, offer some additional clues to the historical background of these texts.

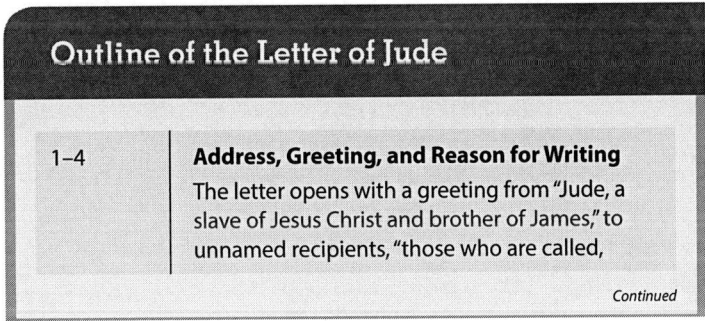

Outline of the Letter of Jude

1–4	Address, Greeting, and Reason for Writing
	The letter opens with a greeting from "Jude, a slave of Jesus Christ and brother of James," to unnamed recipients, "those who are called,

Continued

---

2. Docetism is an umbrella term for different "heresies." But it also refers to one particular Christological debate about the humanity of Jesus.

	Outline of the Letter of Jude *Continued*
1–4	beloved in God the Father and kept safe for Jesus Christ." The author then states his reason for writing: some "intruders" are denying "our only Master and Lord, Jesus Christ."
5–16	**Criticism of False Teachers** The body of the letter is meant to "remind" the recipients of stories from the Old Testament and Jewish apocryphal texts (the *Assumption of Moses* and the *Apocalypse of Enoch*) that speak of divine retribution on those who had gravely sinned (fallen angels, the inhabitants of Sodom and Gomorrah, and even the devil) and of prophesies warning of false teachers who can be identified by their bad moral conduct.
17–23	**Reminder of the Apostles' Warning** The letter then reminds the recipients of the warning, passed on by the original apostles, about those who would "cause divisions" within the community. The letter calls believers to focus on faith, prayer, love, and mercy "on those who waver."
24–25	**Concluding Hymn of Praise** Although not typical of the genre of an ancient letter, the author concludes with a hymn of praise, or doxology, to "the only God, our savior, through Jesus Christ our Lord," the only one who keeps believers from "stumbling."

Author

Both Jude and 2 Peter claim authorship by known figures within the first generation of Christianity. Jude opens with the line "Jude, a slave of Jesus Christ and brother of James" (Jude 1), while 2 Peter begins "Symeon Peter, a slave and apostle of Jesus Christ"

(2 Pet 1:1). In addition to Judas Iscariot, the New Testament writings mention three men with the name "Jude" (Judas): Jude, the "brother" of Jesus and James (Matt 13:55; Mark 6:3); "Judas, the son of James," one of the twelve apostles (Luke 6:16; John 14:22; Acts 1:13); and Judas Barsabbas (Act 15:22, 27, 32). Since only one is recorded as having a familial connection to James, the author seems to present himself as Jude the brother of Jesus and James. Arguing against the inference that the historical Jude wrote this letter, however, is the high quality of the Greek used

Jude 14–15 quotes a passage from *Enoch* as if it were sacred scripture. *Enoch* survives in its entirety only in Ethiopic, as in this elaborate fifteenth-century manuscript. The Ethiopic Church is the only denomination to recognize the book of *Enoch* as canonical.

in the letter, combined with indications of a later date of composition: references to traditions "handed down to the holy ones" (v. 3), and the exhortation to "remember" the past apostles, who, presumably, had died long ago (v. 17). Most scholars conclude that this letter is, in fact, composed by an unknown author writing in the name of Jude; it is another example of New Testament pseudepigraphical writing.[3] The use of Old Testament stories and Jewish apocryphal sources to

---

3. See Daniel J. Harrington, *1 Peter, Jude and 2 Peter*, SP 15 (Collegeville, MN: Liturgical Press, 2003), 182; Helmut Koester, *History and Literature of Early Christianity*, 2nd ed. (New York and Berlin: W. de Gruyter, 1982, 2000), 162; Darian Lockett, *An Introduction to the Catholic Epistles* (New York: T&T Clark, 2012), 77; Udo Schnelle, *The History and Theology of the New Testament Writings*, trans. M. Eugene Boring (London: SCM, 1998), 417; Bart D. Ehrman, *The New Testament: A Historical Introduction to the Early Christian Writings*, 6th ed. (New York and Oxford: Oxford University Press, 2016), 523.

confront the false teachers (who themselves are Christ-believers) suggests that the author is probably a Jewish Christian.[4]

Outline of 2 Peter

1:1–2	**Greeting** The letter opens with a greeting from "Symeon Peter, a slave and apostle of Jesus Christ," to unnamed recipients, "those who have received a faith of equal value to ours."
1:3–21	**Christian Conduct and Peter's Final Witness** The body of the letter begins with a discussion of the divine power and promises bestowed on believers. It then lists various behaviors and dispositions that should supplement one's faith,[5] beginning with virtue and culminating in love. The letter speaks of Peter's impending "departure," implying that the letter serves as a final statement from the Apostle Peter, and reminds its recipients that the apostles did not follow "cleverly devised myths."
2:1–22	**Criticism of False Teachers** The letter then launches into a direct attack against "false teachers" within the congregation who "introduce" destructive ideas. The author cites two Old Testament examples (Noah and the flood, and Lot and Sodom and Gomorrah) as proof of divine retribution for significant sin. The letter continues its denunciation of the false teachers, referring to their return to former ways

Continued

---

4. Harrington, 183; Schnelle, 417.

5. A subtle but significant shift has occurred here with the use of the term "faith." Whereas with Paul, faith referred to "faith in Christ," in 2 Peter (and in Jude), faith refers to "faith in correct teaching."

> **Outline of 2 Peter** *Continued*
>
> | | |
> |---|---|
> | 2:1–22 | of thinking with a proverbial saying, "The dog returns to his own vomit." |
> | 3:1–16 | **Warning against Denial of the Return of Christ**
 A significant portion of the letter is devoted to criticism of a specific false teaching: denial that Christ will return. The letter argues that the "delay" of the Parousia is rooted in God's desire and it advocates patience, so "that all should come to repentance." While waiting, believers should conduct themselves "in holiness and devotion." |
> | 3:17–18 | **Conclusion**
 The letter draws to a close with a warning to "be on your guard not to be led into . . . error" by these false teachers, followed by a short hymn of praise (a doxology). |

The author of 2 Peter clearly intends to portray himself as Peter the apostle who is here making a final statement prior to his death (2 Pet 1:1, 13–15). He presents himself as a witness to Jesus being transfigured and having an encounter with Moses and Elijah on a mountain (1:17–19; see Matt 17:1–8; Mark 9:2–8; Luke 9:28–36) and even appears to refer back to 1 Peter, commenting on the current letter (2 Peter) as "the second letter I am writing to you" (2 Pet 3:1). However, nearly all scholars today agree that 2 Peter, like 1 Peter,[6] is pseudonymous and not written by the apostle himself. The extensive

---

6. Recall from chapter 2 that features in 1 Peter, such as the sophisticated Greek and the rhetorical style of the letter, the citation of Old Testament texts primarily from the Greek translation and not from the Hebrew (as would be expected from a Palestinian Jew), and the letter's lack of direct references to Peter's extended interactions with the historical Jesus (a strange omission from one of Jesus' closest apostles), all point to this letter being a pseudonymous work.

use of the letter of Jude (dated toward the end of the first century or early second century), references to "ancestors" falling asleep *subsequent to* the time of Jesus and the first apostles (3:4), and the significant difference in content and writing style between 1 and 2 Peter all support the inference that an otherwise unknown author wrote in the apostle's name.[7]

The Literary Relationship between Jude and 2 Peter

A strong parallel of content and vocabulary exists between Jude 4–18 and 2 Peter 2:1–3:3, as can be seen by comparing the following passages:

Jude	2 Peter
v. 4	2:1–3
v. 6	2:4
v. 7	2:6
v. 8	2:10a
v. 9	2:11
v. 10	2:12
v. 11	2:15
v. 12	2:13
v. 12–13	2:17
v. 16	2:18
v. 17	3:1–2
v. 18	3:3

Continued

---

7. Harrington, 236; Koester, 299; Schnelle, 426; Ehrman, 524. Harrington (ibid.) and Koester (ibid.) point out, moreover, that the use of Greek proverbs (2:22) and Greek expressions (for example, to "share in the divine nature," 1:4) suggest that the author was a Hellenistic Jewish Christian.

> **The Literary Relationship between Jude and 2 Peter** *Continued*
>
> For example,
>
> > In the last time there will be scoffers who will live according to their own godless desires. (Jude 18)
> >
> > Know this first of all, that in the last days scoffers will come to scoff, living according to their own desires. (2 Peter 3:3)
>
> Many instances of borrowing show a pattern of recycling and adapting the polemics in Jude to fit the social and theological situation addressed in 2 Peter. Most scholars today believe that Jude was composed first and that the author of 2 Peter used some material from Jude when constructing his letter. Scholars base this conclusion on how they believe the author of 2 Peter redacted or edited the letter of Jude.
>
> - 2 Peter 2:4–10 modifies the chronological order of Old Testament examples cited by Jude 5–7, thereby correcting the sequence.
> - 2 Peter 2:4–10 adds material on Noah and Lot to emphasize God's mercy.
> - 2 Peter drops the citations from Jewish apocrypha, specifically the *Assumption of Moses* (Jude 9) and the *Apocalypse of Enoch* (Jude 14–15).
>
> While the author of 2 Peter borrows material about the danger of the "false teachers" from Jude, he criticizes his Christ-believing opponents on different grounds than those invoked in the Letter to Jude.

Date, Audience, and Place of Composition

Most scholars date the composition of the Letter of Jude toward the end of the first century,[8] generally citing three reasons. First, the pseudonym, "Jude, the brother of James" would still have had meaning in the living memory of the early church toward the

---

8. Harrington, 183; Koester, 252; Schnelle, 418; Ehrman, 524.

end of the first century[9] and would have afforded the letter apostolic authority. Second, other New Testament pseudepigraphical literature was being produced during the time period (for example, 1 Peter, Colossians, Ephesians, 2 Thessalonians, 1 and 2 Timothy, and Titus). And third, 2 Peter 2:1–3:3 bears witness to the existence of the Letter of Jude, showing literary dependence; clearly Jude was written before 2 Peter, but it need not have been written much earlier. If, however, one assumes a late date of composition for 2 Peter, that opens up the possibility that Jude may very well date to a later time period, with many arguing for the early second century, roughly 120–140.

The dating of 2 Peter, in turn, is directly dependent on the date of composition of Jude, since it was clearly written after Jude. Internal evidence also supports a rather late date; this includes such evidence as 2 Peter's discussion of the collection of Paul's letters as "scripture" (a process of collection that would have taken some time to develop) as well as its mention of Paul's authority (3:15–16). Further, references in 2 Peter 1:17–18, 3:2 may well reflect an awareness of the written Gospels (dated roughly 70–100). For these reasons, scholars date 2 Peter to the early second century, sometime after the Letter of Jude.[10] This time frame, if accurate, would make 2 Peter the latest of the writings included in the New Testament, dating to perhaps as late as 140.

Neither Jude nor 2 Peter offers any solid internal evidence about intended recipients. Although both pseudonymous authors write about specific concerns (for example, influential false teachers) within their congregations, the communities to which they write cannot be identified with any degree of certainty.[11] Likewise, neither

---

9. Koester, 252; Schnelle, 418.

10. Koester, 300; Schnelle, 426; Harrington, 237; Ehrman, 524.

11. Since one author appears to be a Jewish Christian (Jude) and the other a Hellenistic Jewish Christian (2 Peter), it is possible that the communities are primarily comprised of Jewish Christians (see Lockett, 80). However, if 2 Peter was written for the same congregations as 1 Peter (believers living in five Roman provinces covering much of Asia Minor), then a Gentile Christian community would seem the more likely intended recipients of this letter (Schnelle, 427; Lockett, 83).

letter includes any direct internal evidence about where it was composed. As a result, scholars concede the impossibility of identifying a location for Jude[12] and 2 Peter.[13]

> ### Peter's Letters and the Canon
>
> From very early in Christian tradition, major church figures considered the Apostle Peter the author of 1 Peter but challenged the authenticity of 2 Peter. For example, Origen of Alexandria (as quoted by fourth-century church historian Eusebius of Caesarea) reports that, already in the early third century, some Christians doubted that the Apostle Peter wrote 2 Peter:
>
>> And Peter . . . has left one acknowledged epistle; perhaps also a second, but this is doubtful. (*Church History* 6.25.8)
>
> Eusebius himself also apparently believed that Peter wrote 1 Peter (*Church History* 4.14.9). He classifies 2 Peter as a "disputed book," but acknowledged it "appears useful" to many Christians (*Church History* 3.3.1) even though "we have not received [2 Peter] as canonical" (*Church History* 3.25.3). The differences in vocabulary and style between 1 and 2 Peter, suggesting two different authors, seem to have contributed to the ongoing doubts that the Apostle Peter wrote both of them.

---

12. For the Letter of Jude, Asia Minor, Syria, or Palestine are plausible locations: Asia Minor, given Jude's similar position on angels (vv. 6, 8) to that of Colossians 2:18–19, a letter probably composed in southwest Asia Minor (Schnelle, 418); Syria (Koester, 252); or Palestine (Harrington, 183), with the letter attributed to Jude, the brother of Jesus and James, an area linked to Jesus' family.

13. For 2 Peter, Rome or Egypt are sometimes identified as possible places of composition. In favor of Rome is the pseudonymous use of Peter (2 Pet 1:1), the mention of Paul (2 Pet 3:15–16), and the association of Rome with Peter and Paul (Harrington, 236). Egypt has been suggested because the *Apocalypse of Peter*, which many scholars believe was composed in Egypt, uses 2 Peter (Schnelle, 426–27).

> ## Historical Setting of 2 Peter and Jude
>
> These two pseudonymous writings divulge fewer details about their origin and historical setting than do the early Christian writings discussed in chapters 1–2.
>
> | | |
> |---|---|
> | Author | Jude: unknown person who wrote in the name of Jude two or three generations after the first apostles.

Second Peter: unknown person who wrote in the name of the Apostle Peter three or four generations after the first apostle; this author is to be distinguished from the pseudonymous author of 1 Peter. |
> | Audience | unknown; neither letter provides evidence for its intended audiences. |
> | Date of Composition | Jude: range between end of first century to 140.

Second Peter: after Jude. |
> | Place of Composition | unknown; no internal or external evidence provided. |

Theology and Ethics of Jude and 2 Peter

Even a New Testament letter as short as Jude, which runs just twenty-five verses, presents a distinct theology and ethical vision. The author of Jude appeals to beliefs about Jesus (Christology) and about the church (ecclesiology) to confront what he views as the immoral and unethical behavior of the "intruders." In 2 Peter, another short New Testament letter, the author likewise weaves theology and ethics into the correspondence. Second Peter confronts the "false teachers" about their views on the end time (eschatology) and Christology, and in doing so, presents a set of ethical expectations for believers.

Theology and Ethics of Jude

In terms of its ecclesiology, the Letter of Jude grounds its community in a developing tradition and "faith that was once for all handed down to the holy ones" (v. 3). This tradition has apostolic roots ("remember the words spoken beforehand by the apostles," v. 17) and forms the basis of the congregation's Christian identity ("build yourselves up in your most holy faith," v. 20). The faith and tradition received from the beginning highlights the fact that the teachings of the "intruders," which "deny our only Master and Lord, Jesus Christ" (v. 4), is a destructive and erroneous Christology. Jude counters with a Christology that affirms Jesus' eternal divinity and lordship (vv. 4, 8, 17, 21, 25) and upholds the belief in the return of Christ and impending judgment, especially on the unbelievers (vv. 14–15). In the Parousia, the "mercy of our Lord Jesus Christ" will lead believers to "eternal life" (v. 21). Notably, the pseudonymous author of Jude presents himself as belonging to that first generation of authoritative leaders who "handed down" (v. 3) the orthodox beliefs from which these teachers have strayed and that serve as the basis for critiquing them. Without his recourse to pseudonymity, the author may have, rhetorically speaking, been in a weaker position to voice opposition to rival Christian leaders.

In addition to claiming an ecclesiological precedent, the Letter of Jude also challenges the "intruders" because of their bad moral conduct. The author harshly criticizes the outsiders who "pervert the grace of our God into licentiousness [undisciplined and immoral behavior]" (v. 4), characterizing them as non-believers who "defile the flesh" (v. 8), are self-serving (v. 12), take "advantage" of gullible people (v. 16), and behave as "scoffers who . . . live according to their own godless desires" (v. 18). Although troubling to the author, these very general accusations do not provide modern readers with much insight about what, specifically, the author of Jude viewed as deficient in his opponents' actions.

In response to the danger of their bad example, Jude calls the faithful in his community to be grounded in the faith received by the apostles and to "pray in the holy Spirit" (v. 20). He counsels, "Keep yourselves in the love of God" (v. 21) and "have mercy" on those who "waver" (v. 22), but be cautious about those upon whom you show mercy (v. 23).

> ### The "Intruders" of Jude and "False Teachers" of 2 Peter
>
> Various types of people were causing disturbances and divisions within the communities of Jude and 2 Peter. The names used to identify these trouble-makers ("intruders" and "false teachers") offer some clues as to their identity. Most scholars view these opponents as distinct groups.
>
> In Jude, the "intruders" are presented as an *outside group* that has penetrated and, perhaps, subverted the community. The letter draws a sharp distinction between the insiders and outsiders. For the insiders, the author uses the second person plural pronoun ("you all") and affirmative language, calling them "beloved" (vv. 3, 17, 20) and "unblemished" (v. 24). For the outsiders, however, Jude employs the third person plural pronoun ("they") and dehumanizing, derogatory words: "godless persons" (v. 4), "irrational animals" (v. 10), "waterless clouds" (v. 12), and "disgruntled ones" (v. 16). The author attacks these intruders for their moral and ethical teachings. They are said to reject the moral authority of Christ (vv. 4, 8) and the apostles (vv. 17–18), to engage in immoral sexual behavior (vv. 7–8, 10), and to do so out of greed (vv. 11–12). The illicit and immoral sexual behavior of the "intruders" even impacts their communal meals (v. 12). Historically speaking, it must be acknowledged that whether the opponents actually were outsiders, rather than insiders who competed with this pseudonymous author, is unknowable. The characterization of opponents as recently arrived outsiders who do not stand in line with the apostles' faith (cf. v. 3) could be rhetorical rather than historical.
>
> In 2 Peter, the "false teachers" are presented as an *inside group*, community members who have broken away from the congregation (2:20–22) and have now formed "destructive" factions (2:1). They have abandoned the "straight road . . . and
>
> *Continued*

> **The "Intruders"** *Continued*
>
> have gone astray" (2:15). The author of 2 Peter denounces them as "bold and arrogant" (2:10b). He calls them "stains and defilements," people who "seduce" weaker community members into following their teachings (2:13–14) and have attracted "many" followers from within the community (2:2). The acknowledgement of people who, in the author's view, should be unwelcome at common meals, which likely included the Eucharist, clearly points to an internal problem within this congregation. None other than the Apostle Peter is needed to counteract the threat posed by the rival leaders, which is why the author wrote in Peter's name. The letter views the theological teachings of the false teachers as the real threat. Apparently, because they deny the return of Christ (3:4, 9) and any future divine judgment, followers of these false teachers are "free" to engage in immoral behavior ("licentious desires of the flesh," 2:18–19).

Theology and Ethics of 2 Peter

In the letter's greeting, the author of 2 Peter states his reason for writing: to help the recipients gain "knowledge of God and of Jesus our Lord" (1:2). To that end, much of the letter's theology focuses on events associated with the end times, the eschaton. The supposed "delay" of the end times and doubts about the eventual return of Christ (3:9)—which represented a different eschatology from the author of 2 Peter—lie at the heart of the "destructive" ideas being taught by the "false teachers" (2:1). Second Peter refutes their teachings by asserting, "We [Peter and the apostles] possess the prophetic message that is altogether reliable" (1:19). The author dismisses the "personal interpretation" of scripture by the false teachers as unreliable since it differs from the apostles' message (1:20–21).

As for the delay of Jesus' return, 2 Peter considers this a misperception by the false teachers. While the "scoffers" ask, "Where is the promise of his coming?" (3:3–4), they do not experience time as God does: "With the Lord one day is like a thousand years and a thousand years like one day" (3:8). What feels like a long time for the false teachers is a very brief time for the Lord and for believers. In fact, the so-called "delay" actually reflects God's mercy, since the false teachers have additional time to repent (3:9).

The author of 2 Peter alleges that the false teachers' different eschatology amounts to a "denial" of their common "Master" (2:1). The "false teachers" were apparently Christ-believers who had a different eschatology and who interpreted (some collection of) Paul's letters differently (3:15–16). The author of 2 Peter alludes to the misuse of Paul's letters among the rival leaders: "In them [Paul's letters] there are some things hard to understand that the ignorant and unstable distort to their own destruction, just as they do with the other scriptures" (3:16). Clearly 2 Peter warns others here against the dangers of misinterpretation that exist in Paul's letters. It is precisely because they shared so many common beliefs about Jesus (Christology) that there was friction within the congregation, including at common meals.

> **Views on the End Times**
>
> Different expectations of the end times are evidenced among various New Testament authors. For example, whereas Paul's authentic letters express a keen sense of the imminent return of Christ (see, for example, 1 Thess 4:13–5:11; 1 Cor 15:23–52), the deutero-Pauline First Letter of Timothy views the Parousia as a distant event set in the unknown future (see 1 Tim 6:11–16). The eschatology of 2 Peter, with its position that "the day of the Lord" will arrive in the indeterminate future (2 Pet 3:8–10), is closer to that of 1 Timothy. Even the community to whom 2 Peter writes was divided by their differing views of the end times.

In terms of the ethics espoused in 2 Peter, the letter opens by promoting various behaviors and dispositions that should supplement the believer's faith, beginning with "virtue," including knowledge, self-control, endurance, devotion, and "love" (1:5–8). For 2 Peter, these ethical guidelines ground believers "in the knowledge of our Lord Jesus Christ" (1:8). The author of the letter warns believers, "Be on your guard" against false teachings (3:17). They should conduct themselves in "holiness and devotion" (3:11), be "eager" for the "coming of the day of God" (3:12), and be found "at peace" when Christ returns (3:14).

> ## Summary: Theology and Ethics in First Peter
>
> ### CORE CONCEPTS
> - Both Jude and 2 Peter are pseudonymous writings.
> - Jude attacks his opponents more on ethical grounds than for their theological doctrine.
> - The author's theology in 2 Peter is driven by the desire to correct "false" teachings about Christ and his return.
>
> ### SUPPLEMENTAL INFORMATION
> - The Letter of Jude was composed as late as 120–140, with 2 Peter written sometime after Jude.
> - The author of 2 Peter used and adapted material from Jude's harsh criticisms of some Christians to compose his letter, which likewise criticizes other believers' faulty beliefs about eschatology.
> - Neither Jude nor 2 Peter provides any direct evidence for their place of composition or a profile of their intended audiences.
> - Jude sees the immoral and unethical behavior of the "intruders," who are said to have come from outside the congregation, as the main threat.
> - Second Peter teaches the delay of the Parousia actually reflects God's mercy.
> - The author of 2 Peter asserts that faith should be supplemented with high ethical standards of conduct.

PART 2: THE FIRST, SECOND, AND THIRD LETTERS OF JOHN

The first, second, and third letters of John offer limited internal evidence as to their historical setting in terms of author, audience, date, and place of composition. Scholars have relied in large measure upon external evidence (the witness of the Church Fathers) in establishing the historical context of these three letters. Additionally, virtually all scholars acknowledge literary and thematic parallels between these three Johannine letters and the Gospel of John. The similarities between the Gospel and 1 John are especially striking. It is common today, therefore, for scholars to speak of the Gospel and Letters of John as emanating from a "Johannine school."[14]

The Existence and Location of a Johannine School

A principal reason that scholars argue for the existence of a Johannine school is the common vocabulary found among the four Johannine writings—terms such as "love," "know," "commandment," "hate," "world," and "remain," which are less prominent in other New Testament writings. These texts also speak of church members in similar ways, referring to them as "friends," "brothers/sisters," and "children/children of God." In addition, the Gospel and letters also share certain themes, such as the unity of Father and Son, the dualism between God and the world, the command to love, the images of light and darkness, and knowing the truth.[15] Furthermore, in John 21, which is a later addition to this Gospel, the affirmation that "we know that his testimony is true" (John 21:24b) may well refer to the leader of the Johannine school.

Irenaeus (second-century) and Eusebius (fourth-century) claim the city of Ephesus as the place of composition of the Gospel of John.[16] Polycarp, writing from the city of Smyrna (a neighboring church near Ephesus in Asia Minor), knows of at least two of the Johannine writings; he quotes 1 John 4:2–3 and 2 John 7 in his *Epistle to the Philippians* 7.1. Based on this limited external evidence from tradition, and absent any internal evidence to the contrary, some scholars point to the city of Ephesus as the location of the Johannine school.[17] It is possible

---

14. See, for example, John Painter, *1, 2, and 3 John*, SP 18 (Collegeville, MN: Liturgical Press, 2002), 58–61; Schnelle, 434–39; Ehrman, 196–98.

15. Painter, 61–73, provides an extended discussion and many charts on the literary and thematic parallels between these Johannine writings. See also Schnelle, 434–36.

16. Irenaeus, *Against Heresies* 3.1.2, 2.22.5, 3.3.4; Eusebius, *Church History* 3.23.3–4.

17. Schnelle, 438.

that the Johannine school, which produced the Gospel and letters of John, prepared these writings for a cluster of churches, the "Johannine community" located in various cities of Asia Minor.

The Historical Context of 1, 2, and 3 John
Author and Audience

Both 2 John and 3 John claim to be sent by "the Elder" (or "Presbyter"),[18] and together, these letters offer something of a profile of this author. As implied by his title, he apparently held a leadership position that involved overseeing this community or perhaps several communities. In 2 John he indicates an awareness of potential trouble in at least one of the churches that comprised the larger Johannine community (vv. 7–11). In 3 John the Elder speaks of his authority being challenged in one of the churches (v. 9), his willingness to confront those who challenge him (v. 10a), and the problem of this church's refusal to receive visiting leaders whom he had asked them to welcome (v. 10b).

Outline of the Second Letter of John

1–3	**Greeting and Blessing** The letter opens with a greeting from the "Presbyter" (i.e., the "Elder") to "the chosen Lady and to her children," along with a blessing of "grace, mercy, and peace."
4–6	**Praise for the Congregation** Having heard how some members are "walking in the Truth," the author praises "the Lady" and reminds the congregation to love one another and follow God's commandments.

Continued

---

18. The term "elder" means an "older man," which in the ancient world could have designated a man in his thirties or, as the name suggests, "older."

> **Outline of the Second Letter of John** *Continued*
>
> | | |
> |---|---|
> | 7–11 | **Warning against "Deceivers"**
 The Elder warns against any association with Christ-believing "deceivers" who deny "Jesus Christ as coming in the flesh." He describes them as "deceitful," even using the term "antichrist," and strongly condemns such views as "progressive . . . doctrine." |
> | 12–13 | **Farewell**
 The letter ends with the Elder stating his hope to visit with the community "face to face" and sending a greeting from "your chosen sister" (another Christian congregation). |

> **Outline of the Third Letter of John**
>
> | | |
> |---|---|
> | 1–4 | **Greeting and Praise**
 The letter opens with a greeting from the "Presbyter" (i.e., the "Elder") to its intended recipient, Gaius. The Elder praises Gaius, noting that he has received reports from "the brothers" that Gaius walks "in the truth." |
> | 5–8 | **Support for Missionaries**
 The Elder thanks Gaius for his past support of "strangers" [authorized teachers] who journey and work "for the sake of the Name." The Elder considers them "co-workers in the truth." |
> | 9–12 | **Diotrephes and Demetrius**
 The Elder then openly criticizes a man named Diotrephes, who will not "acknowledge" the |
>
> *Continued*

Outline of the Third Letter of John *Continued*

9–12	Elder's authority or receive any of "the brothers." He accuses Diotrephes of "spreading evil nonsense about us." The Elder asks Gaius to trust Demetrius, a co-worker of the Elder and possibly the letter-carrier.
13–15	**Farewell** The letter ends with the Elder expressing his hope to visit the community "face to face," offering a peace blessing, and extending a final greeting to all the recipients of the letter.

Outline of 1 John[19]

1:1–4	**Prolog** This writing lacks some central features of an ancient letter: it contains no mention of the author or recipients, nor does it include a formal greeting from the author to the addressees. Rather, it opens with a prolog bearing apostolic witness to the humanity of the "Word of life" through the apostles' collective experience of the earthly Jesus.
1:5–2:11	**Light and Darkness** The author speaks of God as light and believers as those who "walk in the light," in contrast to those who "walk in darkness" by denying their sin. Those who love their fellow brother (and

Continued

---

19. Although 1 John is oftentimes referred to as a "letter," it lacks some central features of an ancient letter.

	Outline of 1 John *Continued*
1:5–2:11	sister) remain in the light, but those who hate their brother (and sister) remain in darkness and fail to keep God's commandments.
2:12–3:10	**Community Affairs** The (anonymous) author then directly addresses particular groups within the community (fathers, young men, children), affirming their faith and warning them, "Do not love the world or the things of the world." He turns to the topic of former community members, calling them "antichrists" and accusing them of having left the Christian assembly. He denounces them as "liars" for denying both the claim that "Jesus is the Christ" and the relationship between "the Father and the Son." Referring to believers as "children of God," the author warns them to avoid sin.
3:11–5:12	**God's Commandment to Love One Another** The author reminds the community of Jesus' commandment to love one another and places special emphasis on loving others in "deed" more than in "word or speech." He encourages the community to challenge "false prophets" who may be teaching that Jesus Christ did not come "in the flesh." He assures believers that their faith in Jesus as Son of God "conquers the world" and secures eternal life.
5:13–21	**Epilogue** The writing draws to a close not with a final greeting or blessing, as would be typical in an actual letter, but with a request. The community is asked to pray for sinners—but only for those whose sins are not "deadly" (that is, the grave sin of denying Jesus as the Christ who came "in the flesh"). The author assures believers that they "belong to God" and that Jesus reveals the God of truth.

First John is an anonymous writing and completely lacks the opening greeting where the author of a letter would otherwise identify himself. The biggest clue to the author's identity is his frequent references to himself using the first person singular, "I am writing . . ." (see, for instance, 2:1, 7, 12, 26). In his concluding remarks from the epilog, for example, he writes, "I write these things to you [all] so that you may know that you have eternal life, you who believe in the name of the Son of God" (5:13). In the past, scholars have speculated that the Elder of 2 and 3 John also wrote 1 John,[20] and the similarities in theology and style have convinced many contemporary scholars that the same author wrote all three letters. However, other scholars note differences in content and epistolary form between 1 John and the other two letters. For example, whereas in 1 John the author remains anonymous, in 2 and 3 John the author identifies himself as "the Presbyter." Given such variations, they conclude that 2 and 3 John were written by a different author than 1 John,[21] which is the view also held in this chapter.

Although 2 and 3 John specify their addressees, the targeted readership of 1 John is less obvious. In 3 John, the Elder writes to the "beloved Gaius," a friend and ally to the Elder. In 2 John, the Elder writes to "the chosen Lady and to her children," which most scholars assert is a specific church within the Johannine community.[22] By contrast, the author of 1 John does not clearly indicate the audience. Nevertheless, his widespread use of the second person plural pronoun ("you all") provides a clue. Scholars suspect this more general address is directed to the entire Johannine community rather than to an individual or to a specific congregation.[23] The terms of endearment applied to the addressees ("children" [2:1, 12, 28, 3:7, 18, 4:4, 5:21] and "beloved" [2:7, 3:2, 21, 4:1, 7, 11]) suggest that 1 John is intended for the believers within the Johannine community who align with the author's belief in Jesus as "the Son of God" (5:13).

---

20. See, for example, Raymond E. Brown, *The Epistles of John* (New York: Doubleday, 1982), 14–35, "Problems of Johannine Authorship." Brown, ibid., 19, and Ehrman, 197, argue that the Presbyter wrote all three Johannine letters.

21. Schnelle, 455.

22. Ibid., 443; Ehrman, 197, argues that the same community is the audience for 1 and 2 John, contra Koester, 202, who sees the "elect Lady" as "the church in general."

23. Schnelle, 459–60; Koester, 199–201; Painter, 54, 84; Ehrman, 197.

> ### The Prologs and Conclusions of the Gospel of John and 1 John
>
> The beginning and ending of the Gospel of John and 1 John bear some striking similarities. Both writings open with poetic prologs using the words "In the beginning" and both describe Jesus as "the Word," but the aim of each prolog differs. Whereas the Gospel emphasizes Jesus as the pre-existent and eternal Word (John 1:1–5), 1 John highlights the importance of the apostles' witness to Jesus' humanity as the "Word of life" (1:1–4).
>
> Both writings conclude by reinforcing the belief in Jesus as the Son of God, and a promise of "life" in Jesus' name:
>
> | | |
> |---|---|
> | But these are written that you may [come to] believe that Jesus is the Messiah, the Son of God, and that through this belief you may have life in his name. (JOHN 20:31) | And this is the testimony: God gave us eternal life, and this life is in his Son. Whoever possesses the Son has life; whoever does not possess the Son of God does not have life. (1 JOHN 5:11–12) |
>
> Rather than necessarily being the product of direct literary dependence, these parallels may more broadly reflect the overall theological framework at work in the Johannine school.

Date and Place of Composition

Scholars generally agree that all three letters come from within the Johannine school. The actual place of composition remains uncertain, although the external evidence discussed above suggests that Asia Minor, and possibly the city of Ephesus, may have been the home of the Johannine school.[24]

Most scholars date the three letters toward the end of the first century, around 90–95.[25] Several reasons support this date: First, there is no evidence of any widespread denial of Jesus' humanity

---

24. See also, Schnelle, 442, 448, 459.

25. Schnelle, 442, 448, 459; Painter, 58–61.

(which is denounced in 1 John 2:22, 4:2–3, and 2 John 7) prior to the end of the first century; second, in his *Epistle to the Philippians* 7.1–2, written in the first half of the second century, Polycarp quotes 1 and 2 John; and third, there is a close theological alignment between the letters (especially 1 John) and John's Gospel, which is thought to have been written toward the end of the first century.

Scholars have varying opinions about the order in which the three Johannine letters and the Gospel of John were composed. Some believe the Gospel of John was written first, with 1 John a follow-up text defending John's theology against the interpretation of false teachers.[26] One argument in favor of this position is that the Gospel reflects a (possibly earlier) period of conflict with non-Christ-believing Jews, whereas the Johannine Epistles address a (later) inner-Christian conflict. Others argue that the Gospel of John was composed after the three letters, with the letters exposing the presence of the false teachers and the Gospel offering a comprehensive response to the heresy they espoused.[27] With regard to the order of the letters, scholars have advanced different proposals,[28] but the actual sequence of composition of the Johannine writings remains unknown.

> ### The "Slogans" in 1 John
>
> In the opening verses of this letter, the author of 1 John preserves what may be "slogans" used by the rival Christian teachers who were negatively affecting the Johannine community.
>
> *Continued*

---

26. Koester, 201; Painter, 73–74.
27. Schnelle, 439.
28. Some argue that 3 John 9 is a reference to 2 John and that 1 John is a polemical debate with the false teachers of 2 John, thus suggesting an order of 2 John–3 John–1 John (Schnelle, 439). Others contend that 1 and 3 John were written before 2 John, with the author of 2 John using the title "Presbyter" from 3 John and the phrase "Jesus Christ come in the flesh" from 1 John 4:2, thus proposing the sequence 1-3-2 John (Koester, 201–2). Still others think of 2 John as linking 1 and 3 John in terms of vocabulary and theological expressions. They argue for 1 John being sent simultaneously "under the cover" of 2 John with 3 John sent later to one of the churches targeted by 1 and 2 John, resulting in an order of 1-2-3 John (Painter, 52, 57).

> ### The "Slogans" in 1 John *Continued*
>
> The first three slogans begin with "If we say":
>
> - "We have fellowship with him" (1:6)
> - "We are without sin" (1:8)
> - "We have not sinned" (1:10)
>
> Scholars suspect these sayings may reflect the position of those who eventually "went out from us" (1 John 2:19). According to the author of 1 John, the antichrists' claim of "fellowship" with God was not possible since they "walk in darkness." Their claim of being without sin, simply as believers in Christ, is a dangerous self-deception that makes a "liar" of Christ.
>
> The next three slogans begin with "Whoever says":
>
> - "I know him" (2:4)
> - "[I] abide in him" (2:6)
> - "He is in the light" (2:9)
>
> These sayings, which reflect the claims of the other teachers, indict the Johannine secessionists, since the opponents really do not follow God's commandments, such as the mandate to love one another. For the author of 1 John, the central point is that "fellowship," avoiding "sin," claiming to "know" Christ, and being "in the light" are impossible without a concomitant acknowledgment of Jesus' humanity. The opponents disagreed, and for this reason left the Johannine community, presumably with the goal of continuing to acknowledge Jesus as their Messiah and Savior but without the burden of having to embrace his humanity.

Summary of Historical Setting for 1, 2, and 3 John

Author	First John: unknown, anonymous author Second John: "the Elder" Third John: "the Elder"

Continued

Summary of Historical Setting for 1, 2, and 3 John *Continued*	
Audience	First John: probably the churches within the Johannine community
	Second John: an unknown Johannine congregation ("the chosen Lady and . . . her children")
	Third John: an early Christian leader named Gaius
Date of Composition	90–95, although the order of composition is debated
Place of Composition	probably Asia Minor (maybe Ephesus)

Theology and Ethics of 1, 2, and 3 John

The theology and ethics embedded in 1 John developed in response to the false teachers who had separated from the Johannine community and who, despite the separation, continued to have some influence within the community. In 1 John, it is clear that the author sees the opponents' theology and ethics as a grave threat. Second and Third John reflect the theology and ethics of the Elder and, by extension, of the Johannine school. These letters outline how the community should put its theological and ethical ideas into practice as it confronts false teachers and independent church leaders.

Theology

The prolog of 1 John 1:1–4 presents the basic theological orientation of the letter. First John is driven by a Christology grounded in the real and corporeal existence of Jesus Christ, the "Word of life" (1:1) whom the witnesses, including, purportedly, the author, have heard, seen, and touched. This theology developed in response to the "antichrists" and false teachers within the Johannine community, who denied that Jesus the Christ had been present on Earth "in the flesh" (2 John 7). Despite that crucial difference, the Elder and the rival Christian constituency held many of the same views, which is not

At first the term *antichrist* merely denoted one who taught wrong doctrines about Jesus; in this fifteenth-century woodcut he appears as an ordinary human, though attended by a demon. Today, however, popular culture conceives of the antichrist as an overtly demonic figure.

surprising since they came from the same Johannine "school." Indeed, both sides embraced Jesus as the Messiah who offered the world the saving relationship of God the Father and Son (1 John 2:22–23, 4:2–3, 5:6–8). For the author of 1 John, the presence of the "antichrists" within the community signals the arrival of the "last hour" (2:18).[29] He interprets their arrival as a triggering event leading to the second coming of Christ (2:28), after which, believers, "the children of God," will share in Christ's glory (3:1–3).

In both 2 and 3 John, the Elder links together "truth" and "love." In 2 John, "the teaching of the Christ" (9) embodies the "truth," and the Elder rejoices "greatly," knowing that many are "walking in the truth" (4). Inseparable from the truth is the command of the Father and the Son "to love one another" (5–6). The "many deceivers" who deny "Jesus Christ as coming in the flesh" pose, in the Elder's view, a threat to this fundamental connection between knowledge of the truth and love for one another (7–9) and thus should be avoided altogether (10). The incomplete separation of the two (Johannine) communities lies at the root of the problem. The Elder wants his constituency to have more influence and his rivals to have less.

---

29. Whereas the Gospel of John sees the Jews as the primary opponents (see, for example, John 8:44, where the non-believing Jews are seen as children of "the devil"), the Johannine Epistles see false believers as the primary enemy, along Christological lines. The contrast with enemies between the Gospel of John and 1-3 John is telling about the development of Christianity.

> ### The "Secessionists" of 1 and 2 John
>
> Both 1 and 2 John criticize members of the Johannine community who had separated from the congregations because of theological disagreements:
>
> > They went out from us, but they were not really of our number; if they had been, they would have remained with us. Their desertion shows that none of them was of our number. (1 John 2:19)
> >
> > Many deceivers have gone out into the world, those who do not acknowledge Jesus Christ as coming in the flesh; such is the deceitful one and the antichrist. Look to yourselves that you do not lose what we worked for but may receive a full recompense. (2 John 7–8)
>
> These former members of the Johannine churches clearly had a different understanding of who Jesus Christ was. Their departure from the Johannine community appears to have been quite disruptive, especially to the leadership of the Johannine school.
>
> The reaction to the "secessionists" of 1 and 2 John compared to the reaction to the "false teachers" in Jude and 2 Peter (where the criticisms include the opponents' bad moral behavior) shows how the response to those who left varied from community to community.

The words "truth" and "love" also permeate 3 John. The Elder rejoices that "the brothers" testify that Gaius "walk[s] in the truth" (v. 3) and ministers to visiting "strangers" (visiting leaders) out of "love" (vv. 5–6). The Elder sees himself, Gaius, Demetrius, and the visiting leaders as "co-workers in the truth" (v. 8). He even asserts, "Nothing gives me greater joy than to hear that my children are walking in the truth" (v. 4). The Elder uses the concepts of truth and love to level his criticism against a rival leader in one of the Johannine churches, Diotrephes, who neither welcomes the author nor the visiting leaders of whom the Elder approves (9–10).[30] Rather than

---

30. On the subject of hospitality, 2 John warns against welcoming false believers, while 3 John complains that others are not welcoming true believers.

embracing the truth, Diotrephes is described as "spreading evil nonsense about" the author (v. 10). Although Diotrephes's views about "truth" in relation to "love" remain unknown to modern readers, it seems clear that there is thus a mutual and ongoing conflict between the Elder and Diotrephes.

Ethics

Belief in Jesus Christ as the Son of God and love for one another defines Christian identity in the Johannine community (1 John 1:3, 3:23, 4:8–10, 15–16; 2 John 3; 3 John 5–6). In fact, the central ethical imperative in all three Johannine letters is the command to "love one another" (1 John 2:10, 3:11–18, 23, 4:12, 21; 2 John 5–6; 3 John 5–6). For the Johannine community, the essence of God is love (1 John 4:7, 16b) and when members of the community love one another, "God remains in" them (1 John 4:12, 16b). In fact, anyone who "hates his brother" lives in "darkness" and is a liar (1 John 2:9, 3:10, 4:20). In a community recently rocked by division and conflict between rival leaders, the need for mutual love among those who remained would be particularly strong. Otherwise, those who remain risked additional divisions and attrition.

In addition to the command to love one another, the Johannine letters set forth directives to avoid "sin" [wrongdoing] and to act in "righteousness" (1 John 3:4–10). The community should pray for sinners, providing their sin is not "deadly" (1 John 5:16–17). False teachers and those who deceive the community are to be ignored (2 John 10) and never imitated: "Do not imitate evil but imitate good" (3 John 11).

> ### Summary: Historical Context, Theology, and Ethics of 1, 2, and 3 John
>
> **CORE CONCEPTS**
> - The Gospel of John and the three letters of John are thought to originate from a common "Johannine school."
> - The Christology of the Johannine community is grounded in the real and corporeal existence of Jesus Christ.
>
> *Continued*

> **Summary: Historical Context, Theology, and Ethics** *Continued*
>
> - Love for one another is the ethical imperative of the Johannine community.
>
> **SUPPLEMENTAL INFORMATION**
>
> - The three Johannine letters were probably composed around 90–95.
> - First John includes neither an opening greeting, where an author would usually identify himself, nor any greetings at the end. Thus it lacks central features of an ancient Greek letter.
> - The Johannine school appears to be fighting a particular Christology that denied Jesus had come "in the flesh."
> - At least one church in the Johannine community did not welcome visiting leaders.
> - The Elder of 2 and 3 John links the ideas of "truth" and "love."
> - In 1 John, anyone who hates his brother lives in darkness and is a liar.

PART 3: *FIRST CLEMENT* AND POLYCARP'S *EPISTLE TO THE PHILIPPIANS*[31]

Historical Contexts

These two texts belonging to the writings of the Apostolic Fathers are here grouped together with the canonical texts of Jude, 2 Peter, and 1–3 John because each is an early Christian letter and together they show a range of tensions among rival leaders in the early Christian communities. Although internal evidence helps establish the authors, audiences, dates, and places of composition for these two writings, additional support is needed from external sources such as the writings of the Church Fathers.

---

31. English translations of *1 Clement* and Polycarp's *Epistle to the Philippians* are taken from *The Apostolic Fathers*, ed. and trans. Bart D. Ehrman, 2 vols., LCL (Cambridge, MA: Harvard University Press, 2003).

First Clement

The author of *1 Clement* is unknown. Second-century Church Father Irenaeus, bishop of Lyons, identifies Clement, the third bishop of Rome, as the author of this letter,[32] but no internal evidence supports that claim. The opening address simply states the letter is sent from "the church of God that temporarily resides in Rome."[33] Given the consistent use of first person plural pronouns ("we" and "us") throughout the letter, it seems reasonable to conclude that the letter comes from an unknown author representing the leadership of the church in Rome.[34] Likewise, the opening address identifies the audience as "the church of God that temporarily resides in Corinth." *First Clement* was authored and sent from the leaders in the church in Rome to the church in Corinth, which is about six hundred miles southeast of Rome.

Few scholars doubt that the letter was written in Rome, for this is not a pseudepigraphic writing in which both the author and the depicted audience can be fictitious. Internal evidence from the letter suggests a date of composition toward the end of the first century.[35] This includes references to Peter and Paul as the "heroes nearest our own time" (5.1–7) and to the death of elders. In addition, the fact that successive appointments to leadership positions have already occurred subsequent to when Peter and Paul lived (44.2–3) and that ambassadors had been sent from Rome to Corinth, "who from youth to old age have lived irreproachable lives" (63.3), suggest that a considerable length of time has elapsed since the first apostles.

---

32. Irenaeus, *Against Heresies* 3.3.3. Eusebius identifies Clement as the third bishop of Rome, *Church History* 3.4.10.

33. Koester, 291, identifies Clement of Rome as the author of *1 Clement*. Other scholars, however, point to the lack of any internal evidence and conclude that it is not clear who the author of *1 Clement* was. See Andrew Gregory, "*1 Clement*: An Introduction," in Paul Foster, ed., *The Writings of the Apostolic Fathers* (New York: T&T Clark, 2007), 24.

34. Ehrman, ed., *Apostolic Fathers*, 23, concludes, "it is clear that even though the letter claims to have been written by 'the church' of Rome, it must have been composed by a single author (rather than a group)."

35. Ehrman, *The New Testament*, 521. See also Koester, 292–93, who similarly dates *1 Clement* to 96–97. But the primary reason he cites (the supposed persecution of Christians during the end of the reign of Emperor Domitian, 81–96) is, in the view of many scholars, no longer persuasive given the lack of evidence that Domitian actually persecuted Christians.

Polycarp's *Epistle to the Philippians*

This letter is sent from "Polycarp and the presbyters [elders] who are with him." The consistent use of the first-person singular pronoun ("I") throughout the letter suggests that Polycarp, the bishop of Smyrna, sent it directly after conferring with the elders, or presbyters, in Smyrna. The recipients are "the church of God that temporarily resides in Philippi," a city about four hundred miles north of Smyrna, in the province of Macedonia. Paul, too, wrote to the Christians in Philippi, fifty to sixty years earlier.

Similarly, the place of composition is most likely the city of Smyrna in the province of Asia Minor, where Polycarp resided as bishop. The date of composition is somewhat contested based on questions about the letter's literary integrity. Polycarp makes two references to the martyrdom of Ignatius: one suggests that Ignatius had *already* died (*Phil.* 9.1); the other suggests that Ignatius had *not yet* died (*Phil.* 13.2). This discrepancy raises the possibility that the current *Epistle to the Philippians* is a composite text comprised of two separate letters. According to this theory, chapters 1–12 make up one letter and chapters 13–14 the other.[36] Scholars who consider the *Epistle to the Philippians* a single, unified letter resolve the apparently conflicting statements in 9.1 and 13.2 by inferring that 9.1 is a mere rhetorical comment and therefore not a sound basis for chronology.

This chapter assumes the letter is a single document that dates to around 120. Since Polycarp was likely martyred sometime between 155–160, the letter had to be composed before then. Further, Polycarp received a letter from Ignatius (*To Polycarp*) sometime around 110–117, prior to Ignatius's martyrdom in Rome. Polycarp mentions toward the end of *Philippians* that he is fulfilling the request of the Christians in Philippi by "sending you the letters of Ignatius" that he possessed (13.2). Assuming Polycarp responded soon after the

---

36. Koester, 308. See Michael Holmes, "Polycarp of Smyrna, *Epistle to the Philippians*," in *The Writings of the Apostolic Fathers*, ed. Paul Foster (New York: T&T Clark, 2007), 120–24, for an extended discussion of the literary integrity of the *Epistle to the Philippians*. Holmes views the document as a "single unified letter," 123. If the *Epistle to the Philippians* is a composite of two letters, the actual date of final composition would prove more difficult to determine.

Philippians' request, most scholars conclude that the *Epistle to the Philippians* dates to around 120.[37]

Summary of Historical Settings

Author	Audience	Date of Composition	Place of Composition
First Clement	unknown; leaders	the church in Corinth	end of first century	Rome
Epistle to the Philippians	Polycarp, bishop of Smyrna in Asia Minor	the church in Philippi in Macedonia	uncertain; around 120	Smyrna

Overview of *1 Clement* and Polycarp's *Epistle to the Philippians*

First Clement

Church leaders in Rome wrote *1 Clement* to address their concerns about some things they had heard: "[The] church of the Corinthians is reported to have created a faction against its presbyters, at the instigation of one or two persons" (47.6). Some in Corinth, who sought support from church leaders in Rome, perceived the replacing of one group of leaders with another as controversial. The church in Rome wrote *1 Clement* siding with the old leadership, urging that they be reinstated. The opening chapter of this lengthy letter alludes to the trouble in Corinth: "We realize that we have been slow to turn our attention to the matters causing disputes among you, loved ones, involving that vile and profane faction that is alien and foreign to

---

37. Holmes, 124, suggests "a time closer to Ignatius' martyrdom than to Polycarp's." Ehrman dates the letter "around the year 110 or sometime later," *The New Testament*, 519.

God's chosen people" (1.1). It does not mention further specifics of the situation that prompted the writing of this letter again until chapters 42–44 and 47. Chapters 42–43 speak of Old Testament examples of "rivalry" and "quarreling" that occurred under Moses' leadership and the strategies he employed "so that there might be no disorderliness in Israel" (43.6). Chapter 44 cites the precedent set by the apostles, who themselves anticipated "that strife would arise over the office of the bishop" (44.1), and hence "appointed" the officers (44.2). Therefore, the act of removing an appointed officer is "viewed as a breach of justice" (44.3). In fact, for the leadership in Rome, the "contention and rivalry" in Corinth involves "matters that pertain to salvation" (45.1). Thus, according to *1 Clement*, being "saved" depends not simply on having faith in Christ but on supporting the right group of Christian leaders. Here a clear ecclesiology emerges that seems to support the idea of apostolic succession for church leadership:[38]

> Thus Christ came from God and the apostles from Christ. Both things happened, then, in an orderly way according to the will of God. . . . They [the apostles] appointed the first fruits of their ministries as bishops and deacons . . . and this is no recent development. For indeed, bishops and deacons had been mentioned in writing long before. (*1 Clem.* 42.2–5)

First Clement 47 brings the problem in Corinth into clear focus. The chapter begins by citing the original rivalry in the form of "cliques" and "factiousness" that Paul himself had dealt with in his First Letter to the Corinthians (see 1 Cor 1–4). It describes these earlier community disputes as a "relatively minor sin" (47.4); the current discord in Corinth, however, is far more serious: the "exceedingly shameful" actions of "one or two persons" within the Corinthian church has led the congregation "astray," "diminished" the love within the community, and resulted in "a faction" formed "against its presbyters" (47.5–6). Chapter 47 concludes with comments that may hint at the larger implications of the Corinthian coup: "And this report

---

38. See Francis A. Sullivan, *From Apostles to Bishops: The Development of the Episcopacy in the Early Church* (Mahwah, NJ: Newman, 2001) for a discussion of the history of apostolic succession and its effects on ecumenical relations.

has reached not only us but even those who stand opposed to us." It may well have been the case that Roman leadership feared that a similar rebellion could occur within their congregation. Stopping the attempted overthrow of Corinthian leadership and restoring peace and harmony there were of utmost concern.

The Roman leadership's overriding interest in restoring order to the Corinthian church shaped the letter's form and explains why the actual details of the problems in Corinth take so long to surface. The author(s) are trying to persuade the leadership in Corinth to effectively handle their congregational "quarrels" rather than compel them to do so.[39]

The letter opens with a flattering commentary on the Corinthian church (1.2–3.1), hinting that the success of their congregation has inadvertently led to their current problems of jealousy and rivalry, as seen in the past and present—from Cain and Abel, to David and Saul, to Peter and Paul (3.2–6.4). The letter then suggests that the proper avenue for dealing with the rivalry lies in offering the offenders an opportunity for repentance, once again citing biblical examples (7.1–15.6). It upholds Christ as the model of humility and peace, traits identified as key to effective leadership (16.1–20.12), as well as the importance of right conduct (21.1–23.5). The letter then discusses the future resurrection and calls on readers to strive for holiness and good deeds, citing the example of figures from the Old Testament. It culminates with a focus on the good gifts God provides to believers, especially the salvation received through Jesus Christ (24.1–35.12).

A discussion of proper church order and appropriate community conduct sets the stage for addressing the specific problems reported in the Corinthian congregation (36.1–47.7). The letter urges the community in Corinth to "dispose of this problem quickly," appealing to Christian love, encouraging wrongdoers to seek pardon and calling on the faithful to pray for the dissenters (48.1–56.16). The author then directly appeals to the dissenters, asking that they repent and submit to discipline from the presbyters, which is the necessary

---

39. Scholars have noted that *1 Clement* appears to use a particular type of ancient rhetoric that seeks to offer advice to its readers in order to help them deliberate over an issue. See Gregory, 26–28, for an extended discussion of this ancient literary genre known (in Greek) as *symbouleutikon*.

condition for remaining within the community; failure to do so will result in "no little danger" (57.1–59.1). The letter ends with a closing prayer, a summary of its content, a final warning, and a concluding farewell (58.4–65.1).

First Clement offers an interesting example of how church leaders in one congregation (Rome) sought to support leaders from another congregation (Corinth) and advise them on how to most effectively handle problems. It is unclear if the Corinthian church appealed to Rome for their advice, or if the church in Rome sent their opinion unsolicited.

> ### Abraham in Paul, the Letter of James, and *1 Clement*
>
> Paul, the author of the Letter of James, and the writer of *1 Clement* all refer to the biblical patriarch Abraham. Significantly, all three sources cite Genesis 15:6 as the proof text: "Abr[ah]am put his faith in the Lord, who attributed it to him as an act of righteousness."
>
> Paul cites Abraham as the model of faith in God *before* the Mosaic Law was given to Israel (Gal 3; Rom 6). The Letter of James likewise highlights Abraham as a model of faith in God, albeit with more emphasis on how he put his faith into action, as seen especially in his willingness to sacrifice his son Isaac (James 2). In *1 Clement*, Abraham serves as a model for the elders because he acted as a "friend of God" in terms of obedience, hospitality, humility, and righteousness (10.1–7, 17.2, 31.2). The individuals in Corinth leading the "revolt" against its presbyters had showed themselves to be anything but "friend[s] of God" and therefore cannot claim to belong to the legacy of Abraham and his inheritance.

Polycarp's *Epistle to the Philippians*

Polycarp wrote his *Epistle to the Philippians* in response to their request (3.1, 13.1). He addresses the topic of "righteousness," shares codes of proper Christian conduct for wives, widows, deacons, children, and presbyters; confronts false teachings by rival Christian leaders; offers advice on how to handle the misconduct of one of their elders, Valens; and sends along copies of letters he had received from Ignatius. One of the remarkable features of Polycarp's *Epistle to the Philippians* is his extensive knowledge of the early Christian tradition, which is evident in his use of most of the writings that would eventually make up the New Testament as well as texts now referred to as the Apostolic Fathers (the letters of Ignatius and *1 Clement*).

Polycarp begins with a thanksgiving for the longstanding faith and action of the Philippian community (1.1–3), advising it to abandon "futile reasoning and the error that deceives many" (2.1) and giving a summary of beliefs about Jesus Christ (2.2–3). He then addresses the issue of righteousness, citing "the blessed and glorious Paul" as the expert on the topic, before sharing his view that righteousness is embodied best in those who have "love" and warning against "love of money" (3.1–4.1). He goes on to present codes of conduct: for wives to love their husbands and educate their children; for widows to refrain from evil of all kinds; for deacons to be blameless and servants to all; for children to be pure in thought and deed; and for presbyters to be compassionate, merciful, and attentive to the poor and marginalized (4.2–6.3). Polycarp then warns them to avoid "false teachings" and those who deceive vulnerable community members. He refers to such individuals as "antichrist[s]" and the "firstborn of Satan" (7.1–2), and encourages the Philippians to stand firm in their convictions and their profession of faith, like heroes such as Paul and Ignatius (8.1–10.3). He afterward takes up the matter of Valens ("once a presbyter among you") and his wife, who apparently had stolen money from the congregation (11.1–12.3). He advises the community to forgive Valens and his wife if they truly repent (11.4). He ends this section with an exhortation to pray for all people, whether they are allies or enemies (12.1–3). Polycarp concludes by noting that he has appended the letters of Ignatius to his letter. He identifies Crescens as his letter-bearer; and offers a final blessing and farewell (13.1–14.1).

As bishop of Smyrna, Polycarp served his congregation as both a theologian and a pastor.[40] As a theologian, Polycarp drew extensively on many of the writings that eventually comprised the New

---

40. See chapter 2 for the discussion on the *Martyrdom of Polycarp*, where the church of Smyrna in Asia wrote to the church in the city of Philomelium in Phrygia about the martyrdom of their "blessed" Polycarp.

> ### Diverse Approaches to Appeals among the Early Christian Communities
>
> The letters in this chapter present various approaches used by the authors to exhort others, often fellow believers.
>
> Jude and 2 Peter launch dehumanizing attacks on their opponents:
>
>> But these people revile what they do not understand and are destroyed by what they know by nature like irrational animals. Woe to them! (Jude 10–11)
>
> The Johannine Epistles castigate the secessionists:
>
>> They went out from us, but they were not really of our number; if they had been, they would have remained with us. Their desertion shows that none of them was of our number. (1 John 2:19)
>
> *First Clement* encourages dissenters to seek pardon:
>
>> Thus you who laid the foundation of the faction should be subject to the presbyters and accept the discipline that leads to repentance. (*1 Clem.* 57.1)
>
> Polycarp urges forgiveness for the former presbyter who embezzled community funds:
>
>> Rather than judge such people as enemies, call them back as frail and wayward members, so as to heal your entire body. (Polycarp, *Phil.* 11.4)
>
> One of the values of studying these New Testament letters alongside letters from the Apostolic Fathers is to see the contrasting approaches in challenges to community leadership. The extracanonical texts seem to advocate a more tolerant and forgiving approach to rival leaders than the canonical texts.

Testament. These shaped the theology and ethics discussed in the *Epistle to the Philippians*. Indeed, this epistle not only serves as a prime example of an early bishop who applies the teachings of the Christian tradition to the real and practical concerns of Christian congregations, but also illustrates how the New Testament was received by the early church.

> ### Summary: *1 Clement* and Polycarp's *Epistle to the Philippians*
>
> **CORE CONCEPTS**
> - Church leaders in Rome wrote *1 Clement* in response to attempts to overthrow the presbyters in the church in Corinth.
> - *First Clement* tries to persuade rather than compel the Corinthians to settle their internal rivalries and quarreling.
> - Polycarp's *Epistle to the Philippians* deals with righteousness, codes of conduct, and the misconduct of community members.
>
> **SUPPLEMENTAL INFORMATION**
> - Details of the trouble in Corinth are limited to *1 Clement* 42–44, 47.
> - The Roman leadership considered the discord in the Corinthian church as "exceedingly shameful."
> - The church in Rome recommends that the dissenters seek pardon and submit to the discipline of the presbyters.
> - Polycarp wrote his *Epistle to the Philippians* at their request.
> - Polycarp frequently warns against the love of money.
> - Polycarp offers advice on proper conduct for spouses, children, elders, and deacons.

Questions for Review

1. Who do scholars think wrote Jude and 2 Peter?
2. How does 2 Peter make use of the Letter of Jude?
3. What is Jude's criticism of the moral conduct of the "intruders"?
4. How does 2 Peter explain the delay in the return of Christ? What is the view of the author's Christian opponents?
5. What do scholars mean by the "Johannine school"?

6. Why do some scholars think there were different authors for 1 John and 2 and 3 John?
7. On what grounds do scholars date the writing of the Johannine letters to the late first century?
8. What is the ethical imperative of all three Johannine letters? Why is that important for a community that had recently been split due to differences in Christology?
9. According to *1 Clement*, how should the leaders in Corinth deal with the individuals causing rivalry and quarreling?
10. How does Polycarp recommend the community handle the misconduct of the former elder Valens?

Questions for Reflection

1. How do you think Christians today should react to fellow Christians who voice different theological, political, or ethical viewpoints?
2. Second Peter offers an explanation for the delayed Parousia. Do you view that explanation as compelling? Why or why not?
3. Do you agree with Polycarp's advice in his *Epistle to the Philippians* on how to handle Valens and his wife, who misappropriated money from their congregation? Why or why not?
4. Compare the different approaches to handling rival leaders in the early Christian congregations as seen in the New Testament letters (Jude, 2 Peter, 1–3 John) and the extracanonical texts of *1 Clement* and Polycarp's *Epistle to the Philippians*. Which approach do you think is more effective, and why?

Recommendations for Further Reading

The Letter of Jude and the Second Letter of Peter

Haggmark, Steven A., and Arland J. Hultgren, eds. *The Earliest Christian Heretics: Readings from Their Opponents*. Minneapolis, MN: Fortress, 1998.

Hultgren and Haggmark provide a collection of references from many of the major Church Fathers on the people and movements that they considered "heretical" within the first two centuries of Christianity. This resource is an ideal overview of how the early church dealt with dissenting views within the developing theology of emerging Christianity.

Reese, Ruth Anne. *2 Peter and Jude.* Grand Rapids: Eerdmans, 2007.

Reese provides a very good introduction to the letters of Jude and 2 Peter, examining them from historical, sociological, and literary perspectives. Reese presents the themes of Jude and 2 Peter and analyzes how these themes are present throughout the canon of the New Testament.

The First, Second, and Third Letters of John

Lieu, Judith. *The Theology of the Johannine Epistles.* Cambridge: Cambridge University Press, 1991.

Lieu offers a concise overview of the three letters of John. Beginning with a historical and theological introduction to the Johannine Epistles, Lieu explores how these letters fit within the Johannine tradition and the New Testament. The book concludes with an examination of the significance of the Johannine Epistles for both the ancient and contemporary church.

Culpepper, Alan R., and Paul N. Anderson. *Communities in Dispute: Current Scholarship on the Johannine Epistles.* Atlanta: SBL Press, 2014.

This volume consists of nine essays written by Johannine scholars in honor of Raymond E. Brown, who was an expert on the Johannine writings. The essays explore topics connected to the three letters of John, including the theology and ethics of the epistles, the relationship between the epistles and the Gospel, and between the epistles and the church.

First Clement and Polycarp's Epistle to the Philippians

Sullivan, Francis Aloysius. *From Apostles to Bishops: The Development of the Episcopacy in the Early Church.* Mahwah, NJ: Newman, 2001.

Sullivan offers a historical and theological analysis of the writings of many of the early Church Fathers, including texts of the Apostolic Fathers (*1 Clement*, Polycarp's *Epistle to the Philippians*, the *Didache*, and Ignatius's letters). As the subtitle indicates, Sullivan examines these writings and offers his commentary on the development of the office of the bishop in the early church. He sees the idea of an "apostolic succession" in the episcopate as a "church-dividing issue" between Catholics and Protestants that should be openly discussed and examined.

CHAPTER 4

Hebrews and Early Christian Exhortations

INTRODUCTION

Chapter 4 examines the book of Hebrews and two writings of the Apostolic Fathers: the *Epistle of Barnabas* and *2 Clement*. Each of these three works makes an appeal to its audience, thus serving as examples of early Christian exhortations. Hebrews attempts to rouse its "sluggish" community members to a deeper understanding of the faith and commitment to Christ, hoping that they will not lapse into apostasy. *Barnabas* was written so that the faith of the community would be supported and strengthened through knowledge. *Second Clement* calls its readers to repentance, appealing to the audience to "save" themselves by living in a manner consistent with the Gospel message. Reading Hebrews with the *Epistle of Barnabas* and *2 Clement* gives modern readers an exposure to different approaches used by Christian leaders to appeal to their congregations and highlights the uniqueness of Hebrews.

Part 1 of this chapter provides an overview of the historical context of Hebrews (author, audience, date, and place of composition) and addresses a number of topics, such as the letter's concerns about apathetic believers and the author's use of Jewish theology and Platonic philosophy. In addition, it explores the Christology, soteriology, and eschatology in this exhortation. The chapter also examines the ethics of Hebrews, which includes holding fast to the confession of faith and proper moral conduct. Part 2 presents the historical context of *Barnabas* and *2 Clement* as well as a summary of their contents.

Early Christian Self-Identification

All three writings reveal different ways the early Christians defined themselves in relation to Judaism and other religions. The author of Hebrews views Christianity as the continuation and fulfillment of the promises God made to Israel. Through the suffering, death, Resurrection, and ascension of Jesus into heaven, God established a "new" covenant, making the first covenant with Israel, "obsolete" (Heb 8:13). The author of *Barnabas* likewise discusses Christianity in relation to Judaism, but with a decidedly negative view. He asserts Christianity's supremacy over Judaism by claiming that when the ancient Israelites broke God's covenant and radically misinterpreted God's laws, they ceased to be God's people. Centuries after their disobedience, "the covenant of his [i.e., God's] beloved, Jesus" was established (*Barn.* 4.6–8). The author of *2 Clement* confronts those who "persist in teaching such evil notions [immorality] to innocent people" (*2 Clem.* 10.5) and characterizes the Christian church as a spiritual reality manifested in Christ in the flesh and in the life of its members.

Christian Letters as Sermons

Although all three of these writings carry the label of "letter" or "epistle," none easily fits into this category in either form or function. Formally they lack central features of an ancient Greek letter, such as the name of the author and audience, a greeting, or a thanksgiving, although Hebrews and *Barnabas* do contain some elements of an epistolary postscript.[1] Hebrews, *Barnabas*, and *2 Clement* were composed in order to encourage and support believers. The author of Hebrews, in fact, identifies his text as a "message of encouragement" (Heb 13:22) and the writer of *2 Clement* describes the writing as "a request to pay attention" (19.1).[2] Although *Barnabas* refers to itself as a "brief letter" (*Barn.* 1.5), its content consists largely of a

---

1. Hebrews ends with personal information, final greetings, and a blessing; *Barnabas* concludes with a final exhortation and blessing.

2. It should be noted, however, that *2 Clement* 19 and 20 are a secondary ending, thus raising the question whether the description of *2 Clement* as "a request to pay attention" was the original authorial intent.

persuasive instruction for building up the faith. Given this evidence, many scholars believe that each of the three writings may have functioned as a Christian sermon.[3]

PART 1: HEBREWS
Historical Context

Hebrews offers no internal evidence about its authorship and only limited information about its intended audience and date and place of composition. External evidence about these matters can be gleaned from the writings of the early Church Fathers.

Outline of Hebrews

1:1–4	**Introduction**
	This anonymous writing lacks a formal greeting and any reference to a sender (author) and intended recipients (audience). Rather, it opens with a reflection on God's final and complete revelation in his Son.

Continued

---

3. See Bart D. Ehrman, *The New Testament: A Historical Introduction to the Early Christian Writings*, 6th ed. (New York and Oxford: Oxford University Press, 2016), 477, who states that most scholars think Hebrews "was originally a sermon or homily delivered by a Christian preacher to his congregation." Donald A. Hagner, *Encountering the Book of Hebrews* (Grand Rapids: Baker Academic, 2002), 21, observes, "The document is more of a homily-treatise than an epistle." Helmut Koester, *History and Literature of Early Christianity*, 2nd ed. (New York and Berlin: W. de Gruyter, 1982, 2000), 241, considers *2 Clement* "not a letter at all but a homily, or better, a programmatic theological writing with homiletic features." Christopher Tuckett, *Second Clement: Introduction, Text, and Commentary* (Oxford: Oxford University Press, 2012), 20, cautions against easily classifying *2 Clement* as a sermon: "The lack of comparative material may make it difficult to assess the claim that the text is indeed some kind of 'sermon.'" Koester, 281, sees Barnabas as "not a letter, but a treatise of scriptural gnosis, just like Hebrews." Udo Schnelle, *The History and Theology of the New Testament Writings*, trans. M. Eugene Boring (London: SCM, 1998), 373, argues that Hebrews functions as a "word of exhortation."

Outline of Hebrews *Continued*

1:5–2:18 — **The Son as Higher than the Angels**
The writing then offers seven Old Testament texts proving Jesus' superiority to the angels. It emphasizes Jesus' suffering, which made the salvation of believers "perfect." Through his suffering, Jesus became the "merciful and faithful high priest," who was able to help all believers who are "tested."

3:1–5:10 — **Jesus as the Eternal High Priest**
The author next speaks of Jesus' superiority over Moses, highlighting Jesus as "son" over God's house versus Moses, who was a "servant" in God's house. The hearers are warned to avoid an "evil and unfaithful heart," for that proved the downfall of the Israelites who were disobedient during the desert wanderings under Moses. Jesus is the compassionate and eternal high priest, who learned obedience through suffering and who is now "the source of eternal salvation for all who obey him."

5:11–10:39 — **The Eternal Priesthood and Sacrifice of Jesus**
Leaving "behind the basic teaching about Christ," the author offers further insight into the identity and impact of Jesus Christ, in order to encourage "sluggish" believers. Jesus is a "priest forever according to the order of Melchizedek" and serves as mediator and high priest from heaven. Through his Son, God fulfills the promise of a "new covenant" with the sacrifice of "the blood of Christ." This made the old covenant, which was repeatedly offered with animals' blood, "obsolete."

Continued

> **Outline of Hebrews** *Continued*
>
> | | |
> |---|---|
> | 11:1–12:29 | **Models of Faith, Need for Discipline, Consequences of Disobedience**
 The faith of "the ancients" (figures from the Old Testament) offers believers a model to imitate. This "cloud of witnesses," who are now in Heaven, should uplift believers who may sometimes "grow weary and lose heart." Whatever trials believers currently face should be viewed as "discipline" from God the Father, intended to strengthen faith. Disobedience (falling from the faith and becoming "defiled") can have dire and enduring consequences. |
> | 13:1–25 | **Final Exhortation, Blessing, and Greetings**
 The writing concludes by exhorting believers to maintain right moral conduct toward each other and, in particular, toward their leadership. A final blessing is given, accompanied by greetings from "those from Italy." |

Author and Audience

The author of Hebrews is unknown, and the writing provides no direct information about his identity. Some early Church Fathers believed Paul wrote it, probably because of the reference in the closing to one of Paul's main co-workers, Timothy ("I must let you know that our brother Timothy has been set free. If he comes soon, I shall see you together with him," Heb 13:23), as well as the consistent appending of Hebrews at the end of the thirteen letters of Paul in the manuscript tradition. Although differences in Greek style indicate that Paul did not write Hebrews, the belief in Pauline authorship may have contributed to the inclusion of Hebrews in the New Testament canon.

It appears that the unknown author considered himself a teacher of the church (5:12, 6:1–2), that he had a thorough knowledge of the Jewish Scriptures (1:5–13, 3:1–19, 11:1–40) as well as Jewish culture and traditions (5:1–9, 7:1–28, 9:1–10), and that he was skilled in rhetorical techniques, such as the allegorical interpretation of scripture (9:11–28, 10:1–18).[4] These considerations have led some scholars to conclude that the author was Jewish.[5]

> ## Who Wrote Hebrews?
>
> The early church was divided on the question of who wrote Hebrews. In the second century, some fathers of the Eastern Church attributed the letter to Paul, while certain fathers in the Western Church, such as Irenaeus and Tertullian, challenged Pauline authorship. Tertullian, for example, believed that Barnabas (a co-worker of Paul) wrote Hebrews.[6] Origen of Alexandria (third century) reported that some attributed the letter to Luke (the Gospel writer) or Clement, bishop of Rome (cf. Eusebius, *Church History* 4.14). By the fourth century, both the Eastern and Western Churches upheld the Pauline authorship of Hebrews, perhaps out of the desire to ensure its canonical status.[7] Questions arose again in the sixteenth century as Reformers challenged the authorship, and, as a result, its status as a part of Scripture. In response, the Council of Trent (1545–1563) affirmed the canonical status of Hebrews.
>
> Speculations about the identity of its author continues to the present day, with theories ranging from Apollos, a learned Hellenistic Jew from Alexandria (see Acts 18:24–28), to Priscilla, a teacher
>
> *Continued*

---

4. The word "allegory" comes from the Greek *allos* ("other") and *agoreuein* ("proclaim"). The allegorical method of interpretation argues that the Bible has several different levels of meaning that can be uncovered in the reading of the text.

5. Hagner, 23. See Paul Ellington, *The Epistle to the Hebrews*, NIGTC (Grand Rapids: Eerdmans, 1993), 3–21, who discusses various possible authors at length. Ellington sees Apollos as "the least unlikely of the conjectures" of possible authors. Daniel J. Harrington, *What Are They Saying about the Letter to the Hebrews?* (New York and Mahwah, NJ: Paulist, 2005), 37–38, discusses the theory that Prisca, a female, wrote Hebrews. Numerous contemporary scholars do not even hazard a guess as to the identity of the author of Hebrews. See, for example, Schnelle, 367: "The issue of authorship is not important for a theological understanding of this writing, since the theologically significant content of Hebrews speaks for itself."

6. See Tertullian, *On Modesty* 20.

7. See Ellington, 34–36, for a brief and informative discussion on the history of the canonization of Hebrews.

> **Who Wrote Hebrews?** *Continued*
>
> of Apollos (Acts 18:26), who, along with her husband, Aquila, were companions of Paul (Acts 18:1–4) and leaders within the Corinthian community (1 Cor 16:19). Nearly all modern scholars side with (and often quote) the conclusion of Origen on the subject of the authorship of Hebrews: "But who wrote the epistle, in truth, God knows."[8]

The audience of Hebrews, like the author, is never directly identified. Clues within the writing suggest a mostly Jewish-Christian audience. Discussions about such matters as the relationship between the old and new covenant (8:7–13), which models of faith from Israel's history and tradition should be emulated (11:1–38) and which avoided (12:15–17), and the fact that some believers had ceased attending the Christian assembly (6:4–6, 10:26–29) support the idea of a mostly Jewish-Christian audience.[9] Scholars remain uncertain whether the author of Hebrews writes to a specific Christian community of believers or a cluster of communities.

The author of Hebrews was very concerned about the faith, behavior, and attitude of the intended audience. The Christian community addressed in the letter seems in danger of ignoring "so great a salvation" (2:3). It has become "sluggish in hearing" (5:11, 6:12), does not assemble as a community (10:25), is not upholding its original confession of faith (4:14, 10:23), and not only needs to hear the fundamentals of the faith again, but also to reflect further on the Christian message (5:12–6:2). The author warns the Christian community not to repeat the sin of infidelity committed by the ancient Israelites, as evidenced by their disobedience to God in the desert wanderings under Moses' leadership (3:7–19).

---

8. Origen of Alexandria as quoted by Eusebius, *Church History* 4.25.14.

9. However, some scholars argue that the author may also have had Gentile Christians in view when he warns against forsaking "the living God" (3:12) and reverting back to "dead works" (9:14), possibly referring to a return to paganism. It seems probable that the audience for Hebrews was mostly Jewish Christian, with some Gentile members. See for example, Schnelle, 369; Ellington, 21–27; contra Hagner, 23, who sees the audience as Jewish Christians, and Ehrman, 478, who asserts Hebrews is directed to Gentile Christians.

Date and Place of Composition

Scholars date Hebrews from anywhere in the mid- to late-60s to the end of the first century. The limited internal evidence could support either range of dates. First, the author implies at least a generation (perhaps two) has lapsed since the time of Jesus: "Announced originally through the Lord, it was confirmed to us by those who had heard" (2:3). Second, the author mentions "days past" when the community "endured a great contest of suffering," ranging from public abuse to imprisonment and confiscation of property (10:32–34). This could refer to any number of spontaneous, local protests against that Christian community or, possibly, to either the expulsion of Jews from the city of Rome by the Emperor Claudius around 49 (Acts 18:2) or to the persecution of Christians in Rome under Nero in 64. Since the writing includes greetings from the Christians in Italy, it presumably was sent elsewhere, where the actions of Claudius and, later, Nero had no effect.

The references to persecution, combined with the fact that the author makes no mention of the destruction of the Temple in Jerusalem in 70 CE[10] and even consistently speaks in the present tense

The Jerusalem Temple, represented by this scale model, was destroyed in 70CE. Why does the author of Hebrews not cite this event as proof of his assertion that God had now replaced the traditional system of sacrifices with Christ's sacrificial self-offering?

---

10. Some see Heb 8:13 as a possible reference to the destruction of the Temple.

about priestly functions and the sacrificial system of the tabernacle ("tent") associated with the Temple (see, for example, Heb 5:1, 7:5, 9:1–7, 13, 22, 10:8, 11, 13:11), has led some scholars to date the composition of Hebrews to sometime in the mid- to late 60s.[11]

Most scholars, though, argue for a later date of composition because of the writing's apparent connection to the developing Pauline theology and tradition—for example, the discussions of Jesus' death in atonement for sins as the "new covenant"[12] (Heb 8–10; cf. 1 Cor 11:24–25) and of the "foundation" of faith resting upon the belief in the resurrection from the dead and the final judgment (Heb 6:1–2; cf. Rom 1:4, 2:1; 1 Cor 15:12–28, etc.). External evidence supporting a later date for the composition of Hebrews is the "days past" reference, which could apply to various time periods (beyond the days of Claudius and Nero), given the fact that persecution of Christians in the first century occurred on a sporadic and informal basis. These factors have thus led other scholars to date the composition of Hebrews toward the end of the first century.[13]

The closing remarks of Hebrews offer the only internal evidence for the writing's place of composition: "Greetings to all your leaders and to all the holy ones. Those from Italy send you greetings" (Heb 13:24). This suggests the writing was composed in Italy, quite possibly Rome.[14]

Summary of Historical Setting for Hebrews

Author	unknown, anonymous
Audience	mostly Jewish Christians with a good knowledge of comparatively obscure Old Testament characters, such as Melchizidek

Continued

---

11. Ellington, 33; Hagner, 25.

12. *Atonement* in this sense means that through the new covenant in Christ, sinful humanity has been provided a way to be reconciled with God.

13. Koester, 275–76; Schnelle, 368.

14. Schnelle, 367; Hagner, 24; Ellington, 28–29.

Summary of Historical Setting for Hebrews *Continued*	
Date of Composition	probably late first century, possibly earlier
Place of Composition	probably the Italian peninsula, possibly Rome

Another Threat to Early Christian Communities

Previous chapters identified a variety of threats to the well-being and survival of the early Christian communities. The recipients of 1 Peter suffered from external forces: non-believers who discriminated against them (1 Pet 3:16–17), abused them verbally and even physically (1 Pet 2:12, 15, 3:9, 14, 4:4), and brought false accusations against them before the courts (1 Pet 4:15–16). The church in Corinth faced "revolt" by some individuals who were attempting to overthrow the current presbyters (*1 Clement*). The Johannine churches faced Christ-believing "dissenters" who had left the community (1 John) and opposed the Elder's leadership (2 John). Additionally, the authors of Jude and 2 Peter complained about "intruders" who were dividing the faithful.

The book of Hebrews presents a different challenge to the continued existence of the Christian congregation. The author does not indicate that he is responding to an external threat or to internal power struggles. Rather, he addresses the apathy and disinterest of its current members who have "drooping hands" and "weak knees" (12:12). The author tries to shame the community into facing that problem:

> Although you should be teachers by this time, you need to have someone teach you again the basic elements of the utterances of God. You need milk and not solid food. Everyone who lives on milk lacks experience of the word of righteousness, for he is a child. But solid food is for the mature, for those whose facilities are trained by practice to discern good and evil. (5:12–14)

Those addressed in Hebrews face possible dissolution because of their own lack of fervor. As opposed to being targeted by an enemy from without, the community addressed in Hebrews is threatened by a danger of its own making.

Jewish and Platonic Influences in Hebrews

The writing's distinctiveness derives in part from the way it combines Jewish theology and Greek philosophy in an effort to convince the congregation not to abandon its Christian faith. The author of Hebrews constructs a sermon about Jesus Christ, balancing the idea of Christ as the fulfillment of the Jewish Scriptures (which makes the new covenant superior to the old) with the concepts of the cross (Jesus' suffering death) and Christ's ascension and exaltation in heaven as eternal high priest as the fullest expression of "reality."

> ### The Influence of Plato
>
> Plato was a Greek philosopher and mathematician who lived about four hundred years before Christ (roughly 428–348 BCE). His ideas helped lay the foundation for Western philosophy and science. One of his most famous teachings was the idea that the world as humans experience it is merely a "shadow" of the "reality" that lies just beyond human reach and understanding. This led to the development of a system of thought known as "Platonic idealism": all forms have an absolute and eternal reality, of which the phenomena of the world are but an imperfect and transitory reflection.
>
> This idea was part of the Hellenistic thought-world of first-century CE Jews and Christians. In Hebrews 8:1–6, the understanding of Israel's cultic tabernacle and annual animal blood sacrifices as "shadows" of the "real" heavenly sanctuary and Jesus' one-time blood sacrifice on the cross highlights the enduring impact of Plato's ideas.

Hebrews quotes numerous Old Testament prophets to demonstrate how Jesus fulfills the Jewish Scriptures (for example, Isa 8:17–18 in Heb 2:13; Psalm 110:4 in Heb 6:20). Among the prophetic writings quoted, Jeremiah 31:31–34 takes center stage: that entire text is quoted in Hebrews (8:8–12) as part of its argument for how Jesus, as the heavenly high priest and eternal mediator, fulfills Jeremiah's prophecy that God would establish a "new covenant." That fulfillment results in the replacement of the first covenant with Israel and renders it "obsolete" (8:13). Hebrews returns to Jeremiah 31:31–34 in a later discussion of how Jesus' sacrificial death on the cross atoned for sin forever (10:11–18).

The author of Hebrews also discusses the tabernacle and Jewish Law within a Greek philosophical (Platonic) framework, according to which all that is in the material world is merely a "shadow" or dim reflection of another, more true "reality." Hebrews speaks of the original tabernacle constructed by Moses and the Israelites during their forty-year journey in the desert as a "copy and shadow of the heavenly sanctuary." Jesus, "who has taken his seat [as high priest] at the right hand of the throne of the Majesty in heaven" (8:1–6), now presides over the real, heavenly sanctuary. Hebrews also contrasts the yearly blood sacrifices of animals prescribed in the Law as "only a shadow of the good things to come" (10:1), referring to Jesus' sacrifice of his blood on the cross; his "offering . . . has made perfect forever those who are being consecrated" (10:14). Notably, the author never criticizes the religious practices described in the Old Testament, highlighting instead their incompleteness.

Summary: Historical Context of Hebrews

CORE CONCEPTS

- Hebrews is an anonymous writing composed in the latter half of the first century.
- Hebrews addresses the apathy of members of one or more mostly Jewish Christian congregations.
- The author of Hebrews combines Jewish theology and Platonic philosophy to persuade the community not to abandon its Christian faith.

Continued

> **Summary: Historical Context of Hebrews** *Continued*
>
> **SUPPLEMENTAL INFORMATION**
> - The unidentified author of Hebrews considers himself to be a teacher within the church and demonstrates a thorough knowledge of the Jewish Scriptures.
> - Scholars are uncertain if Hebrews targets a specific Christian community of believers or a cluster of communities.
> - The city of Rome is often cited as the writing's place of composition.
> - Scholars debate whether Hebrews was written before or after 70.
> - The author of Hebrews tries to shame his target audience into "maturing" in the faith.
> - Hebrews sees Jesus fulfilling the prophecy in Jeremiah 31:31–34.

Theology and Ethics of Hebrews

The theology of Hebrews is deeply rooted in the Old Testament; its Christology, soteriology, and eschatology are governed by the idea of Jesus' "superiority" to the figures and institutions found in the Old Testament. The ethics of Hebrews is presented in the form of exhortations to the community of believers to remain faithful to Christ and to exhibit proper moral conduct.

Christology

From the opening lines (1:1–4), the author sets forth the superiority of Christ, referring to God's *partial* prophetic revelations in the past as compared to God's *complete* revelation in Christ, who is the "very imprint of his [God's] being." Even beyond the prophets, Christ is superior to the angels (1:4–11, 2:5–18), to Moses (3:1–6) and Joshua (4:1–11), and even to the Jewish priesthood (4:14–5:10, 7:1–28).[15] In addition to these Old Testament figures, Jesus also

---

15. See Harrington, 45–55, for a discussion on how contemporary scholars see the treatment of Moses and Melchizedek in Hebrews.

surpasses Jewish institutions: he is the minister of a superior covenant (8:1–13) and tabernacle (9:1–28) and even offers a superior sacrifice (10:1–18).

The Christology of Hebrews can also be seen in its numerous titles for Jesus. The letter uses over a dozen, many of which are unique within the New Testament (for example, "high priest," "forerunner," and "minister of the sanctuary and of the true tabernacle").

The most frequent title applied to Jesus in Hebrews is "high priest," which appears ten times in various contexts. Hebrews is the only New Testament writing to refer to Jesus as "high priest." The writing refers to Jesus as the high priest "forever" in the likeness and order of Melchizedek (5:5, 10, 6:20, 7:11, 15). As high priest, Jesus atones for sins (2:17), hears our confession (3:1), sympathizes with our weaknesses (4:14–15), intercedes for us in heaven (7:25–26, 8:1), and brings all good things (9:11).

The descriptions of Jesus as "leader to their salvation" (2:10), "minister of the sanctuary and of the true tabernacle" (8:2), and "a great priest over the house of God" (10:21) speak to his role as the eternal and heavenly high priest. Other references reinforce the notion that in Jesus God establishes a new covenant with believers,

Melchizedek greets Abraham in this fifteenth-century woodcut. By tracing Jesus' priesthood to Melchizedek, the author of Hebrews overcomes a potential objection to seeing Jesus' saving work as a priestly offering for sin: Jesus was not of the priestly tribe, Levi, but the royal tribe, Judah.

a covenant that, according to Hebrews, replaces Israel's "first" and original covenant (8:13). In addition, Hebrews contains other, more common titles for Jesus, such as "Son" (1:2, 3:6, 5:8, 7:28), "Son of God" (4:14, 6:6, 7:3), and "Lord" (7:14, 13:20).

Melchizedek

Melchizedek, a somewhat mysterious figure, is introduced in Genesis 14:17–20 as the king of Salem and "a priest of God Most High." It is notable that Genesis mentions Melchizedek's priesthood before the giving of the Law and the establishment of the Levitical priesthood in Exodus. Melchizedek gives a blessing to Abraham in thanksgiving for Abraham's victory over enemy kings in the region. In response, Abraham offers Melchizedek ten percent of everything he owns. The other Old Testament reference to Melchizedek occurs in Psalm 110, where God appoints David as both king, to rule over the enemies of Israel, and as priest: "You are a priest forever in the manner of Mechizedek" (v. 4). The Old Testament offers no further information about Melchizedek.

The author of Hebrews picks up on those two arcane Old Testament traditions and further develops the figure of Melchizedek. He speaks of Melchizedek as a forerunner (or type) of Christ: "Without father, mother, or ancestry, without beginning of days or end of life, thus made to resemble the Son of God, he remains a priest forever"(7:3). According to Hebrews, God declared Jesus an eternal and perfect "high priest" in the "order of Melchizedek" through his obedience and suffering on the cross:

> Son though he was, he learned obedience through what he suffered, and when he was made perfect, he became the source of eternal salvation for all who obey him, declared by God high priest according to the order of Melchizedek. (5:8–10)

Jesus' high priesthood through the order of Melchizedek is higher even than the priesthood that derives from the order of Abraham and Levi (7:1–28), since, according to Hebrews, the priesthood of Jesus and Melchizedek predate that of Abraham and the Levites.

Soteriology

Much of the soteriology of Hebrews (how Jesus "saves") is found in chapters 6–10, a section discussing how believers should deepen their understanding of the faith (6:1). The salvation Jesus offers to believers is connected to the establishment of a new and everlasting covenant based on his cross, ascension, and enthronement in heaven.

Hebrews speaks of Jesus' sacrificial death as an everlasting atonement for sin (2:17, 5:1–9). Jesus' blood sacrifice on the cross renders unnecessary the yearly animal sacrifice performed by the Jewish high priest (7:27, 9:11–15).[16] Furthermore, his ascension and enthronement in heaven assure believers of Jesus' continuing intercession, advocacy, and mercy on their behalf (4:16, 9:24).

Jesus' death and ascension into heaven mark God's establishment of a new covenant. Jesus, as the "mediator of a new covenant" (9:15), offers an "even better covenant" than the first (7:22, 8:6). He alone can offer redemption and salvation to believers. For Hebrews, salvation is immediate and permanent in Christ.

Eschatology

The book of Hebrews is replete with references to the return of Christ and the age to come. In the opening verses, the author speaks of the present time as "these last days" (1:2), signaling the writing's end-time orientation. In terms of the eschaton, Hebrews mentions the "good things" to come (6:5, 9:11, 10:1), hope for the future (6:11, 10:25), and fulfillment of a long-awaited salvation (9:27–28). But Hebrews also speaks of future judgment (6:1–2), especially for enemies of Jesus (10:27, 30) and those who have fallen from the faith (6:4–8, 12, 10:29, 12:25).

In addition to a future eschaton, Hebrews also speaks of the eschaton in the present. Believers are already "partners of Christ" (3:14); they have now "entered into [Sabbath] rest" (4:3–4, 10) and "tasted the good word of God and the powers of the age to come" (6:5). Hebrews contrasts the experience of Moses and the ancient Israelites, who in fear and trembling approached God (12:18–21), with those believers in Christ who now approach God without fear

---

16. See Harrington, 71–77, for a brief survey of what scholars are saying about the themes of priesthood and sacrifice in Hebrews.

because they have already arrived at the place of salvation in the new covenant with Jesus (12:22–24). The author's eschatology may well have served to motivate believers out of their complacency, since access to God is already available through Christ.

> ### Paul and the Authorship of Hebrews
>
> Although many during the history of Christianity accepted the Pauline authorship of Hebrews, today the scholarly consensus is that Paul did not write this work. The line of argument is generally twofold, centering on the writing's form and content. First, Paul used the literary form of an ancient letter. Hebrews, however, lacks most of this form's standard elements: salutation (sender, receiver, and brief greeting), thanksgiving, and closing (peace wish, greeting, and benediction). Moreover, the book of Hebrews employs a more sophisticated style of Greek than that found in the Pauline and deutero-Pauline letters.
>
> Second, the theological content of Paul's letters differs significantly from that of Hebrews. For example, Hebrews never mentions two of Paul's major theological concepts: justification by faith, and the relationship between faith and works of the Mosaic Law. Similarly, important themes in Hebrews, such as Jesus as the perfect high priest and the "mediator of a new covenant" who is enthroned in heaven, are altogether missing from Paul's theological framework.

Holding Fast

One of the overriding concerns for the author of Hebrews is the apathy and "sluggish" response of some contemporary Christ-believers: "Let us hold unwaveringly to our confession that gives us hope, for he [Christ] who made the promise is trustworthy" (10:23). The author expresses unease over those who would "sin deliberately" by abandoning the faith (10:26) and warns them of the impending divine judgment that awaits them (10:29–31, 12:14–17). He reminds wavering believers that faith is "the realization of what is hoped for and evidence of things not seen" (11:1) and lists numerous Old Testament figures (a "cloud of witnesses") who modeled believing without seeing and never lost hope (11:2–12:1).

Members of the Christian congregation addressed in Hebrews had experienced trials that challenged their faith (10:32–34). The author encourages his community to view these trials as "discipline" from God who, like a loving parent, disciplines a child for his own "benefit" so that he may later experience "the peaceful fruit of righteousness" (12:7–11). He concludes with a stern appeal expressing his concern that believers keep the faith: "So strengthen your drooping hands and your weak knees. Make straight paths for your feet, that what is lame may not be dislocated but healed" (12:13–14).

Moral Conduct

The author of Hebrews concludes with a series of exhortations (13:1–19), which cover a range of topics pertaining to the well-being of the Christian congregation. These exhortations include advice about what virtues to imitate and what behaviors to avoid. On the positive side, the author of Hebrews instructs believers to love one another, to be mindful of prisoners and those who are mistreated, to honor the "marriage bed," to remember past leaders who shared the faith, to obey and defer to current leaders, to share their possessions with others, and to pray for "us" (including the sender of Hebrews). Behaviors to avoid include love of money, attraction to "strange teaching," and failure to do good to others.

Summary: Theology and Ethics in Hebrews

CORE CONCEPTS

- Jesus as the perfect and eternal high priest is foundational to the Christology of Hebrews.
- Jesus "saves" believers through his death on the cross and his ascension and exaltation in heaven.
- Believers must hold fast to their confession of faith.

SUPPLEMENTAL INFORMATION

- In Hebrews, Jesus is superior to the angels, the prophets, Moses, the Levitical priesthood, and Joshua.

Continued

> **Summary: Theology and Ethics in Hebrews** *Continued*
>
> - Hebrews applies many unique titles to Jesus, including "high priest" and "forerunner."
> - According to Hebrews, Jesus' sacrificial death on the cross reconciles believers with God.
> - Hebrews speaks of both a future and present eschatology.
> - The author views the trials of believers as "discipline" from God meant to strengthen faith.
> - The author encourages proper moral conduct by listing behaviors to avoid and to emulate.

PART 2: THE *EPISTLE OF BARNABAS* AND *2 CLEMENT*

Historical Context of the *Epistle of Barnabas*

There is limited internal evidence from *Barnabas* to assist in establishing the letter's author, audience, date, and place of composition. External evidence is needed to determine its historical context.

> **Outline of the *Epistle of Barnabas*[17]**
>
> | Chapter 1 | **Introduction** |
> |---|---|
> | | The writing begins with a brief greeting. The author indicates that the recipients know him personally, although he never directly identifies himself by name. The author, who describes his writing as "a brief letter," writes "not as a teacher but as one of your own" in the hopes of strengthening and supplementing the recipients' faith with additional "knowledge." |
>
> *Continued*

---

17. English translations of the *Epistle of Barnabas* and *2 Clement* are taken from *The Apostolic Fathers*, ed. and trans. Bart D. Ehrman, 2 vols., LCL (Cambridge, MA: Harvard University Press, 2003).

Outline of the *Epistle of Barnabas* Continued

Chapter 2–16	**Christian Interpretation of the Jewish Scriptures** The author next launches into an extended discussion of his interpretation of a wide range of Jewish teachings and practices as presented in the Jewish Scriptures, arguing that many of them have been erroneously applied and historically misunderstood. The author clearly favors a non-literal—in his words, "true"—interpretation of the Jewish Scriptures, arguing that Jews have historically interpreted many aspects of the Mosaic Law too literally. Throughout this section, the author intersperses his interpretation of numerous Christian ideas, ranging from baptism to the death of Christ.
Chapter 17	**Summary and Transition** The author offers a brief transition before turning to a new subject, stating his hope that he has not "omitted anything that pertains to salvation."
Chapters 18–20	**The "Two Ways"** The writing turns now to the "two paths of teaching and authority, the path of light and the path of darkness." The path of light is guided by the angels of God; the path of darkness by "the other angels of Satan." The letter presents the two ways in terms of contrasting moral behavior for believers. Whereas believers, guided by the light, strive to live virtuous lives and repent when sin occurs, non-believers, directed by darkness, engage in immoral acts and are destined for damnation.
Chapter 21	**Final Exhortation** The writing concludes with a series of final exhortations in anticipation of the coming day of judgment.

Author and Audience

The title eventually given this writing implies that someone named Barnabas wrote it, presumably Paul's co-worker Barnabas, which then connects him to the first apostles. However, no internal evidence supports that claim. Writing in the late second century, Clement of Alexandria was the earliest Church Father to cite Barnabas as the author of this text.[18] Later Church Fathers affirmed Barnabas's authorship, but this attribution implies that *Barnabas* would have been written in the mid- to late-first century. The internal evidence does not support such an early date, and the negative disposition toward the Jewish Law in this writing does not correspond to what is known about the historical Barnabas, who was an advocate of the Jewish Law (Acts 15:22–29; Gal 2:1–10). Most modern scholars conclude that the author of this work is unknown.[19] Even whether the author is Jewish or Gentile remains uncertain.

Such phrases as "newcomers" against the Law (*Barn*. 3.6) and "before we believed in God" (*Barn*. 16.7) suggest a Gentile audience. The use of an allegorical method of scriptural interpretation (*Barn*. 10), however, could suggest that the author is Jewish or a Gentile who had had close contact with Judaism.

Date and Place of Composition

Two passages in *Barnabas* offer possibly divergent clues about its date of composition (4.3–5, 16.3–4). The former passage, which suggests an earlier date, cites two Jewish writings, *1 Enoch* 98 and Daniel 7, to describe the role of Jesus ("the master") at the end of time:

> The final stumbling block is at hand, about which it has been written, just as Enoch says. For this reason the Master [Jesus] shortened the seasons and the days, that his beloved may hurry and arrive at his inheritance. For also the prophet

---

18. See Clement, *Miscellanies* 2.6.31, who quotes from the *Epistle of Barnabas*, citing "the apostle Barnabas" as the author.

19. See James C. Paget, "The *Epistle of Barnabas*" in *The Writings of the Apostolic Fathers*, ed. Paul Foster (New York: T&T Clark, 2007), 74; Koester, 280; Ehrman, *Apostolic Fathers*, 6.

> [Daniel] says, "Ten kingdoms will rule the earth and a small king will rise up afterwards; he will humble three of the kings under at one time." So, too, Daniel speaks about the same thing: "I saw the fourth beast, wicked and strong, and worse than all the beasts of the sea, and I saw how ten horns rose up from him, and from them a small horn as an offshoot; and I saw how he humbled three of the great horns at one time." (*Barn.* 4.3–5)

Some scholars consider the phrase "fourth beast" a reference to Emperor Vespasian (60–79) who succeeded three emperors: Galba, Otho, and Vitellius.

Another passage in *Barnabas* would seem to refer to a later date, during the reign of Emperor Hadrian (117–138), who had a Roman shrine in honor of Jupiter Capitolinus built over the ruins of the Jerusalem Temple, which had been destroyed in 70 CE:

> Moreover he says again, "See, those who have destroyed this temple will themselves build it." That is happening. For because of their war, it was destroyed by their enemy. And now the servants of the enemies will themselves rebuild it. (*Barn.* 16.3–4)

A "developing consensus" among scholars favors this later date, around the year 130, for the composition of Barnabas.[20]

Barnabas provides no direct or conclusive evidence for its place of composition. However, scholars tend to support the location of Alexandria, Egypt, for numerous reasons.[21] First, the city of Alexandria had a large Jewish population, and some Alexandrian Jews (like the well-known Jewish philosopher and historian, Philo, 25 BCE–50 CE) employed an allegorical interpretation of scripture, which is also

---

20. Paget, 75; Ehrman, *Apostolic Fathers*, 7. See James C. Paget, *The Epistle of Barnabas*, WUNT (Tubingen: Mohr, 1994), 9–28, for an extended discussion on the plausibility of a Vespasian or Hadrian date of composition. Paget (in 1994) hypothesized a date of composition during the reign of Nerva, 96–98, when hope for a rebuilt temple was still alive for the Jewish people.

21. Paget, *Apostolic Fathers*, 75; Koester, 280–81; Ehrman, *Apostolic Fathers*, 7–8. Paget, *Barnabas*, 30–42, presents an extended discussion on three possible places of composition for *Barnabas* (Alexandria, Asia Minor, and Syria-Palestine), concluding that Alexandria is the "most probable" location.

seen throughout *Barnabas* (see, for example, *Barn.* 3, 10). Second, *Barnabas* 9.6 mentions Egypt by name ("indeed, even the Egyptians belong to the circumcision"). And third, Clement of Alexandria cites *Barnabas* in his writings.

> ### Is *Barnabas* Anti-Jewish?
>
> The main section of the *Epistle of Barnabas*, chapters 2–16, consists of the author's interpretation of Jewish scriptures. He makes what appear to be some rather startling anti-Jewish claims, implying that Judaism is a false religion. For example:
>
> - *Barnabas* 4.6–8 The Jews permanently broke their covenant with God in worshipping the golden calf in the desert (see Exod 32), and now God's covenant belongs to Christians alone.
> - *Barnabas* 9.1–9 An "evil angel" tricked the Jews into interpreting the Jewish Law literally (for example, with the Jewish practice of male circumcision; see Gen 17) rather than figuratively, as God intended. Therefore, many of the Jewish cultic practices are illegitimate.
>
> It seems clear that the author of *Barnabas* wants to prove the supremacy of Christianity by delegitimizing the Jews as God's chosen and covenantal people. However, the author's appropriation of Jewish symbols, such as covenant (*Barn.* 4) and land (*Barn.* 6), for establishing Christian identity, combined with the fact that he never actually uses the term "Jew" or "Jewish," shows that his goal is to build up and edify his Christian community, not tear down the Jewish community. But clearly *Barnabas* views non-Christian Judaism as rejected by God. Scholars are divided over whether this second-century writing signals a definitive split between Jews and Christians or whether it "reflects a more complex form of interaction"[22] and aims to actualize such a split. On the whole, it may be the *Epistle of Barnabas* is less anti-Jewish than it is pro-Christian.

---

22. Parvis, 80.

Summary of Historical Setting for the *Epistle of Barnabas*

Author	unknown
Audience	unknown, but likely Gentiles
Date of Composition	around 130
Place of Composition	possibly Alexandria, Egypt

Overview of *Barnabas*

Barnabas is divided into two main parts: chapters 2–16 (the author's Christian interpretation of the Jewish Scriptures) and chapters 18–20 (the "two ways": the way of light and the way of darkness). Chapter 1 serves as the introduction; chapter 17 as a summary of part one and transition to part two; and chapter 21, the final exhortation.

In the introduction, the author greets the unnamed recipients in generic terms ("sons and daughters," 1.1), and the greeting presents an author who knows them ("since I spoke among you," 1.3). The author then states his purpose for writing: "in order that your knowledge may be perfected along with your faith" (1.5).

Much of part 1 (*Barn.* 2–16) is devoted to the author's teachings on the Jewish Scriptures. Certain chapters focus on the Jewish Bible and the author's Christian interpretation of it: sacrifice (ch. 2), fasting (ch. 3), circumcision (ch. 9), the dietary laws prescribed by Moses (ch. 10), the Sabbath (ch. 15), and the Temple (ch. 16). The author pointedly disagrees with the traditional Jewish literal interpretation of these commandments and advocates instead for non-literal (Christian) interpretations.[23] The discussion on sacrifice in chapter 2 provides a good example of how, in his view, the Jews "misunderstood" God's intent for the sacrificial system:

---

23. It should be noted that Jewish interpretation at this time was also often non-literal (e.g., Philo of Alexandria, 25 BCE—50 CE).

> And again he says to them, "Did I command your fathers who came out of the land of Egypt to offer whole burnt offerings and sacrifices to me? No, this is what I commanded them: Let none of you bear a grudge against your neighbor in your heart, and do not love a false oath." And so, since we are not ignorant, we should perceive the good intention of our Father. For he is speaking to us, wanting us to seek how to make an offering to him without being deceived like them. (*Barn.* 2.7–9)

Other chapters in part 1 address more strictly Christian teachings. Chapters 5–7 discuss the death of Christ and its significance. Chapters 11–12 discuss the meaning of baptism and the cross. Chapters 4, 13, and 14 take up the topic of the covenant, emphasizing the Jewish loss and Christian claim to the covenant using "us" versus "them" language:

> Now let us see whether it is this people [Christians] or the first one [Jews] that receives the inheritance, and whether the covenant is for us or them. Hear what the Scripture says concerning the people: "Isaac prayed for Rebecca his wife, because she was infertile. And then she conceived." Then, "Rebecca went to inquire of the Lord and the Lord said to her: 'There are two nations in your womb and two peoples in your belly, and one people will dominate the other and the greater will serve the lesser.'" You ought to perceive who Isaac represents and who Rebecca, and whom he means when he shows that this people is greater than that one. (*Barn.* 13.1–3)

This citation offers a good example of the author's pro-Christian language, which seems designed to establish and reinforce Christian identity.

Barnabas 17 serves as a summary to part 1 (*Barn.* 2–16): "Insofar as I have been able to set forth these matters to you simply, I hope to have fulfilled my desire not to have omitted anything that pertains to salvation" (17.1). Part 1 consists largely of the author's appeal to Christian theology and interpretation of the Jewish Scriptures.

Part 2 (*Barn.* 18–20) begins with a simple transitional phrase: "But let us turn to another area of knowledge and teaching" (18.1). The writing then presents a discussion of the "two ways" of light and darkness, with literary parallels to the "two ways" from the beginning of the *Didache* (chs. 1–6). Rather than a direct dependency of one upon the other, some scholars suspect the authors of the *Didache* and *Barnabas* used a common source.[24]

The author presents the "way of light" using a list of behaviors designed to help believers live a virtuous life. Some behaviors have parallels to the Ten Commandments: for example, do not commit adultery (19.4), do not take the name of the Lord in vain (19.5), and do not covet a neighbor's goods (19.6). This "moral" interpretation of the Ten Commandments contrasts with the letter's allegorical treatment of the rest of the Law in regard to circumcision, kashrut, and sacrifice, as seen earlier in *Barnabas* 2–16.

Other behaviors designed to promote right living include a proper mental disposition, being "humble minded in all things" (19.3), and not being of "two minds" (19.5). Some encourage confession of sins and praying (19.12), while still others address prohibitions against abortion and infanticide (19.5) and quarrelling (19.12).

Those who follow the "way of death" are non-believers and will suffer "eternal punishment" (20.1). The author provides a list of behaviors that "destroy [the] soul" and warrant damnation. These include virtually every bad deed imaginable, from idolatry, adultery, and murder to ignoring the widow and orphan and showing no pity on the poor. In short, it encompasses all negative behaviors, those that are "altogether sinful" (20.1).

The writing concludes with a final appeal to follow the teachings outlined in the writing, since this will lead to "resurrection" (21.1). A brief reference to the eschaton (end times) is followed by a series of directives for community members to be "good lawgivers" and "faithful counselors," and to avoid "hypocrisy" (21.4). Then comes a prayer that the Lord would give the community members "wisdom, understanding, prudence, knowledge, and patience" (21.5). The author then reminds "the faithful" of the coming "day of Judgment" (21.6) and asks the audience to remember him in prayer (21.7) and remain "diligent" in fulfilling "every commandment" (21.8).

The author's self-described "brief letter" (1.5) appears designed to persuasively argue for the supremacy of the Christian religion. In

---

24. Koester, 280.

highlighting the errors and insufficiency of Judaism, the author of *Barnabas* hopes to support and build up the Christian community.

Historical Context of *2 Clement*

Similar to *Barnabas*, *2 Clement* provides only limited internal evidence to establish its historical context and external evidence is needed to answer questions of author, audience, date, and place of composition.

Outline of *2 Clement*

Chapters 1–18	**Believers' Debt and Response to God for Their Salvation**
	The author opens with the assertion, "Brothers, we must think about Jesus Christ as we think about God, as about the judge of the living and the dead. And we must not give little thought to our salvation" (1.1). The author often returns to the theme of believers being grateful for God's mercy, which is offered through the gift of eternal life, as well as the debt owed for this gift. That debt is paid by repenting from sins (8.1–2, 9.8, 13.1, 16.4, 17.1), detachment from the sinful world (5.1, 6, 6.5, 17.4), and acts of righteousness and self-control (4.3, 10.1, 12.1, 15.1, 3) in anticipation of the end times and God's final judgment (5.5, 10.3, 16.1, 18.2).
Chapters 19–20	**Later Addition**
	The final chapters appear to be a later addition to this writing and emphasize paying attention to what has been written and the importance of the salvation of believers. They focus on upright living and hope for the resurrection of the dead and the life to come at the end of time. This secondary ending concludes with a doxology (a hymn of praise to God).

Author and Audience

Second Clement contains no direct internal evidence indicating its author or audience. It lacks an opening address that, in an ancient Greek letter, would disclose the identity of the author and the intended audience. Furthermore, many scholars agree that *2 Clement* is not even a letter, but a homily, delivered by a presbyter whose identity is no longer known.[25]

Some clues within the text indicate it was intended for a Gentile audience who came to Christian faith from polytheism (belief in many gods), rather than from a monotheistic Jewish background: "We were maimed in our understanding, worshipping stones and pieces of wood and gold and silver and copper—all of them made by humans" (1.6); "For he called us while we did not exist, and he wished us to come into being from nonbeing" (1.8); "He has shown us such mercy since, to begin with, we who are living do not sacrifice to dead gods or worship them; instead, through him we know the Father of truth" (3.1).

At the Academy of Athens stands Athena, Greek goddess of heroic endeavor and wisdom. In ancient times, Jews and Christians often contrasted the lifeless idols worshipped by polytheists with the true, living God (see Isa. 44:9–20). *Second Clement* continues this polemic.

---

25. Parvis, *Apostolic Writings*, 34; Koester, 241. But see J. A. Kelhoffer, "If *Second Clement* Really Were a 'Sermon,' How Would We Know, and Why Would We Care? Prolegomena to Analyses of the Writing's Genre and Community," in Mark Grundeken and Joseph Verheyden, *Early Christian Communities between Ideal and Reality*, WUNT 342 (Tübingen: Mohr Siebeck, 2015), 83–108, who questions whether "sermon" or "homily" is a helpful genre designation.

Date and Place of Composition

Scholars usually date the composition of *2 Clement* to around the middle of the second century,[26] in large part based on the sources used. The text is not only informed by two of the New Testament Gospels (*2 Clem.* 8.5 seems to cite Luke 16:10–12; *2 Clem.* 9.11 may cite Matt 12:50), but also, and with equal authority, by noncanonical gospels, such as *Gospel of Thomas* 22 (cf. *2 Clem.* 12.2) and the so-called *Gospel of the Egyptians* (cf. *2 Clem.* 13.2). The list of gospels accepted as part of the official church's accepted "canon" of scripture was still fluid.[27] Furthermore, *2 Clement* appears to also draw from images in two of Paul's authentic letters: the athlete and his crown in *2 Clem.* 7.1–3 (see 1 Cor 9:24–27) and the potter and the clay in *2 Clem* 8.1–2 (see Rom 9:19–24).

Scholars remain uncertain about the place of composition of *2 Clement*. Some scholars favor Egypt, given the author's use of the *Gospel of the Egyptians*.[28] Others favor the city of Corinth, due in part to the manuscript tradition that attaches *2 Clement* with *1 Clement*, which was clearly addressed to Corinth.[29]

Summary of Historical Setting for 2 Clement

Author	unknown
Audience	Gentile Christians
Date of Composition	around 150
Place of Composition	unknown; possibly Corinth or Egypt

---

26. Parvis, 26–27; Koester, 242; Tuckett, 62–64.

27. It was only later, around 180, that Irenaeus argued for the acceptance of only the four Gospels now found in the New Testament. See Irenaeus, *Against Heresies* 3.11.8.

28. Koester, 242–43. The *Gospel of Thomas* was discovered at Nag Hammadi, Egypt, in 1945. It is written in Coptic, an Egyptian language.

29. Parvis, 37; Tuckett, 62: "Probably any claim about the geographic origin can be, at the end of the day, no more than an educated guess."

Overview of *2 Clement*

Most scholars question the literary integrity of *2 Clement*. There seems to be a break dividing chapters 1–18 and chapters 19–20.[30] Chapters 1–18 address the intended audience as "brothers," while the final two chapters speak to "brothers and sisters" (19.1, 20.2). In fact, the opening to *2 Clement* 19–20 serves as somewhat of an introduction to the entire text and could reflect the eventual use of *2 Clement*, if not both *1 Clement* and *2 Clement*, in a liturgical setting:

> So then brothers and sisters, now that we have heard this word from the God of Truth, I am reading you a request to pay attention to what has been written, so that you may save yourselves and the one who is your reader. (*2 Clem.* 19.1)

Second Clement 1–18 is dominated by moral imperatives, such as the ongoing obligation to God incurred when believers received the gift of faith (8.1–4, 9.8, 13.1, 16.1, 17.1), concern over false teachers (9.1, 10.4, 13.3, 14.4, 17.6), and teaching about the final judgment (12.1–6, 16.1–4, 17.3–7) and the church (14.1–5).

The call to repentance heard throughout *2 Clement* often carries a sense of urgency not only in anticipation of the return of Christ, but also the reality of facing God's judgment of both believers and unbelievers:

> For after we leave the world we will no longer be able to make confession or repent in that place. (*2 Clem.* 8.3)

> And so we should repent from our whole heart, lest any of us perish. (*2 Clem.* 17.1)

Although he often mentions repentance from sin, the author of *2 Clement* also exhorts his readers to embody virtues, such as loving one another (9.6), practicing charity, fasting (16.4), and praying often (17.3).

The author also shows much concern about false teachers who endangered the congregation on both a doctrinal and, especially, on a moral level. The false teachers (who are never directly identified)

---

30. Parvis, 34–35.

apparently denied that Christ-believers, too, will face the final judgment (9.1), accused Christians of teaching myths and being delusional (13.3), and perverted the "commandments of Jesus Christ" (17.6). Furthermore, these false teachers were encouraging immorality by preferring "the pleasure of the present to the promise that is yet to come" (10.3) and "teaching such evil notions to innocent people" (10.5). In response, the author of *2 Clement* emphasizes Christ in the flesh as the source of salvation (9.5), the necessity of loving one's enemies (13.4), and the need for readiness to patiently endure the "torments" prior to the day of judgment (17.6).

The author of *2 Clement* mentions the second coming of Christ a number of times. The belief in the indeterminate arrival remains strong: "For this reason, we should await the kingdom of God with love and righteousness every hour, since we do not know the day when God will appear" (12.1). The catastrophic events leading to the end times are still anticipated: "But you know the day of judgment is already coming like a blazing furnace, and some of the heavens and all of the earth will melt like lead in the fire" (16.3). However, believers welcome the eschaton, for they will experience the "mercy of Jesus" (16.2) and his redemption: "And this is what he calls the 'day of his appearance,' when he comes to redeem each of us, according to our deeds" (17.4).

The Assessment of *2 Clement* throughout History

From an early date, some did not hold *2 Clement* in high regard. Eusebius, the fourth-century church historian and Bishop of Caesarea, refused to "recognize" *2 Clement* as an authoritative part of scripture, which, along with *1 Clement*, was apparently considered part of the New Testament by some Christians in the fourth century:

> But it must be observed also that there is said to be a second epistle of Clement. But we do not know that this is recognized like the former, for we do not find that the ancients have made any use of it. (*Church History* 3.38.4)

Continued

> ### The Assessment of 2 Clement throughout History *Continued*
>
> Photius, the ninth-century Patriarch of Constantinople and a prolific writer, offered commentary (summary and analysis) on many of the writings of the Church Fathers. Regarding *2 Clement*, Photius observed:
>
>> Certain passages are strangely interpreted. The sentiments are somewhat poor and at times inconsistent. (*Bibliotheca*, cod. 126)
>
> Even some modern scholars comment on its quality:
>
>> *Second Clement* is not a profound theological text. . . . It is neither well written nor well organized. (Parvis, *Apostolic Writings*, 41)
>
> Other contemporary scholars find this negative assessment of *2 Clement* both unfortunate and unfair:
>
>> *Second Clement* is probably the most overlooked and least appreciated of the writings of the Apostolic Fathers. This is somewhat to be regretted, as it is in some ways a historically significant work. (Ehrman, *Apostolic Fathers*, 154)
>
> *2 Clement* is significant for several reasons. First, assuming the date (around 150) and genre are correct, *2 Clement* is the earliest example of a Christian homily outside of the New Testament. Second, the author's use of the Greek translation of the Jewish Scriptures (the Septuagint) along with oral sayings attributed to Jesus and use of Pauline images provides early evidence that second-century Christians viewed both sources (the Septuagint and the teachings of Jesus and the apostles) as equally authoritative for Christian education and formation. Third, *2 Clement* offers us a comparative homily with Hebrews, underscoring the richness and depth of the theology and ethics of Hebrews.

In terms of ecclesiology, the author of *2 Clement* speaks of a pre-existent church to which believers now belong: "So, then, brothers, if we do the will of God our Father we will belong to the first church, the spiritual church, the church that was created before the moon and the sun" (14.1). That spiritual church was "manifest in Christ's flesh" (14.3) and now exists as "the living church" so that believers might be "saved" (14.2). Christ and the church coexist as spirit and flesh: "the flesh is the church and the Spirit is Christ" (14.4).

Another central theme in *2 Clement* is the necessity of reciprocity: "repayment" or "exchange" must be given to Christ and God. Readers are challenged throughout *2 Clement*: "What can we pay in exchange for what we have received?" (1.5); "While we have time to be healed, let us give ourselves over to the God who brings healing, paying him what is due" (9.7). This payback does not entail the purchase of salvation but the maintaining of a divine-human relationship, like the mutual obligations between a patron and a client.[31]

The later addition to this writing (chs. 19–20) takes up the theme of repentance and being open to admonishment because one has "two minds" and lacks faith (19.1–2). The "pious" person can anticipate resurrection to new life in heaven, where "a more fortunate time awaits him" (19.4). *Second Clement* urges faith in God's providence (20.1–4) and concludes with a brief benediction (20.5).

The unknown author of *2 Clement* offers this writing to his community as "a request to pay attention" (19.1) in order to "save" themselves. It is an appeal to live out one's faith in Christ in the community of believers, the church.

Summary: *Barnabas* and *2 Clement*

CORE CONCEPTS

- *Barnabas* views both ancient Israelite religion and the Judaism of his time in a very negative light.
- *Barnabas* devalues a literal interpretation of scripture.

Continued

---

31. For further discussion, see James A. Kelhoffer, "Reciprocity as Salvation: Christ as Salvific Patron and the Corresponding 'Payback' Expected of Christ's Earthly Clients according to the *Second Letter of Clement*," *New Testament Studies* 59 (2013): 433–56. Kelhoffer argues that *2 Clement* presents Christ as a salvific benefactor and patron who offers salvation to those who accept the terms of his patronage, terms that include the obligation to render various forms of "payback," including praise, witness, loyalty, and almsgiving. A failure to accept these terms would jeopardize the relationship between Christ and his earthly clients and thus call their salvation into question. For Kelhoffer, then, a likely purpose for *2 Clement* was to convince a Christian audience that the benefits of salvation come with recurring obligations to Christ, their salvific patron.

> **Summary: *Barnabas* and *2 Clement*** *Continued*
>
> - *Second Clement* is held together by moral imperatives and concerns about false teachers, with some discussion on eschatology, ecclesiology, and the need for "payback" to God and Christ so as to ensure salvation.
>
> **SUPPLEMENTAL INFORMATION**
>
> - The authors of *Barnabas* and *2 Clement* remain unknown.
> - Much of the content of *Barnabas* is devoted to a reinterpretation of the Jewish Scriptures.
> - Because *Barnabas* and the *Didache* contain similar material on "the two ways," some scholars believe that the authors drew from a common source.
> - Chapters 1–18 comprise the main body of *2 Clement*, with chapters 19–20 a secondary ending.
> - The call to right moral conduct is repeated often in *2 Clement*.
> - *Second Clement* is concerned about teachers who allegedly pass on false doctrine and encourage immoral behavior.

Questions for Review

1. What can be gleaned from Hebrews about its unknown author?
2. What new threat to the early Christian communities does Hebrews reveal?
3. How does Hebrews show the influence of Platonic thinking in its discussion of the "heavenly sanctuary"?
4. According to Hebrews, what is Jesus now able to do for believers in his role as perfect high priest in heaven?
5. How does the author of Hebrews explain how Jesus' death on the cross saves believers?
6. According to *Barnabas*, how should the Jewish Scriptures be interpreted?
7. What are some characteristics of "the two ways" in *Barnabas*?
8. How does *2 Clement* speak about the church and Christ?

9. What are some of the moral imperatives in *2 Clement*?
10. How does *2 Clement* emphasize the need for reciprocity?

Questions for Reflection

1. How does Hebrews describe "sluggish" believers? What, according to Hebrews, prevents believers from becoming lazy in their faith?
2. Why, according to Hebrews, is Jesus "superior" to the angels, the prophets, Abraham, and Moses? Do you feel this line of argument is compelling? Why or why not?
3. In your view, is *Barnabas* anti-Jewish?
4. How would you compare the way Hebrews treats Jewish traditions and practices versus to the ways the *Epistle of Barnabas* and *2 Clement* treat them?

Recommendations for Further Reading

Hebrews

Ellington, Paul. *The Epistle to the Hebrews*. NIGTC. Grand Rapids: Eerdmans, 1993.

> Ellington presents a verse-by-verse commentary on Hebrews. He begins with a thorough discussion of its historical setting and its theology and includes discussions of the canonization of Hebrews and influences from such sources as the Old Testament, Philo, and Qumran.

Harrington, Daniel J. *What Are They Saying about the Letter to the Hebrews?* New York and Mahwah, NJ: Paulist, 2005.

> Following the format of the popular WATSA series, Harrington gives an up-to-date analysis of what contemporary scholars are saying today about Hebrews. This short book is divided into four parts: reading Hebrews today, the mysteries of Hebrews, Hebrews and the "Old Testament," and the theology of Hebrews.

Schenck, Kenneth. *Understanding the Book of Hebrews: The Story behind the Sermon*. Louisville and London: Westminster John Knox Press, 2003.

> As the subtitle indicates, Schenck unpacks the storyline of Hebrews through its events, settings, and characters. In identifying the narrative framework of this sermon, Schenck is able to present the rhetorical force

of Hebrews. The book features sidebars and charts designed to help readers better understand the story world of Hebrews.

Barnabas

Paget, James C. *The Epistle of Barnabas.* WUNT. Tübingen: Mohr, 1994.

Paget provides an in-depth analysis of *Barnabas*, beginning with an introductory chapter examining its author, date, provenance, and form. Paget then spends two chapters looking at various theories of possible sources used by the author of *Barnabas*. The volume concludes with an analysis of the theology of *Barnabas* in relation to Judaism and Christianity, including a section on how *Barnabas* was positively received by the early Church Fathers.

Second Clement

Tuckett, Christopher. *2 Clement: Introduction, Text, and Commentary.* Oxford Apostolic Fathers. Oxford: Oxford University Press, 2012.

Tuckett offers an extended introduction on the historical, literary, and theological context of *2 Clement*. Tuckett also includes discussion of such topics as the writing's opponents and the manuscript evidence. In his commentary, Tuckett offers many insights into the debates associated with *2 Clement*, such as the author's use of Matthew and Luke.

CHAPTER 5

Revelation and Early Christian Apocalypses

INTRODUCTION

This final chapter discusses the three earliest Christian apocalypses: the Revelation of John, the *Shepherd of Hermas*, and the *Apocalypse of Peter*. The term "apocalypse" (from *apokalypsis*, Greek for "unveiling") refers to the literary genre. As indicated by the term, each of these apocalypses claims to unveil or reveal something hidden, often involving heavenly or otherworldly mysteries. In these three apocalypses early Christian writers sought to reveal things that were hidden from all people, including their fellow believers. The Revelation of John is the final book of the New Testament; the *Shepherd of Hermas* is one of writings of the Apostolic Fathers; and the *Apocalypse of Peter* belongs to the broader category of extracanonical writings from early Christianity often referred to as "New Testament Apocrypha." Exposure to other early Christian apocalypses in addition to the Revelation of John allows contemporary readers to see the popular impact that the apocalyptic worldview held within the early Christian communities.

The chapter provides an overview of the historical context of each of these apocalyptic writings as well as each writing's theology and ethics. Part 1 of this chapter focuses on the Revelation of John, which presents a series of visions the prophet John purportedly experienced while exiled on the island of Patmos. Part 2 discusses two other extracanonical early Christian apocalypses: the *Shepherd of Hermas*, a story that narrates revelations and angelic messages received by a man named Hermas, and the *Apocalypse of Peter*, written in the Apostle Peter's name, which reveals the pleasures of heaven and the tortures of hell. The chapter also presents a summary of each text's content.

The Ancient Apocalyptic Worldview

The surviving ancient Jewish and Christian apocalypses reflect what is termed an "apocalyptic" worldview, which perceives the world as subject to the dual forces of good and evil. The authors of these apocalypses believed that God ultimately controls human history and maintained that God must intervene to deliver the covenant people—for example, by sending one or more messianic figures to conquer the forces of evil, set up God's kingdom on Earth, raise the dead, and judge the world. Many ancient apocalypses, including the Revelation of John, anticipated an imminent end (the eschaton) to this age.

Most scholars argue that each of these apocalypses was written during a time of (perceived) crisis and was intended for an audience experiencing some level of duress and suffering on account of its faith. These writings offer a message of hope, for they assert that, contrary to all appearances, God is in control and will soon intervene on behalf of the righteous and bring their suffering to an end. The apocalypses also offer a message of support to believers, encouraging them to remain firm in their beliefs in the face of persecution and to resist the temptation to become lax in their practice of the faith. They also come with a warning to those Christ-believers who do not heed the prophet or apostle's message and who are not prepared to face the final judgment.

Jewish and Christian Apocalypses

Both ancient Jews and Christians produced apocalypses. Jewish apocalypses were produced during a period of about three hundred years, from around 200 BCE to 100 CE. Many Christian apocalypses were written between the first and third centuries CE, with some dating to as late as the Middle Ages (for example, the twelfth-century *Apocalypse of Golias*). Apocalyptic may be defined as

> a genre of revelatory literature with a narrative framework, in which a revelation is mediated by an other-worldly

being to a human recipient, disclosing a transcendent reality, which is both temporal, insofar as it envisages eschatological salvation, and spatial insofar as it involves another, supernatural world.[1]

Five major Jewish apocalypses either predate or are roughly contemporary to the Revelation of John: *1 Enoch*, Daniel (chs. 7–12), *4 Ezra*, *2 Baruch*, and the *Apocalypse of Abraham*.[2] Of these, only the book of Daniel is counted as scripture.[3] Scholars commonly refer to the series of visions in Daniel 7–12 (dated around 165 BCE) as the foremost example of apocalyptic literature in the Old Testament. The author of the Revelation of John likely drew upon some of the visions from Daniel as well as earlier visions in the prophetic books of Ezekiel and Zechariah. *First Enoch* is thought to date to sometime before Daniel 7–12, around the year 200 BCE.[4] The three other major Jewish apocalypses—*4 Ezra*, *2 Baruch*, and the *Apocalypse of Abraham*—were probably composed near the end of the first century CE, around the same time as the Revelation of John.

The Revelation of John is the New Testament's only apocalypse. Although the Gospels and Letters of Paul contain apocalyptic sections or motifs,[5] no other New Testament text belongs to the genre. Some apocalypses were mediated through a vision, while others were mediated through a journey; the Revelation of John is considered a vision apocalypse.[6]

---

1. John J. Collins, *The Apocalyptic Imagination: An Introduction to Jewish Apocalyptic Literature*, 2nd ed. (Grand Rapids: Eerdmans, 1998), 5.

2. For historical and literary information on these five Jewish apocalyptic texts as well as on apocalypticism in early Christianity, see ibid.

3. Following the Septuagint (the Greek translation of the Hebrew Bible), Christian Bibles commonly group the book of Daniel with the Prophets, but the Hebrew Bible classifies it among the Writings. The Ethiopic Orthodox Church, uniquely among Christian denominations, accepts *1 Enoch* as canonical.

4. *First Enoch* is actually a composite work consisting of five parts that were not all written at the same time. Only the first part, known as the "Book of the Watchers" (*1 Enoch* 1–36) is apocalyptic.

5. See, e.g., Matt 24; Mark 13; 1 Thess 4:13–18; and 2 Thess 2.

6. For further discussion on the unseen orders of heaven and hell in the Jewish and Christian traditions, see Martha Himmelfarb, *Tours of Hell: Apocalyptic Form in Jewish and Christian Literature* (Minneapolis: Augsburg, 1985), and *Ascent to Heaven in Jewish and Christian Apocalypses* (New York: Oxford University Press, 1993).

PART 1: THE REVELATION OF JOHN

Some internal evidence exists for establishing author, intended audience, and date and place of composition. External sources, including the writings of the early Church Fathers, assist in determining the historical context.

Historical Context

John does not present a *linear* series of predictions in his apocalypse, but rather a *circular* or *spiraling* series of overlapping predictions. This movement will be highlighted in the outline below.

Outline of the Revelation of John

1:1–3	**The Prolog** The prolog identifies the "servant John" as the source of this writing and states he is reporting the visions shown to him by an angel of the Lord. The content is the "revelation of Jesus Christ, which God gave to him [Jesus]." A blessing is offered to the reader and the audience, those who hear and heed its "prophetic message."
1:4–8	**The Greeting** The prophetic message—sent from John, Jesus Christ, and "the seven spirits before his throne" to the "seven churches of Asia"—includes an assurance of the imminent return of Christ.
1:9–20	**Opening Vision** The author (John) identifies himself, his location and circumstances (exiled on the island of Patmos because he preached about Jesus), and some details about his initial vision, which included a command to write down what he sees and send it to seven specific churches. John

Continued

Outline of the Revelation of John *Continued*

1:9–20	then describes his opening vision, using striking imagery to depict Jesus. Jesus reassures John and again commands him to "write down" all he sees. The vision concludes with Jesus interpreting the "secret meaning" of some of the images in John's initial vision, meanings that those seven churches would have understood.
2:1–3:22	**Prophetic Oracles to the Seven Churches** John follows Jesus' instructions and writes a prophetic oracle to each of seven churches of Asia Minor: Ephesus, Smyrna, Pergamon [Pergamum], Thyatira, Sardis, Philadelphia, and Laodicea. These messages follow the pattern Jesus commanded in the initial vision: to write "what you have seen, and what is happening, and what will happen afterwards." Thus each oracle includes some aspects of John's first vision of Jesus, details of the community's current circumstances (good and bad), and directives for them to prepare for the cataclysmic end times.
4:1–5:14	**The Vision of Heaven** John next sees a vision of heaven where God is seated on a throne. Surrounding God are twenty-four "elders" on their thrones and "four living creatures," all of whom sing praises and glory to God. John sees God holding a sealed scroll whose contents only Jesus, depicted as the slain and resurrected "Lamb," can reveal. All those in heaven, including "countless" angels, worship and offer praise to God and Jesus.
6:1–8:1	**The Vision of the Seven Seals** Still in heaven, John now witnesses the Lamb (Jesus) breaking the seven seals of the scroll in turn. The breaking of each of the first six seals in heaven corresponds to cataclysmic events

Continued

	Outline of the Revelation of John *Continued*
6:1–8:1	that are to occur on Earth in the near future to all unbelievers. Before the seventh seal is broken, John sees two other visions: the 144,000 "marked" (saved) from the twelve tribes of Israel and those who kept the faith, those who faithfully endured and "survived the time of great distress," and who now receive their reward in heaven. After the breaking of the seventh seal, there commences "about half an hour" of silence in heaven.
8:2–11:19	**The Vision of the Seven Trumpets** After the breaking of the seven seals, a series of overlapping predictions begins anew. John now sees an angel burning incense and the "holy ones" who offer prayers to God in anticipation of the blowing of the seven trumpets. As the first four trumpets are blown in heaven, once again the inhabitants on Earth experience calamity. When the fifth and sixth trumpets sound, only non-believers and those who persecute believers suffer disasters on Earth. Before the blowing of the seventh trumpet, John again has two additional visions: a vision of an angel who bears a small scroll containing "the mysterious plan of God," and a vision of two witnesses (unnamed prophets and witnesses to the faith) who, as a result of testifying to God's plan on Earth, were martyred, raised, and ascended to heaven, whereupon they exacted vengeance on their enemies. The sounding of the seventh trumpet marks God's final victory over evil and the restoration of God's reign on earth.
12:1–13:18	**The Enemies of God** Yet another series of overlapping predictions begins with John's vision of a "great sign . . . in the sky": the woman and the dragon. John sees

Continued

Outline of the Revelation of John *Continued*

12:1–13:18	a woman giving birth to a son while a "huge dragon," "who is called the Devil and Satan," waits to devour the newborn child. God rescues both the son, who was "destined to rule all the nations," and his mother, but "war" breaks out in heaven between the dragon and the archangel Michael and his angels. The angels win the war, and the dragon is cast "down to earth." Failing to destroy the woman, who remained on Earth after being saved, the dragon attacks "her offspring" (believers in Jesus). John then sees two beasts (the second worse than the first). Empowered by the dragon and depicted as enemies of God, the beasts prevail even over faithful Christians and deceive many others on Earth.
14:1–20	**The Lamb and the Saved** John next sees Jesus (the Lamb) assembled with those martyred for the faith and the saved (the 144,000) singing a "new hymn" of praise before God, the twenty-four elders, and the four living creatures. Afterward, three angels announce the coming reign of God and the fall of "Babylon the great" and warn against worshipping the beast or its image. The vision concludes with images of fields ready for harvest, a reference to the approaching end times.
15:1–16:21	**The Vision of the Seven Plagues and Seven Bowls** John sees another sign: seven plagues "through [which] God's fury is accomplished." This is followed by two more visions, one in which those who are saved sing God's praises, and the other in which the heavenly temple fills with God's glory. Angels then pour "the seven bowls of God's fury" upon the earth. Non-believers and the unrepentant undergo great suffering.

Continued

Outline of the Revelation of John *Continued*

17:1–19:10 — **Babylon and the Pagan Nations**

An angel next explains to John that "the great harlot" (Babylon) will face judgment and punishment for persecuting and martyring "witnesses to Jesus." The angel interprets for John much of the symbolism associated with the woman and the beast empowered by the dragon. John then sees another angel announcing the fall of Babylon and the nations associated with her, followed by a victory song from the "great multitude" in heaven proclaiming the establishment of God's reign and the arrival of the "wedding feast" of the Lamb.

19:11–22:5 — **Closing Visions**

John has a final vision in which he sees a "rider" (Jesus) on a white horse battling both the beast (the "false prophet") and the kings of the Earth aligned with the beast and defeating them. Satan and the forces of evil are locked in "the abyss" for a thousand years, after which they will be released for a final battle in which they will lose. The devil and the beast will be "tormented day and night forever and ever." John then sees the final judgment of the living and the dead. His final vision is of a new heaven and a new earth where God and humans dwell together in everlasting peace. The new, heavenly Jerusalem is beautifully adorned, and the faithful live in perfect union with God and the Lamb.

22:6–21 — **Epilogue**

The "prophetic message" ends with both John and Jesus testifying to the truth of the visions, along with a stern warning not to add or remove anything from this "prophetic . . . book."

Author and Audience

There is little reason to doubt that someone named John, a Christian prophet who was exiled for his "testimony to Jesus" (1:9), wrote this apocalypse. Unlike most apocalypses, the Revelation of John is not a pseudonymous text (claiming to be written in someone else's name and drawing upon another's authority).[7] Although some early Church Fathers attributed the text to the Apostle John,[8] others doubted this identification.[9] Today most scholars take the statements in Revelation 1:1–4, 9 and 22:8 at face value and believe that someone named John authored this work.[10]

Given the author's familiarity with Old Testament texts, such as Daniel 7–12, Ezekiel 1–3, and Zechariah 9, and the idea of a "new Jerusalem" at the end times (21:2, 9–27), most scholars conclude that John was probably a Jewish Christian. His exact status within in the community is not clear. John does not claim a leadership position among the congregations of Asia Minor to whom he is writing, simply referring to himself as a "brother" among the believers in the seven churches in Asia (1:9). Presumably the Roman authorities who exiled him considered John a leader in the community. John refers to his writings as a "prophetic message" (1:3) and "prophetic words" (22:18), so it can be assumed he viewed himself as a prophet. He likely does this to distinguish himself from Christian "false prophets," who were among his opponents in at least three of the churches to which he writes: the Nicolaitans in Ephesus (2:6, 15), those who follow the

---

7. As will be seen, the *Shepherd of Hermas* is likewise not pseudonymous but the *Apocalypse of Peter* is.

8. See Justin Martyr, *Dialog* 81.4 for the earliest attestation in the mid-second century; see also Irenaeus, *Against Heresies* 5.30.1.

9. Eusebius, *Church History* 3.25.2.

10. See Wilfrid J. Harrington, *Revelation*, SP 16 (Collegeville, MN: Liturgical Press, 1993), 8–9; Udo Schnelle, *The History and Theology of the New Testament Writings*, trans. M. Eugene Boring (London: SCM, 1998), 523; Helmut Koester, *History and Literature of Early Christianity*, 2nd ed. (New York and Berlin: W. de Gruyter, 1982, 2000), 253; Craig R. Koester, *Revelation and the End of All Things* (Grand Rapids: Eerdmans, 2001), 47; Leonard L. Thompson, "Ordinary Lives: John and His First Readers," in *Reading the Book of Revelation*, ed. David L. Barr (Atlanta: SBL Press, 2003), 25–47; Bart D. Ehrman, *The New Testament: A Historical Introduction to the Early Christian Writings*, 6th ed. (New York and Oxford: Oxford University Press, 2016), 536.

teachings of "Balaam" in Pergamon (2:14), and "Jezebel" in Thyatira (2:20–23). Beyond this general sketch, though, who exactly this "John" was and his position within the churches to whom he wrote remains unknown. Clearly his authority would have been disputed by at least some of those loyal to the "false prophets" he repeatedly criticizes.

The text identifies the intended recipients as seven churches located in the western cities of the Roman province of Asia: Ephesus, Smyrna, Pergamon, Thyatira, Sardis, Philadelphia, and Laodicea (1:11). Geographically, these Christian congregations were in close proximity; most were between thirty and fifty miles apart from each other, with the greatest distance, about one hundred miles, between Ephesus and Laodicea. Ephesus was also the city closest to Patmos, the island in the Aegean Sea where John was exiled. Patmos lies about fifty miles southwest of Ephesus.

> ### The Prophetic Oracles Sent to the Seven Churches of Asia Minor[11]
>
> The prophetic oracles John sent to the Christian communities at Ephesus, Smyrna, Pergamon, Thyatira, Sardis, Philadelphia, and Laodicea provide a snapshot of the successes and challenges those congregations faced. The specific details provided in each letter create the impression that John had first-hand knowledge of these communities. In fact, after the address, most of the letters begin with the phrase, "I know your works." Some of the prophetic proclamations serve as a dire and divine warning against following the teachings of John's opponents or assimilating into the larger Roman pagan culture.

The prophetic oracles in Revelation 2–3 offer clues about the circumstances in each of them. Some of the churches are discussed in

---

11. James A. Kelhoffer, *Persecution, Persuasion and Power: Readiness to Withstand Hardship as a Corroboration of Legitimacy in the New Testament*, WUNT 270 (Tübingen: Mohr Siebeck, 2010), 148–49, argues these messages to the churches are better described as "prophetic oracles" rather than letters since they really function as prophetic proclamations.

both positive and negative terms. For example, the author talks about how Ephesus has endured trials and discovered "imposters," but also points out the community's need to repent for having fallen away from their original zeal for the faith. While the community in Pergamon remained faithful even in the face of the killing of one of its members, Antipas, some have now been led astray by false Christian teachers, identified cryptically as those who "hold to the teaching of Balaam." Thyatira excels in faith, love, and service, but some members follow the teachings and actions of the false prophet "Jezebel," who refuses to repent of her ways. Other churches are portrayed largely in a negative light. The faith of the community in Laodicea has become "lukewarm," and the congregation deceives itself by boasting of its material wealth. Instead, Jesus denounces them as "wretched, pitiable, poor, blind, and naked" (3:17). Sardis has largely stopped practicing the faith, with only a few members remaining faithful. Still other churches receive mostly praise. Philadelphia, for instance, has kept the faith and endured hardships admirably. Smyrna, while facing "poverty" of material goods, is, according to John, actually "rich" in the faith, with believers there enduring slander, suffering, and imprisonment.

Details from the letters provide a window onto the diversity of these early Christian communities. It seems clear that the Christians in these churches have been exposed to competing theologies from rival leaders and have responded in a variety of ways to those challenges. John identifies three opponents (the Nicolaitans, those who subscribe to the teachings of "Balaam," and the followers of "Jezebel," the latter two being derogatory terms applied by John), but he does not provide enough detail for modern scholars to differentiate the beliefs or practices of these rival leaders.[12] In addition to these different views, the community members seem to be unduly influenced, as John sees it, by the larger imperial cult, which was devoted to honoring the Roman emperor as a god and as humanity's protector and benefactor. Concerns over Christians adopting polytheistic practices, such as eating meat offered to idols (Rev 2:20), suggests that there was an ongoing debate regarding how far Christians might legitimately assimilate into the wider pagan society. What John deemed

---

12. Kelhoffer, 152.

compromise with pagan Rome and over-assimilation led some (perhaps many) church members to become "lukewarm" (3:16), "fallen" from their original zeal for the faith (2:5), and even "dead" in their faith (3:1).

> ### Antipas of Pergamon
>
> The prophet John held Antipas in high regard. Apparently Antipas was killed in the city of Pergamon, presumably by the Roman authorities, for publically witnessing to his faith in Jesus. John refers to Antipas as a "faithful witness" (2:13), which is the very same title John had applied to Jesus (1:5).
>
> From John's perspective, the death of Antipas serves a very important function: Antipas models faithful endurance in the face of persecution. In addition, his mistreatment at the hands of the authorities foreshadows the widespread persecution of Christians sure to come in anticipation of the end times. In being a faithful witness to Jesus, Antipas resisted assimilation—for example, by not participating in the imperial cult—and offered to all believers an example in view of the catastrophes to come. Like John himself, who bore testimony to Jesus and suffered for it (1:9), Antipas never denied or compromised his faith (2:13). Both Jesus and Antipas, who remained faithful unto death, serve as examples to Christians, who must be prepared to be persecuted by believers and unbelievers alike.

Date and Place of Composition

The prophet John indicates that he received his visions during the time of his exile on the island of Patmos (1:9). The reference leaves it somewhat ambiguous as to whether John actually composed his writing while still exiled on Patmos or at some later point.[13] Most scholars infer that John composed this work while still in exile.[14]

---

13. Schnelle, 523–24, notes that the aorist verb tense (John says he *was* on the island called Patmos) suggests John may have composed the writing later, subsequent to his return from exile.

14. Harrington, 52; Koester, *History and Literature of Early Christianity*, 253–55; Thompson, 26.

The limited internal and external clues point to a date of composition between 90–110.[15] Some Jews began using the term "Babylon" for Rome (see Rev 14:8, 16:19, 17:1–6, 18:2) after the destruction of Jerusalem and the Temple in 70. The letters to the seven churches attest to other troublesome issues, such as the presence of false teachers and the laxity of faith (2:4, 6, 14–15, 20, 3:9, 15). These same problems are mentioned in letters written in the late-first and early-second century (for example, the deutero-Pauline letters, 1 Peter, 2 John, and 3 John) by other authors to other Christian communities.

> ### The Island of Patmos as a Roman Penal Colony
>
> The rather small island of Patmos encompasses about thirteen square miles, seven miles north to south and six miles east to west. One of twenty-four islands of the Sporades, it sits off the east coast of the modern Greek mainland in the Aegean Sea and about thirty-five miles from the west coast of Asia Minor (in modern-day Turkey). Patmos is a volcanic island with a mostly rocky landscape. The Roman historians Pliny (*Natural History* 4.69–70) and Tacitus (*Annals* 4.30) note that Roman authorities routinely sent prisoners found guilty of offenses such as magic and astrology to three of the Sporades islands (Donusa, Gyarus, and Amorgus) but neither of them specifically mentions Patmos. It may be that Patmos was not one of the Romans' preferred islands for housing political prisoners.

---

15. Kelhoffer, 144, offers the range between 90–110 "or possibly later." See also James A. Kelhoffer, *Conceptions of "Gospel" and Legitimacy in Early Christianity*, WUNT 324 (Tübingen: Mohr Siebeck, 2014), 233–45, for an extended discussion of the dating of Revelation. Harrington, 9, argues for a narrower dating: 90–95. Ehrman, 537, argues for a different date of composition, believing John initially composed Revelation during the reign of Nero in the sixties (Nero being the most probable reference to the beast "666" in Rev 13:18) and completed it during the reign of Domitian, around 95. By contrast, Schnelle, 530–31, argues in favor of the literary integrity of the Revelation of John, and argues for a date of composition between 90–95, 524.

Summary of Historical Setting for the Revelation of John

Author	John, a Christian prophet
Audience	seven churches in Asia Minor: Ephesus, Smyrna, Pergamon, Thyatira, Sardis, Philadelphia, and Laodicea.
Date of Composition	around 90–110
Place of Composition	the island of Patmos

Theology and Ethics

John's theology and ethics are shaped by his apocalyptic worldview. For John, the world was soon to be the site of a cosmic battle between good and evil, with God in ultimate control of the battle and its outcome. In the present, John would maintain that he and the churches to which he writes live in a time of crisis and anticipation; they face significant challenges ranging from persecution by outsiders to the presence of false Christian teachers (rival leaders) and disillusioned believers within their communities. Most significantly, they will face an unprecedented level of persecution by the forces of evil operative in and throughout the Roman Empire. John weaves together a message of encouragement and a stern warning for beleaguered believers who may be tempted to compromise their faith or who have already done so, according to John.

John's beliefs about God as the one on the throne (theology) and Jesus as the slain Lamb (Christology) influence his views of the end times (eschatology), how believers are saved (soteriology), and the role of the church (ecclesiology) in God's master plan for salvation. The ethical imperative of this apocalypse emerges in the directives for faithful endurance and right conduct in the anticipation of the imminent and catastrophic end times.

God

The plan (and wrath) of God in the coming tribulation serves as the driving force behind John's theology. The author of Revelation portrays God as the one who sits on the throne in a heavenly court and "whose appearance sparkled like jasper and carnelian" (4:3).[16] God is frequently characterized as the "Lord God almighty" (4:8, 11:17, 15:3, 16:7, 21:22; cf. 19:6, 15), who is eternal (4:8), who reigns in heaven and on earth (11:17, 19:6), and whose judgments are just and true (15:3, 16:7, 19:2). As king and judge of all, God deserves praise, honor, and glory (4:11, 5:13, 7:12, 15:4, 19:7).

In Revelation, God has total control and orchestrates history toward salvation. In John's visions, as prelude to the return of Christ and the final judgment, God is about to unleash events that will trigger the end times: "the appointed time is near" (1:3). John prophesies at a time of an anticipated widespread persecution, when the devil will soon roam the earth in the form of a dragon (12:9) and inflict enormous pain and suffering on the Christian

Satan appears as a dragon in this medieval commentary on the book of Revelation. Revelation 12:9 identifies Satan with "the ancient serpent" that tempted Adam and Eve, a connection not actually present in the temptation story in Genesis.

---

16. At times, it is unclear whether God or Christ is on the throne—or if John is particularly concerned about distinguishing them. (See, e.g., Rev 7:9–10, 17).

The Patriarchs and Apostles, wearing crowns, worship the Lamb in this fifteenth-century manuscript illumination. If Revelation were penned by the Apostle John, as was once thought, this vision becomes awkward: he was looking at himself.

congregations (2:10). The devil, in fact, is fully embedded in the power and authority structures of the Roman Empire (13:2). The pagan society, its leadership, and its structures are corrupt and corrosive. Believers must stay away to remain pure. The author of Revelation also points out, though, that God will be coming soon (1:4, 8, 4:8, 22:7) to overthrow the devil (12:12), to exact judgment upon the nonbelievers, especially those who openly oppose and oppress Christians (18:10), and even "erase" the names of Christ-believers from "the book of life," which lists those who resist temptation and endure the coming tribulation (3:5). As heavenly king, God is moving history toward its end when all will experience the divine new creation: "The one who sat on the throne said, 'Behold, I make all things new'" (21:5).

Decoding the Revelation of John

In apocalyptic literature, colors, numbers, and images often have a symbolic or allegorical meaning connected to real events and people, and contemporary political and religious institutions during the author's lifetime. The events, people, politics, and religion

Continued

> **Decoding the Revelation of John** *Continued*
>
> to which the book of Revelation alludes are those of the Roman Empire around the turn of the first century.
>
> Scholars have identified how John's ancient audience likely would have understood the meaning behind many of the symbols in the Revelation of John:
>
> COLORS: **white** (divine world, resurrection, victory, dignity); **black** (disaster, distress); **red** (bloody power, violence); **green** (death); **purple** and **scarlet** (wickedness)
>
>> Then I watched while he broke open the sixth seal, and there was a great earthquake; the sun turned black as dark sackcloth and the whole moon became like blood. (Rev 6:12)
>
> NUMBERS: **one/first** (exclusiveness, primacy); **half/three and a half** (limited time, restricted period); **four** (universality); **six** (imperfection); **seven** (perfection, fullness); **twelve** (the twelve tribes of the chosen people, continuity of the old with the new); **thousand** (large number)
>
>> The seven angels who were holding the seven trumpets prepared to blow them. (Rev 8:6)
>
> IMAGES: **the lamb** (Christ); **the one who sits on the throne** (God); **the twenty-four other thrones and elders** (the twelve tribes of Israel and the twelve apostles); **the four living creatures** (all of creation); **the scroll** (the prophetic message); **the two witnesses** (unnamed prophets and witnesses to the faith); **the woman and the child** (presumably Mary and Jesus and/or the church); **the dragon** (the devil); **the two beasts** (the Roman Empire and false prophets); **666** (Caesar Nero); **144,000** (12 X 12,000—large numbers from the tribes of Israel); **Babylon, the harlot** (Rome); **the new Jerusalem** (both heaven and earth united after evil is expelled).
>
>> The beast I saw was like a leopard, but it had feet like a bear's, and its mouth was like the mouth of a lion. To it the dragon gave its own power and throne, along with great authority. I saw that one of its heads seemed to have been mortally wounded, but this mortal wound was healed. Fascinated, the whole world followed after the beast. They worshiped the dragon because it gave its authority to the beast; they also worshiped the beast and said, "Who can compare with the beast or who can fight against it?" (Rev 13:2–4)

Christology

In the Revelation of John the dominant image of Christ is that of the "lamb" of God;[17] John uses it twenty-eight times as a title for Jesus. He introduces Jesus as the "slain" Lamb (5:6), from the lineage of King David (5:5, 22:16), who is now exalted in heaven (5:9–14). The Lamb alone has the authority to break the seals of God's scroll in heaven (5:2–5, 6:1), unleashing the wrath of God upon unbelievers on earth as the end times unfold (6:16–17). As the "Lamb" and God's "Anointed" one, Jesus will bring salvation to the world (7:10, 12:10). In the aftermath of the end times, a new creation is born: Jerusalem is adorned as the bride of the Lamb (21:2, 9), and "the Lord God almighty and the Lamb" (21:22) replace the Temple in Jerusalem as the source of divine presence among the people.

John's Christology is also encapsulated in the greeting of this apocalypse, where Jesus is "the faithful witness, the firstborn of the dead and ruler of the kings of the earth" (1:5). Through the blood of his cross, Christ has "freed" believers from their sins and has made them "into a kingdom [and] priests for his God and Father" (1:5b–6). The greeting also includes an affirmation of Christ's imminent return (1:7). The coming Parousia is critical to arrival of the end times because Christ, crucified and raised from the dead, serves as God's agent to accomplish the plan of salvation. As "the Alpha and the Omega" (1:8, 21:6), God has total control. And God's will is fulfilled through Christ not only in the past savings acts of his death, Resurrection, and ascension, but also in the upcoming cosmic battle between the forces of good and evil.

The opening vision reported by John portrays Jesus in graphic imagery as the "son of man" ready for battle (1:12–16). Jesus will return from his place seated on a heavenly throne and will be instrumental in battling the forces of evil (5:1–14, 6:1–8:1). As the resurrected and ascended Christ, Jesus stands next to God, who is enthroned in heaven; both receive worship and praise from the heavenly creatures and the "elect" who were martyred for their faith (5:9–14, 7:9–17, 19:5–8).

---

17. The image of Christ as "Lamb of God" is also used in the Gospel of John as a title for Jesus (see, for example, 1:29, 36).

Finally, Revelation also presents an angelic Christology.[18] The exalted Jesus is portrayed at times as a supernatural being (1:13–16). At other times Jesus is presented as a human-like figure who is temporarily separated from the divine throne but with angelic form and function (14:14–16). Jesus is even portrayed as the heavenly warrior and angelic figure serving as the commander of God's army, ready to release "the fury and wrath of God the almighty" (19:11–16).

Eschatology

In Revelation, the end times are "revealed" to the reader during the unfolding of the narrative. In fact, the opening line of the Revelation of John signals its apocalyptic, eschatological orientation: "The revelation [Greek: *apokalypsis*] of Jesus Christ, which God gave to him, to show his servants what must happen soon" (1:1).[19] According to John, the end times are near (1:3, 12:12) and the return of Christ is imminent (1:8). This dualism and accompanying pessimism are part of the apocalyptic worldview.

The events associated with the end of the age are orchestrated to defeat the forces of evil in the world (11:15–19, 20:10). God and the Lamb (6:16) will unleash their wrath upon the world to avenge the blood of the martyrs (6:10). All those who opposed God and who persecuted believers in Christ will face God's "fury" (11:18, 14:19, 15:1, 7, 16:1) in the final battle.

In the aftermath, only "a new heaven and a new earth" (21:1) will remain. God will dwell "with the human race" (21:3) and the "old order," characterized by tears, pain, mourning, and death, will be "no more" (21:4). Only those names "written in the Lamb's book of life" will enjoy the new, eternal life (21:27), where the reign of God will last "forever and ever" (22:5). For the "unfaithful," the "cowards," a different destiny awaits. Their future involves a "burning pool of fire and sulfur, which is the second death" (21:8). The pessimistic eschatological scenario (all

---

18. See Peter R. Carrell, *Jesus and the Angels: Angelology and the Christology of the Apocalypse of John* (New York: Cambridge University Press, 1997) for a thorough study of the angelic Christology in the Revelation of John. Carrell, 220–32, offers a comprehensive summary conclusion.

19. See Scott M. Lewis, *What Are They Saying about New Testament Apocalyptic?* (New York: Paulist Press, 2004), 7–21, for an introduction and scholarly survey of New Testament apocalyptic literature, which Lewis, concurring with the late German scholar Ernst Käsemann, describes as "the mother of all theology."

will be destroyed except what God saves) is a warning for believers to choose sides and not to compromise with the evil world. According to John, the whole (pagan) world, including the Roman Empire, will be destroyed soon: within three and one-half years (11:2).[20]

> ## Satan in the Revelation of John
>
> Given its apocalyptic perspective, with its view of the world as a duality of good and evil, it is not surprising that Satan plays a prominent role in the Revelation of John. John accentuates the influence of Satan and demonic forces both within the seven churches of Asia Minor and as a threat from outside the communities. The prophetic oracles in Revelation 2–3 expose the presence of Satan as an internal threat, for example, in the churches of Smyrna and Philadelphia, where some in the community "claim to be Jews and are not" but actually are "members of the assembly of Satan." They bring significant distress to these churches. This likely reflects a conflict between Jews who did, and did not, trust in Christ. In his letter to the Christians of Pergamum, John acknowledges that the congregation (unfortunately) lives "where Satan's throne is," a likely reference to the cult devoted to the Roman emperor that flourished there. In Thyatira, some community members are drawn to "the so-called deep secrets of Satan."
>
> John also speaks of Satan as an external threat, portraying him as "the huge dragon, the ancient serpent" (12:9) who seeks to deceive the world and destroy Christians. Expelled from heaven, the Devil brings to earth "great fury" (12:12). Satan empowers "the beasts" (the Roman Empire and the false prophets) to attack and murder Christians and to mislead the inhabitants of the earth.
>
> Part of the message of hope and encouragement communicated in the Revelation of John is that while Satan is real and adversely affects the lives of Christians, God is sending Christ as the slain and resurrected "Lamb" in the final and definitive battle with Satan and the forces of evil. In the battle at the end times, Satan will be defeated. Therefore, Christ-believers need not fear the threats posed by the synagogue or the imperial cult, but must refrain from participating in their religious rites.

---

20. John's prediction was indeed realized 350 years later with the fall of the Roman Empire in 476.

Soteriology

Salvation in the Revelation of John requires an active and ongoing response by believers and a readiness to remain faithful to Christ during the coming tribulation. Faith alone in Jesus as the crucified and resurrected Christ sent by God to free believers from their sins is insufficient for one's salvation. Believers must also repent from various sins: negligence in the practice of the faith (2:4), promoting and supporting false teachings (2:21, 9:20), insincere and inadequate works (2:5), as well as arrogance and self-deception (3:17–19). With the return of Christ imminent and the battle between the forces of good and evil soon to commence, believers who have not been faithful must "repent" in order to be saved (2:5, 16, 22, 3:3, 9:21).

But faith and repentance do not automatically secure salvation. Believers must actively resist both internal and external threats in anticipation of the final tribulation. In this way, salvation in the Revelation of John is actually conditional and not assured. Salvation is assured to those who resist compromise but is also contingent upon such resistance. It is not simply assured by the believer's past and present faith in Christ.

Salvation within the Johannine Writings

Both the Revelation of John and the Johannine writings speak of salvation in terms of "conquering" the world. In the Gospel of John and in 1 John, Jesus has *already* "conquered" the world, and faith in Jesus allows believers to participate in that victory:

> I have told you this so that you might have peace in me. In the world, you will have trouble, but take courage, I have conquered the world. (John 16:33)

> For whoever is begotten by God conquers the world. And the victory that conquers the world is our faith. Who indeed is the victor over the world but the one who believes that Jesus is the Son of God? (1 John 5:4–5)

In Revelation, the resurrected Christ has also "conquered" the world (3:21, 5:5). However, the believer's salvation is not solely dependent

Continued

> **Salvation within the Johannine Writings** *Continued*
>
> upon Christ's victory; the believer must also "conquer" the world by remaining faithful under duress and by resisting rival leaders in the community who promote pagan practices:
>
>> Do not be afraid of anything you are going to suffer. Indeed, the devil will throw some of you into prison that you may be tested, and you will face an ordeal for ten days. Remain faithful until death, and I will give you the crown of life. (Rev 2:10)
>>
>> Yet I hold this against you, that you tolerate the woman Jezebel, who calls herself a prophetess, who teaches and misleads my servants to play the harlot and to eat food sacrificed to idols. (Rev 2:20)
>
> In the Gospel and Epistles of John, salvation is a present and unconditional reality for believers because of their faith in Christ. This is not the case in the Revelation of John. In fact, salvation in Revelation is a future, conditional reality, based on how effectively the *believer* "conquers" the world in terms of faithful endurance and resistance to the practices of the imperial cult while waiting for the coming tribulation of the end times.[21] In Revelation, Christ is the model for believers to follow: he conquered, and those who wish to be saved must do the same.

Ecclesiology

The prophetic oracles sent from John to the seven churches of western Asia Minor (Rev 2–3) imply the existence of organized groups of believers. However, John's oracles make no mention of any formal leadership structure, such as bishops or elders, among those believers. John refers to himself simply as a "brother" (1:9) and "servant" (19:10, 22:9) among fellow believers of these Christian congregations. The designation of "servant," in fact, applies to all members of the church (2:20, 7:3, 19:2, 5, 22:3) and even the angels in heaven (22:9). Although John refers to himself as a brother and servant to fellow church members, the recording of the visions, which are

---

21. See further Kelhoffer, *Persecution, Persuasion and Power*, 160–63.

characterized as a "prophetic message" (1:3) and are described by John as "prophetic words" (22:18), implies that John considered himself to be a prophet (22:9). How the Christian leaders whom John criticizes would have regarded John is unknown.

One distinctive aspect of John's ecclesiology is the direct communication that exists between the churches and the resurrected and ascended Christ. No hierarchical structures or church offices are needed to mediate between the human and the divine. In the letters sent to the congregations, John presents himself as simply relaying a message from Christ himself. An intimate tone pervades the letters and each one begins with a personal greeting to the community members ("I know your works" or a similar phrase 2:2, 9, 13, 19, 3:1, 8, 15).

Faithful Endurance

The prophetic oracles sent to the churches communicate the ethical standards that all believers are expected to uphold. Community members should avoid false teachers who pass along erroneous ideas (2:14, 20). The letters specifically name some teachers (the Nicolaitans, 2:6, 15) and indirectly identify others (the false prophet "Jezebel," 2:20; those promoting the "secrets of Satan," 2:24). John also cautions the communities to avoid the trappings of wealth and riches (3:17).

The Revelation of John consistently expresses two ethical imperatives: faithful endurance in the face of persecution (2:10, 3:11) and remaining true to their faith (2:4, 25, 3:2, 15). For some believers, repentance is needed (2:5, 16, 21, 3:3, 19); for all believers, perseverance in times of duress and suffering is required (2:10, 7:14, 13:10). Some of the Christian congregations are fortunate enough to have members who model this behavior (2:24, 3:4) for others.

Right conduct

Embedded within the letters to the churches is an underlying message from the resurrected and ascended Christ: "Remain faithful until death, and I will give you the crown of life" (2:10). Being "faithful" involves the avoidance of eating food offered to idols (2:14, 20) and not worshipping the beast or becoming involved with the harlot (13:4, 17:6).

The apocalypse lays out additional moral guidelines toward the end of the text, calling on believers to be courageous, chaste, honest, and truthful, and to avoid murder and idol worship[22] (21:8, 22:15).

> ### Summary: Historical Context, Theology, and Ethics of Revelation of John
>
> **CORE CONCEPTS**
>
> - John wrote the book of Revelation to seven churches in western Asia Minor from his exile on the island of Patmos.
> - Apocalyptic eschatology pervades the Revelation of John: the end times are unveiled to the reader in the unfolding of the narrative.
> - Faithful endurance and openness to repentance are central moral imperatives in the Revelation of John.
>
> **SUPPLEMENTAL INFORMATION**
>
> - The Revelation of John was composed toward the end of the first century, around 90–110.
> - The author, "John," presents himself as a Christian prophet. He is different from the author(s) of the Gospel and Epistles of John.
> - God is portrayed as the judge of the universe.
> - The "Lamb" of God is the most frequently used title for Jesus.
> - Believers' salvation is dependent upon their continued resistance to pagan practices and faithful endurance during the chaos of the end times.
> - The Revelation of John contains no references to hierarchical church structures or to church leadership. John criticizes certain church leaders who, in his view, advocate compromise with the world and thereby jeopardize their followers' salvation.
> - Church members are expected to give heed to John's warnings and to be courageous, chaste, honest, and truthful.

---

22. John's concerns over the dangers of idol worship were clearly not shared by other Christians who did not view the worship of idols as compromise with Satan.

PART 2: THE *SHEPHERD OF HERMAS* AND THE *APOCALYPSE OF PETER*

The Historical Context of the *Shepherd of Hermas*

The *Shepherd of Hermas* offers some internal evidence that helps establish the text's author and audience as well as its date and place of composition. In addition, numerous early Church Fathers mention the *Shepherd of Hermas*; these external sources shed light on the historical questions.

The *Shepherd of Hermas* is comprised of three different types of revelations: visions, commandments ("mandates"), and parables ("similitudes"). The abbreviations *Vis.*, *Mand.*, and *Sim.* refer to these three parts of the *Shepherd of Hermas*. Compared to the Revelation of John, the *Shepherd of Hermas* is a very long and repetitive text. A central theme of repentance emerges throughout.

Outline of the *Shepherd of Hermas*[23]

1.1–25.7	**The Five Visions** The author of the text, Hermas, begins with some autobiographical information. He then reports a series of visions he receives from an angelic being whom he addresses throughout the visions as "Lady" (*Vis.* 1.1, 5, 2.3, 3.1, 4.3), "elderly woman" (*Vis.* 2.3, 3.1), and "young woman" (*Vis.* 4.1). In the fifth vision, another angelic mediator, called "the Shepherd" (*Vis.* 5.3), replaces the "Lady" and communicates twelve commandments and ten parables to Hermas. The Shepherd directs Hermas, "Write the commandments and parables—that you may read them regularly and so be able to keep them" (*Vis.* 5.5).

Continued

---

23. English translations of the *Shepherd of Hermas* are taken from *The Apostolic Fathers*, ed. and trans. Bart D. Ehrman, 2 vols., LCL (Cambridge, MA: Harvard University Press, 2003), 2:174–473.

Outline of the *Shepherd of Hermas* *Continued*	
26.1–49.5	**The Twelve Commandments ("Mandates")** Following the directives of the Shepherd, Hermas records twelve "commandments," which consist primarily of moral teachings on how to live a righteous life as a believer. Throughout this process, Hermas is in dialog with the Shepherd, often asking clarifying questions or engaging in further discussion (*Mand.* 3.3, 4.1.4, 6.2.2, 8.1–2, 12.3.1). The first commandment—to believe that "God is one" and to "fear him [God]" (*Mand.* 1.1–2)—grounds each of the remaining commandments. The subsequent commandments urge, for example, "do not slander anyone" (*Mand.* 2.2), "be patient and understanding" (*Mand.* 5.1), "refrain from evil . . . from adultery and sexual immorality, from lawless drunkenness, from evil luxury, from an abundance of food, extravagant wealth, boasting, pride, and haughtiness" (*Mand.* 8.2–3), and "do not be of two minds" (*Mand.* 9.1; see also *Vis.* 2.2.4, 3.2., 3.7.1).[24] The eleventh commandment takes up how to discern true Christian prophets from false prophets and concludes with an exhortation to "trust the spirit that comes from God and has power" (*Mand.* 11.17). The final commandment lists a series of virtues and vices, laying out how to avoid evil and do what is good (*Mand.* 12.1–6).
50.1–114.5	**The Ten Parables ("Similitudes")** With no transition, Hermas begins to report ten parables the Shepherd relayed to him. Most begin by identifying a simile (comparison) between the parable and the underlying topic addressed. For example, the first similitude, the

Continued

---

24. The theme of not being of two minds is prominent throughout the *Shepherd of Hermas*.

Outline of the *Shepherd of Hermas* *Continued*	
50.1–114.5	parable of the man living in a foreign city, addresses the reality that believers, as "slaves of God" (*Sim.* 1.1), are aliens on a journey in the world. The second similitude, the parable of the elm tree and the vine, speaks to the coexistence and mutual dependence between the rich and the poor in the community of earthly and heavenly riches. In *Similitudes* 9.1–33, the church is symbolized as a mighty tower that is still under construction and is anticipating the coming kingdom of God at the end times.[25] The tenth parable serves as a final warning to Hermas to do good and avoid evil until the end time arrives.

Author

The author of the *Shepherd of Hermas* was a Christian who probably lived near Rome in the first half of the second century. He is identified at the beginning of the work in the context of an opening vision, where he is called by name, "Hermas, greetings!" (1.4). Like the Revelation of John, and uncharacteristically for the genre, this apocalypse is not pseudonymous (written in someone else's name and authority).[26] The text reveals that Hermas was a former slave (now free) from the city of Rome (*Vis.* 1.1), married with children (*Vis.* 1.3.1–2), possibly a farmer (*Vis.* 3.1.2), who professes that people regard him as a pious, cheerful, and simple man (*Vis.* 1.2.1–4). Although he never claims the status of prophet, it is reasonable to assume he enjoyed or at least felt entitled to some type of privileged status as the recipient of divine revelations. The writing does not

---

25. *Similitude* 9, the building of the tower, is by far the longest and expands upon an earlier vision reported by Hermas (*Vis.* 3).

26. As mentioned above, most apocalypses, including *1 Enoch*, the Old Testament book of Daniel, and the *Apocalypse of Peter* (discussed below) are pseudonymous. See Carolyn Osiek, *The Shepherd of Hermas: A Commentary* (Minneapolis: Augsburg Fortress, 1999), 10–12, who raises the question "Is Hermas an Apocalypse?" Osiek argues, "*Hermas* forces the question of the limits of apocalyptic genre," 11.

specify that he held any formally recognized leadership role within his community, however.[27]

Audience, Place, and Date of Composition

The text offers little direct information about the place of composition or the intended audience. A few early references to the city of Rome (*Vis.* 1.1–2) and to the "Via Campania" (*Vis.* 4.1.2) suggest that city as the place of composition and may also indicate the Christian community in Rome was its target audience. In addition, the Muratorian Canon (an early listing of books belonging to the New Testament) mentions that Hermas composed his work in the city of Rome.[28] The Christian community to whom Hermas wrote appears already to have had a leadership structure in place, with bishops, presbyters, deacons, teachers, and apostles (*Vis.* 2.4.2–3, 3.5.1); faced some level of persecution (*Vis.* 3.2.1); and contained both rich and poor members (*Sim.* 2.1–10).

The writing provides few clues that point to a firm date of composition. Hermas appears to have had access to Jewish and Christian writings from the first and early-second centuries CE; he even refers to a now-lost Jewish writing known as the *Book of Eldad and Modat* (*Vis.* 2.3.4). More common are parallels to New Testament materials, such as Pauline images of the church and parables from the Synoptic Gospels.[29] In terms of external sources, early Church Fathers from the second and third centuries knew of the *Shepherd of Hermas*, and it was included on the list of canonical books in the Muratorian Canon.[30] While some Church Fathers freely quoted

---

27. This lack of reference to any specific leadership role within the community is also true for John in the Revelation of John.

28. Muratorian Canon, 73–74. This same source claims Hermas was the brother of Pope Pius I (140–155). For additional information and historical context for the Muratorian Canon, see Bruce M. Metzger, *The Canon of the New Testament: Its Origin, Development, and Significance* (New York: Oxford University press, 1987), 191–201.

29. Compare, for example, Herm. *Sim.* 9.13.5, "one spirit and one body," with Rom 12:4–5; 1 Cor 12:12–13; Eph 2:16–18; Herm. *Sim.* 5.2 with Matt 13:24–30, the parable of the weeds among the wheat; and Herm. *Vis.* 2.2.4 with Jas 1:8 about not being of "two minds."

30. See James S. Jeffers, *Conflict at Rome: Social Order and Hierarchy in Early Christianity* (Minneapolis: Fortress, 1991), 106–20, for an extended discussion on the use of the Muratorian Canon as a source for dating the *Shepherd of Hermas*. The *Shepherd of Hermas* is also listed among the canonical books in numerous surviving manuscripts, including the fourth-century Codex Sinaiticus and the sixth-century Codex Claromontanus.

from the *Shepherd of Hermas*,[31] others cast doubt upon its authority.[32] Furthermore, references to church offices, such as bishops, deacons, and presbyters, indicate a development in ecclesial structures that, generally speaking, was more prominent in the early second century. The *Shepherd of Hermas*, therefore, likely was composed somewhere in the first half of the second century, around 110–140.[33]

Summary of Historical Setting for the *Shepherd of Hermas*

Author	Hermas, a freedman
Audience	probably Rome
Date of Composition	early second-century, 110–140
Place of Composition	probably Christian communities in Rome

Overview of the *Shepherd of Hermas*

The *Shepherd of Hermas* is an apocalypse because the story recounts a series of revelations and angelic communications granted to Hermas by two different divine messengers: the "Lady" and the "Shepherd." The revelations are grouped into three categories: five "Visions," twelve "Commandments" and ten "Parables." The "Lady" reveals the first four visions. The fifth vision and all the commandments and parables are then conveyed to Hermas by the Shepherd, who is "the

---

31. Irenaeus, *Against Heresies* 4.20.2, quotes *Mand.* 1.1; Clement of Alexandria, *Miscellanies* 1.17, quotes *Mand.* 11. Cf. Origen, who quotes from the *Shepherd* in his *Commentary on Romans* and identifies the "Hermas" mentioned in Paul's Letter to the Romans (see 16:4) as the author of the *Shepherd*.

32. Tertullian, *Modesty* 10.12.

33. Jeffers, 119–20; Ehrman, *Apostolic Fathers*, 169; Koester, 263: "The date should not be moved too far into the 2nd century." Osiek, 18–20, argues for the date of composition to extend over a period of time, beginning perhaps as early as the last few years of the first century, "but stretching through most of the first half of the second century," 20.

angel of repentance" (*Sim.* 9.1). The dialogs and revelations, both those that occur initially between Hermas and the Lady and later exchanges between Hermas and the Shepherd, clearly show that these divine messengers offer not only revelations but also instruction. The work's title stems from the figure who gave most of the revelations to Hermas.

The major theological and ethical themes of this apocalypse (in regard to the church, the end times, and the reality of sin and importance of repentance) are communicated through the various visions, commandments, and parables. The apocalypse does not develop these themes in any systematic way; rather, they are touched upon repetitively in this very long work. Nevertheless, the central features of this genre (for example: a narrative framework; revelation mediated to humans by an other-worldly being; transcendent realities involving the end times and salvation) are all present in the *Shepherd of Hermas*.

Vision 3 and *Parable* 9 exemplify the theology and ethics embedded in the writing, in particular Hermas's ideas about the church (ecclesiology), the end times (eschatology), and the importance of repentance for salvation (soteriology). In *Vision 3*, for instance, Hermas recounts what the Lady revealed to and interpreted for him. He initially sees an "ivory couch," "six young men," a "great tower built upon the water," and "stones" (*Vis.* 3.1–2). Each of these heavenly objects, the Lady informs Hermas, represents another reality: the ivory couch stands for divine judgment, the six young men for the holy angels of God, the tower and the water for the church comprised of the baptized faithful, and the stones for all Christ-believers (both those who will be saved and those who will ultimately be rejected).

This vision includes both a present and future (end time) reality: the tower (the church) is still under construction by the six young men (the angels), but will soon be completed (*Vis.* 3.4.2). The completion of the tower will mark the arrival of the end times (3.5.5). In the meantime, the tower continues to be built with "stones" of varying quality: square and white stones are church leaders (3.5.1); hewn stones drawn from the sea are those who have suffered and died for the faith (3.5.2); stones simply taken from dry land are those who are upright and follow the Lord's commandments (3.5.3); stones tossed aside are sinners who need to repent (3.5.5); and stones broken off and cast far from the tower are unrepentant sinners who, ultimately, will have no place in the church (3.6.1). While the righteous believers can take comfort in God's control, salvation is by no means guaranteed; for those who sin, repentance is essential to ultimately securing a place in the kingdom of God (3.13.4).

On the right side of the couch are believers who have suffered and been martyred for the faith and who await their reward at the end times; due to their faithfulness amid oppression, they have "already pleased God" (3.1.9). Those seated on the left, including Hermas, have yet to earn their position on the right. In order to be "cleansed" of their "sins" (3.2.2), they must not be of "two minds."

In *Parable 9*, the Shepherd reveals additional images about the ongoing construction of the tower (the rock, the gate, and the virgins, *Sim.* 9.5.3). The rock and the gate are "the Son of God" through whom all enter the kingdom of God (*Sim.* 9.12.1–5). The virgins are the "holy spirits" who possess "the powers of the Son of God" and offer them to believers (*Sim.* 9.13.1–4). The symbolism is consistent with the fundamental idea, introduced in *Vision 3*, that the tower and the various stones represent the church still under construction until the divine judgment of all believers.

> ### The Dragon and Beast of Revelation and the Monster of the *Shepherd*
>
> A hallmark of apocalyptic literature is the inclusion of violent and strange creatures. The Revelation of John, for example, speaks of the "dragon" (ch. 12) and the two "beasts" (ch. 13). The dragon represented "the Devil and Satan" (12:9), and the two beasts were the Roman Empire and false prophets, all of whom were sent to destroy Christians in the catastrophic events associated with the imminent end times.
>
> The *Shepherd of Hermas* likewise describes an encounter with a "monster":
>
>> The sun began to shine a bit and suddenly I saw a wild beast, something like a sea monster, with fiery locusts spewing from its mouth. The beast was nearly one
>
> *Continued*

> **The Dragon and Beast of Revelation** *Continued*
>
> hundred feet long, and its head looked like a ceramic jar. And I began to weep and ask the Lord to save me from it. Then I remembered the word I had heard: "Do not be of two minds, Hermas." And so, putting on the faith of the Lord, brothers, and remembering the great things he had taught me, I courageously gave myself over to the beast. And so it came on with a roar, enough to lay waste a city. But when I approached it, the enormous sea monster stretched itself out on the ground and did nothing but stick out its tongue; otherwise, it did not move at all until I had passed by. (*Vis.* 4.1.6–9)
>
> In the *Shepherd of Hermas*, the monster represents the coming "great affliction" that will devastate believers who are of "two minds" and who fail to repent of their sins once and for all and trust the Lord (*Vis.* 4.2.4–6). Both the Revelation of John and the *Shepherd of Hermas* call believers to be ready for anticipated difficulties in the form of these strange creatures. Whereas Revelation anticipates an imminent arrival to the troubles that lie ahead for Christians, the *Shepherd* contains more of an indefinite future to these troubling times.

Hermas's ethics are set within the twelve "Commandments" or mandates, with the first setting the foundation for the others:

> First of all, believe that God is one, who created and completed all things, and made everything that exists out of that which did not, who contains all things but is himself, alone, uncontained. And so believe in him and fear him, and in your fear be self-restrained. Guard these matters and you will cast all wickedness from yourself and clothe yourselves with every righteous virtue, and you will live to God—if you guard this commandment. (*Mand.* 1.1–2)

Commandments 2–10 and 12 consist primarily of long lists of virtues and vices, advice and warnings that all believers should heed. The moral teachings in this section lack the symbolism and allegory that dominate the visions and parables.[34] Much of the material focuses on ethical challenges in daily life, ranging from unethical business practices to arrogance, hypocrisy, irritability, and "double-mindedness." One virtue in particular is held in high regard: self-restraint, especially in the area of sexual morality (*Mand.* 4.1, 6.1, 8.1–3, 12.2). Hermas himself confronts sexual temptation in the opening vision when he sees his beautiful former master, Rhonda, naked (*Vis.* 1.1–9) and again in *Parable* 9 when he spends the night with twelve heavenly virgins "as a brother, not a husband" (*Sim.* 9.11.3).

The theme of repentance from sin, repeated throughout the visions and parables, is also mentioned in several commandments (*Mand.* 4.2.1–4, 10.2.3, 12.3.2). Such repentance was a prerequisite for baptism. In the *Shepherd of Hermas*, repentance *after* baptism is also possible, but may occur only once. There is no hope for sinners who continue to sin after a post-baptismal repentance (*Mand.* 4.2–3); they are the "stones" cast far away from the tower. The discourse between Hermas and the Shepherd continues throughout the giving of the commandments, but now moves on to moral dilemmas. Should a man who is a believer continue to live with an adulterous wife? (*Mand.* 4.1.4–9). Hermas is advised that if the adulterous wife is unrepentant, the man can divorce her, but he should "live alone" in hopes of a future repentance. But if the adulterer never repents, that person should be avoided and not allowed to live in the community of believers.

The eleventh commandment breaks the pattern of moralistic exhortations and takes up the topic of discerning true and false prophets. Believers of "two minds," who exalt themselves and indulge in many luxuries (*Mand.* 11.12), are susceptible to the false prophets (*Mand.* 11.1–4). The true prophet shows the presence of the "divine spirit by his way of life"; he is "meek and humble" and "abstains from all evil and the vain desires of this age" (*Mand.* 11.8). Significantly, the very same problem—competition with other Christian prophets who held competing viewpoints—is begrudgingly acknowledged in the Revelation of John (see, for example, Rev 2:14–15, 20). Hermas's

---

34. In this way, the genre of apocalypse is stretched here, just as the oracles in Rev 2–3 stretch the genre.

teachings may not have been obviously correct to his hearers, since those teachings are part of a larger discourse that encompassed competing views, including views about morality and who will ultimately be included in the church after the final judgment. Hermas hopes that his hearers will be ready for that judgment. Some of them may have wondered why he was so worried about repentance and the coming judgment.

The *Apocalypse of Peter*

Historical Context

The *Apocalypse of Peter* offers almost no internal evidence to establish the text's author, audience, date, or place of composition. However, references to the *Apocalypse of Peter* by some early Church Fathers help to date its composition.

Outline of the *Apocalypse of Peter*[35]

1–2	**The End Times and the Fig Tree**
	The *Apocalypse of Peter* opens with Christ explaining to Peter and the other disciples the signs of the end times that will precipitate his return: Christ will "judge the quick and the dead and recompense every man according to his works." Peter then asks Christ to interpret the parable of the fig tree,[36] so he can understand the mystery of the end times. Christ

Continued

---

35. English translations of the *Apocalypse of Peter* are taken from J. K. Elliott, *The Apocryphal New Testament: A Collection of Apocryphal Christian Literature in an English Translation* (Oxford: Clarendon, 1993), 600–612. Elliott, 612, also offers a summary of the Ethiopic text of the *Apocalypse of Peter*, where it is revealed that Peter "appeals to Christ to have pity" on those suffering in hell and Christ shows them mercy and eventually releases them.

36. See Matt 21:18–20; Mark 11:12–26; Luke 13:6–9, 21:29–33 and the discussion below of the eschatological discourse in the Synoptic Gospels.

Outline of the *Apocalypse of Peter* Continued

1–2	explains to Peter that "the fig tree is the house of Israel," meaning that Israel, like the unproductive fig tree, has been cut off from God's salvific plan. Christ then warns Peter of "false Christs" who, upon being exposed and rejected, will create "many martyrs" from the "twigs of the fig tree."
3–14	**Divine Judgment at the End Times for the Sinner and the Righteous** Christ then shows Peter and the disciples how "the righteous and the sinners" are "separated" on judgment day. All those who saw the punishment that awaits the sinners "wept." Christ next reveals to Peter the transformation of creation on judgment day: the "whole creation dissolves" into fire—the sea becomes fire and even the stars melt. The elect who have done good are spared death by the devouring fire, but the unrighteous and sinners face eternal punishment, each according to their particular "transgressions." Many sins and their corresponding punishments are listed: blasphemers, who sinned in what they said, are hung by their tongues over fire for eternity; murderers are thrown into a fire with "venomous beasts" and "tormented without rest"; women who aborted their children are "swallowed" up to their necks in "foulness and excrement," tormented with "great pain"; female fornicators will be hung by their breasts, and male fornicators by their "loins" (testicles); and disobedient children are eaten for eternity by "flesh-devouring birds." The unrighteous and sinners repent in hell, but their confession is denied since God's judgment has already been rendered. Comparatively little is said of the reward that awaits the elect and

Continued

	Outline of the *Apocalypse of Peter* Continued
3–14	the righteous. They are taken by Christ into his "everlasting kingdom" and shown the "eternal good things."
14–17	**Peter's Commission and the Encounter with Moses and Elijah** After Peter's vision of heaven and hell, Christ commissions him, "Spread my gospel throughout all the world in peace." The scene then switches to the encounter between Peter and the disciples and Jesus, Moses, and Elijah on the "holy mountain." There they hear a voice from heaven proclaim, "This is my beloved Son in whom I am well pleased." After the encounter, Peter and the disciples descend the mountain, "glorifying God."

Author and Date of Composition

The author of this apocalypse is unknown. It claims to be written by the Apostle Peter: "And, I, Peter, answered and said to him [Christ]" (*Apoc. Pet.* 2). The text, however, is another example of early Christian pseudonymous writing. As is common for the genre of apocalypse, someone wrote this in another person's name (in this case, the Apostle Peter's) and drew upon his authority when composing it. In the Synoptic Gospels, the eschatological discourse discusses the signs of the end times prior to the appearance of the Son of Man (compare Mark 13; Matt 24||Luke 21:5–36). The author's use of the eschatological discourse in his opening chapter and the inclusion of the story about the Transfiguration of Jesus (see Matt 17:1–13; Mark 9:2–8) in chapters 16–17 dates this writing to a point in time after the writing of these Gospels, at least the end of the first century, decades after the death of Peter.

The text offers few clues to the date of composition. Some scholars infer that the phrase "false Christs" in the discussion of the parable of the fig tree (*Apoc. Pet.* 2) is a reference to the Bar Kokhba revolt of 132–135.[37] External evidence includes a citation of the *Apocalypse of Peter* 8 by the early third-century Church Father Clement of Alexandria, which would date the text to before about 225.[38]

Given the internal and external clues, scholars commonly date the composition of this text to the middle of the second century.[39] This apocalypse is thus roughly contemporary to the *Shepherd of Hermas* and somewhat later than the Revelation of John. Together, these three writings attest to the variety of symbolism in and numerous functions of apocalyptic literature.

Audience and Place of Composition

Especially since the actual author is unknown, it is quite difficult to say much with certainty about the intended audience or place of composition. If references to false messiahs in the *Apocalypse of Peter* 2 point to events associated with the Jewish revolt of Bar Kokhba, then Palestine is possible.[40] Alternately, Clement of Alexandria's knowledge and use of the *Apocalypse of Peter* could suggest Egypt as a possible location for its composition.[41] The identity of the text's original audience remains equally uncertain and subject to scholarly speculation. Inclusion of the *Apocalypse of Peter* in the list of canonical books found in the mid- to late-second-century Muratorian Canon and the fact that a number of early Church Fathers seem to be aware of this writing[42] suggests that it quickly moved beyond the original audience to circulate among Christians throughout the Roman Empire.

---

37. See Elliott, 595; Wilhelm Schneemelcher, *New Testament Apocrypha*, trans. R. M. Wilson, rev. ed. (Louisville: Westminster John Knox, 1991), 2:622.

38. See Clement of Alexandria, *Extracts from the Prophets* 41:1–2, 48:1.

39. Elliott, 595; Schneemelcher, 2:622.

40. Elliott, 595.

41. Schneemelcher, 2:625; Koester, 168, identifies Syria as the place of composition for the *Apocalypse of Peter.*

42. Elliott, 598–600, lists numerous Church Fathers who cite the *Apocalypse of Peter*, including Clement of Alexandria, Methodius of Olympus, and Theophilus of Antioch.

Summary of Historical Setting for the *Apocalypse of Peter*

Author	unknown
Audience	Christians of unknown identity and location
Date of Composition	middle of the second century, between 130–150
Place of Composition	unknown, possibly Egypt or Palestine

Overview of the *Apocalypse of Peter*

Unlike the Revelation of John and the *Shepherd of Hermas*, both of which have complex storylines and dramatic images and symbols, the *Apocalypse of Peter* is considerably shorter and has a relatively easy to follow narrative: on the Mount of Olives, Jesus explains to Peter and the disciples about the judgment to come at the end times. The world will be consumed by fire, followed by the final judgment of all people. There are only two possible ultimate destinations for all humanity: heaven or hell. Most of the story describes the horrors awaiting those condemned to hell. For example:

> Other men and women whose works were done in deceitfulness shall have their lips cut off; and fire enters into their mouth and their entrails [bowels]. These are they who caused the martyrs to die by their lying. (*Apoc. Pet.* 9)

It offers comparatively few details about what happens to those destined for their reward in heaven, beyond that they live in eternal bliss:

> I [Jesus] will cause the people to enter into my everlasting kingdom, and show them eternal good things to which I have made them set their hope, I and my Father in heaven. (*Apoc. Pet.* 14)

At the end of this apocalypse, Peter and the disciples witness Jesus' Transfiguration and the appearance of Elijah and Moses, and then hear a voice from heaven proclaiming of Jesus, "This is my beloved Son in whom I am well pleased: he has kept my commandments" (*Apoc. Pet.* 17). Peter and the disciples then descend from the Mount of Olives, praising and glorifying God.

In effect, the apocalypse inserts into the teaching of the earthly Jesus information about future rewards and, especially, punishments. The pseudonymous author of the *Apocalypse of Peter* presents a straightforward theological message: at the end times, severe divine judgment awaits those who sin against the "Most High" and squander the gift of life God has given (*Apoc. Pet.* 3). Jesus himself does not pass judgment; rather, God alone either condemns the sinner to hell or rewards the "elect and righteous" with "entry into my [Jesus'] everlasting kingdom" (*Apoc. Pet.* 14). God offers no mercy to those who die in a state of sin. In fact, judgment day is characterized as "the judgement of wrath" (*Apoc. Pet.* 5). The "sinners" in hell will suffer an eternal torment that corresponds to their particular sin: murder, fornication, or whatever it happens to be. The "righteous" experience "eternal good things" in heaven without any differentiation or degrees of reward in heaven (*Apoc. Pet.* 14).

The "tour of hell" motif found in works like the *Apocalypse of Peter* would have a powerful effect on the Christian imagination in subsequent centuries, as evident in this fifteenth-century illumination. The motif would find its fullest expression in *Dante's Inferno*.

> ## The Angels of the *Apocalypse of Peter*
>
> The *Apocalypse of Peter* mentions the many angels present in both heaven and hell, for example, those who "weep" at the site of the condemned (*Apoc. Pet.* 3). Four angels singled out by name for particular mention are Uriel (*Apoc. Pet.* 4, 6, 12); Ezrael (*Apoc. Pet.* 7, 9–12); Temlakos (*Apoc. Pet.* 8); and Tatirokos (*Apoc. Pet.* 13). These names do not occur in the Old or New Testaments.
>
> The "great" Uriel, described as "the angel of God," is in charge of "the resurrection of the dead at the day of judgment" (*Apoc. Pet.* 4). *First Enoch* 9, a Jewish apocalypse, also mentions the archangel Uriel; there it is said that he protected humanity from the "Watchers" (a group of fallen angels). Ezrael is the "angel of wrath" who summons the sinners in hell to face their torment. In *Apocalypse of Peter* 8, the angel Temlakos, whose name means "care-giver," protects the children aborted by their parents. Tatirokos, the "keeper of hell," offers no mercy to the unrighteous in hell, who suffer without end.

In the *Apocalypse of Peter*, the ethical imperative, like the theological message, is direct: Christians are called to put their faith into action by living a moral life. The apocalypse does not lay out particular ethical guidelines for believers; rather they are given a stark warning about sins that warrant eternal damnation, including murder, blasphemy, abortion, disobedience to parents and masters, and adultery. That warning implies ethical guidelines in terms of grievous sins to avoid. As in Revelation and the *Shepherd of Hermas*, repentance of sins is possible in this life, but once the end times arrive, the sinner's atonement is no longer accepted by God (*Apoc. Pet.* 13).

Questions for Review

1. Where was the Revelation of John composed? What kind of place was it? Was that John's original home or place of ministry?
2. What are some of the challenges and difficulties faced by the seven churches to which John wrote?

3. What does it mean to say that the Revelation of John has an apocalyptic eschatology? What is the relationship of the genre apocalypse to the worldview known as apocalypticism?
4. What is one distinctive feature of the ecclesiology in the Revelation of John?
5. How is Jesus portrayed in the Revelation of John?
6. When and where was the *Shepherd of Hermas* composed, and what can be said of the intended audience?
7. What autobiographical details are revealed about its author, Hermas?
8. What are some of the major theological and ethical themes of the *Shepherd of Hermas?*
9. What is the historical setting claimed in the *Apocalypse of Peter?*
10. According to the *Apocalypse of Peter,* what are some of the tortures of hell? In what ways do the punishments fit the crimes?

Questions for Reflection

1. What impressed you most in your reading of the Revelation of John? What makes Revelation different from other New Testament writings and from the *Shepherd of Hermas* and the *Apocalypse of Peter?*
2. John is concerned about Christians who have assimilated too much into the surrounding pagan culture. How does this compare or contrast to ways that modern people of faith balance their religious beliefs with the beliefs of the larger secular world? Is it always possible to distinguish clearly between what is religious and what is secular? Can people of (the same) faith have different views about where to draw the line?
3. What do you think modern Christians should do with the Revelation of John? What does it mean for Christians in a post-modern world to engage this apocalyptic vision?
4. What is your reaction to the graphic images of hell in the *Apocalypse of Peter?*

Recommendations for Further Reading

The Revelation of John

Barr, David L., ed. *Reading the Book of Revelation: A Resource for Students.* Atlanta: SBL Press 2003.

This book is a collection of essays designed to present various aspects of the Revelation of John. Each essay stands on its own, with some essays more historically oriented ("Ordinary Lives: John and His First Readers") and others addressing such areas as ethics ("Doing Violence: Moral Issues Reading John's Apocalypse") and contemporary application ("The Lion/Lamb King: Reading the Apocalypse from Popular Culture").

Koester, Craig R. *Revelation and the End of All Things.* Grand Rapids: Eerdmans, 2001.

Koester offers an introduction to the Revelation of John that balances the cultural context of the first-century readers to whom it was addressed with the contemporary world of current readers. Koester begins by presenting the various ways others have interpreted "the mystery" of this apocalypse, and then walks through the storyline of the Revelation of John while offering literary and historical analysis.

Lewis, Scott M. *What Are They Saying about New Testament Apocalyptic?* New York: Paulist Press, 2004.

In this survey, Lewis presents different methodological approaches to the study of the Revelation of John. Lewis covers a wide range of areas, from "Jesus and the End of the Ages" to "Apocalyptic, the World, and the Church," and brings the reader up to date on the latest scholarly research on ancient apocalyptic literature.

The *Shepherd of Hermas* and *Apocalypse of Peter*

Elliott, J. K. *The Apocryphal New Testament: A Collection of Apocryphal Christian Literature in an English Translation.* Oxford: Clarendon, 1993.

In one volume, Elliot introduces and translates a large number of early Christian extracanonical gospels, acts, epistles, and apocalypses, including the *Apocalypse of Peter.* This volume shows how literary forms of expression in the New Testament continued to develop even centuries later in subsequent (often pseudonymous) Christian literature.

Osiek, Carolyn. *Shepherd of Hermas: A Commentary.* Hermeneia. Minneapolis: Augsburg Fortress, 1999.

Osiek presents a verse-by-verse commentary on the *Shepherd of Hermas*. She begins with an analysis of the literary, historical, and theological character of this writing. In this introduction, Osiek examines topics such as the text's integrity and reception, its main characters, and the role of "doublemindedness."

INDEX

Note: The abbreviations *c*, *cap*, *i*, *s*, *m*, *n* that follow page numbers indicate charts, captions, illustrations, sidebars, maps, and footnotes, respectively.

A

Abel and Cain, 128
abortion, 49, 160, 205*s*, 210, 210*s*
Abraham
    as church leadership role model, 129*s*
    as faith and works model, 21*s*, 28, 29, 36
    as faith model, 28–29, 129*s*
    Melchizedek and, 148*i*, 149*s*
    Old Testament references for audience theories, 25
abrupt endings, 48
Academy of Athens, 162*i*
action (works), 114*s*. *See also* faith in action
Acts of Peter, 66*s*
Acts of Peter and Andrew, 66*s*
Acts of Peter and Paul, 67*s*
Acts of Peter and the Twelve Apostles, 67*s*
Acts of the Apostles, 22, 24*s*, 67
Adam, 23*n*5, 89
adelphoi, 11*s*, 30*s*
adultery, 160, 196*s*, 203, 210
Agabus (prophet), 51*i*
Ahab, king of Judea, 37*n*15
Alexandria, Egypt, 26, 27*m*, 156–57
aliens (term usage), 56, 62, 69, 70, 197*s*
allegorical biblical interpretation, 140*n*4, 155, 156–57
ambition, 21*c*

Amorgus (Sporades island), 183*s*
Ananias the Younger, 23
anarchy, 40*s*, 47
Andrew (apostle), 66*s*
angels, 138*s*, 154*s*, 176–78*s*, 200, 210*s*
animal sacrifices, 145, 146, 150
Anointing of the Sick, 37, 37*s*
antichrists, 94, 114*s*, 117–18*s*, 119–20, 120*i*, 130. *See also* dissenters; false teachers and teachings
Antioch, Syria, 41, 42–43, 76
Antipas of Pergamon, 181, 182*s*
apathy, 144–45, 151–52, 181, 182
Apocalypse of Abraham, 173
Apocalypse of Enoch, 96*s*
Apocalypse of Golias, 172
Apocalypse of Peter
    audience, intended, 207
    authorship, 13*s*, 197*n*26, 206
    date of composition, 12, 206–7
    as extracanonical writing, 12
    historical context methodology, 204
    historical setting, summary, 208*c*
    literary genre of, 16*c*, 171
    outline and contents descriptions, 204–6*s*, 208–10
    place of composition, 103*n*13, 207
    Second Peter references in, 103*n*13

apocalypses, overview. See also
Apocalypse of Peter; Revelation of
John; *Shepherd of Hermas*
  audiences for, indented, 172
  authorship traditions, 197n26
  Christian, and dating, 172
  genre definition and description, 16c, 172–73
  as genre type, 12, 171
  historical contexts for, 172
  Jewish, 172, 173
  mediation methodology, 173
  purpose, 172
  worldview and themes of, 172, 189
Apollos of Alexandria, 140s
apologies, 13, 15c, 55, 57. See also
Apology of Quadratus; *Epistle to Diognetus*; First Peter; *Martyrdom of Polycarp*
Apology of Quadratus
  audience, intended, 78, 86
  contents descriptions and themes, 86–87, 86s
  date of composition, 12, 57, 78
  early church acceptance and copies of, 86
  as extracanonical writing, 12
  historical context and writing purpose, 55
  historical setting, summary, 80c
  literary genre of, 15c
apostolic age, 13s
Apostolic Canons, 12
Apostolic Fathers
  definition and description, 13s
  least appreciated, 166s
  themes/genres of books of, 14–16s
  title origins, 12n4
  writings of, 12, 93, 124, 135, 171
Aquila, 140–41s
Arezzo, Thomas d', 79s

arrogance, 35, 191, 203
Asia Minor
  communication networks in, 63m
  as composition location of extracanonical texts, 77ms, 78, 80n27, 84, 110, 125
  as composition location of New Testament texts, 103n13, 116
  as intended audience, 57s, 62
  Johannine community in, 111
  Revelation audience and churches in, 175s, 180, 180s, 181
  Satanic presence in, 190s
Assumption of Moses, 23n5, 96
astrology, 49, 183
Athanasius of Alexandria, 30
Athena (goddess), 162i
atonement
  Christological symbols of, 70, 146, 149s, 150, 153s, 188
  of sins, 143, 146, 148, 150, 151s, 191, 210
Augustine of Hippo, 30

B

Baal, 37n15
Babylon, 59s, 63, 64, 177s, 178s, 183, 187s
Balaam, 180, 181
baptism
  catacomb paintings illustrating, 19i
  as Christian identity foundation, 58s
  instructions for, 18–19, 50
  Noah's Ark analogies of, 69i
  path of life and, 48
  theology, 69–70
  visions as symbolism for, 200
Bar Kokhba revolt, 207

Barnabas (associate of Paul), 140*s*, 155
beasts
    extracanonical apocalyptic imagery of, 205
    New Testament apocalyptic imagery of, 178*s*, 183*n*15, 187*s*, 190*s*, 201*s*, 202*s*
    Old Testament and apocalyptic imagery of, 156
bishops, 19, 40*s*, 51, 82, 127
Bithynia (Asia Minor), 56, 57*s*, 62, 63*m*
black (color symbolism), 187*s*
blasphemy, 210
boasting, 181, 196*s*
Book of Eldad and Modat, 198
bowls of God's fury, 177–78*s*
Bryennois, Philotheos, 41*s*

C

Cain and Abel, 128
Calvin, John, 31
Cappadocia (Asia Minor), 56, 57*s*, 62, 63*m*
charity, 164
chastity, 194
child (title), 46–47
children
    conduct codes for, 130
    of the devil, 120*n*29
    of God, 110, 111*s*, 114*s*, 115, 120
    murders of, 49, 160, 205*s*, 210, 210*s*
chosen, the, 56, 70, 71, 111*s*, 115, 157*s*, 187*s*
Christ (title), 47, 68, 105, 114*s*, 119–20, 147–48
Christ-believers. *See also* Christian conduct, exhortations on
    as children of God, 110, 111*s*, 114*s*, 115, 120
    eschatological fate of righteous, 105, 189–90, 205–6*s*, 208, 209
    identity of, 56, 58*s*, 105, 136, 157*s*, 160–61
    reciprocity and obligation of, 161*s*, 164, 167
Christian church, early. *See also* Christian church leadership and organization
    apathy within, 144–45, 151–52
    canonical debates in, 9–10, 25, 30–31, 103*s*
    eschatological parables symbolizing, 197*s*, 200
    Jewish practices continued for legitimacy of, 84*s*
    legitimacy of, 84*s*, 86, 86*s*, 87, 136, 157*s*
    rules for path of life, 48
    unity symbols, 47*s*
Christian church leadership and organization
    challenges to (*see* dissenters)
    conflict and factiousness within, 25, 94, 126–29, 129*s*
    descriptions, 59*s*, 62, 192–93, 198, 199
    direct communication to Christ, 193
    instructions on, 40*s*, 50–51, 82–83, 127
    moral conduct of, 129, 130
    moral conduct toward, 152
Christian communication networks, 63*m*
Christian conduct, exhortations on. *See also* faith in action; love; repentance; wealth
    avoidance of evil and sin, 73, 122, 130, 196*s*, 197*s*, 205*s*, 210
    of church leaders, 130
    devotion, 99*s*, 108, 109

discipline and self-control,
72–73, 108, 131s, 139s, 152,
161s, 203
end times anticipation, 72, 165
faithfulness, 161s, 164, 167,
193–94
fear of God, 196s, 200
holiness, 73, 73s, 99s, 109
hospitality, 58s, 121n30
household codes, 48, 73, 75s, 130
humility, 21s, 35, 73, 128
life, path of, 39s, 48–49, 49s,
154s, 159–60
patience and perseverance, 34,
38s, 99s, 196s
poor, preferential treatment of,
20s, 32, 33, 36, 160
prayer, 19, 22s, 37, 50, 114s, 122,
164
rituals and practices, 18–19, 39s,
50
sexual morality, 106s, 194, 196s,
203
social conformity, 58s, 74, 88, 88s
tongue/speech, control of, 20s,
21s, 33, 35, 38s, 44s
virtues, 98s, 108–9, 154s, 164,
196s, 202–3
worldly abstinence, 20s, 33, 35,
38s, 73, 114s, 161s
Christian identity, 56, 58s, 105, 136,
157s, 160–61
Christocentricity, 18
Christology. *See also* cross of Jesus
Christ; Parousia
cornerstone of faith, 58s, 71
eternal divinity, 105
false teachings on, 104–5,
120n29
high priest and superiority, 138s,
148–49
humanity of Jesus, 83–84, 95,
114s, 118s, 120

Lamb of God, 175s, 177s, 184,
186i, 188–89
Messiah, 41, 116s, 120
Passion of Christ, 46, 84–85, 150
Son of God, 46–47, 88–89, 114s,
149, 201
suffering, 48–49s, 70, 74s, 82
supernatural descriptions, 189
Word and Word of life, 113s,
116s, 119
Christs, false, 205s, 206–7
Church Fathers. *See also specific
names of Church Fathers*
Apocalypse of Peter awareness, 207
Didache knowledge and usage,
39, 41
Epistle of Barnabas authorship
attributions, 13c, 155
First Peter authorship acceptance, 59
Hebrews authorship theories,
139
James, authenticity debates, 25
Letter of James canonical
acceptance, 30
Revelation of John authorship
acceptance, 10
Shepherd of Hermas citations by,
198–99
Church History (Eusebius of
Caesarea)
Apology of Quadratus citations in,
78, 78–79n26, 86s
Didache references in, 41s, 45
Gospel of John composition
location, 110
Hebrews authorship theories, 140s
James of Jerusalem references
in, 24s
Letter of James authenticity
debates in, 9–10
Second Peter authenticity
debates in, 103s

Index   219

Claudius, emperor of Rome, 142
Clement of Alexandria
    Apocalypse of Peter citations, 207
    Didache canonical acceptance, 45
    Epistle of Barnabas authorship
        theories, 155
    Epistle of Barnabas citations, 157
    Peter-associated texts as
        quotations, 67*s*
Clement of Rome, 124*n*33, 140*s*
cloud of witnesses, 139*s*, 151
Codex Alexandrinus, 12
Codex Claromontanus, 198*n*30
Codex Hierosolymitanus, 41*s*
Codex Sinaiticus, 9*n*1, 12, 198*n*30
Colossians, 75*s*, 102, 103*n*12
commandments, 48, 160, 195, 196*s*,
    199–200, 202–4
Commentary on Romans (Origen),
    199*n*31
confession
    of faith, 135, 141
    of sins, 37, 148, 160, 164, 205*s*
conversion of sinners, 37
Coptic Apocalypse of Peter, 66*s*
Corinth (Greece), 124, 126–29,
    163
couches, 200
Council of Trent, 31, 32*s*, 37*s*, 140*s*
covenant, 136, 138*s*, 145–46,
    148–49, 150, 157*s*, 159
    Christian claim to new, 136,
        138*s*, 145–46, 148–49, 150,
        157*s*, 159
    Gentile inclusion in, 28
    with Israel, 136, 138*s*, 141, 146,
        149, 157*s*
creatures. *See also* beasts
    dragons, 176–77*s*, 185, 185*i*,
        187*s*, 190*s*, 201–2*s*
    four living, 175*s*, 177*s*, 187*s*
    sea monsters, 201–2*s*
Crescens, 130

cross of Jesus Christ
    atonement/salvation symbolism,
        70, 146, 149*s*, 150, 153*s*, 188
    instruction on, 159
    Jewish Scripture and Platonic
        influence, 145, 145*s*, 146
    theme omissions, 18, 46, 50

D

Daniel, book of, 155–56, 173, 179,
    197*n*26
Dante's Inferno, 209
darkness *versus* light, 110, 113–14*s*,
    118*s*, 122, 154*s*, 159–60
day of the Lord. *See* end times
deacons, 19, 40*s*, 51, 82, 127, 130
dead, raising, 86, 86*s*
death, path of, 39*s*, 48–49, 154*s*,
    159–60
Decius, emperor of Rome, 65
Demetrius, 112–13*s*, 121
devotion, 99*s*, 108, 109
Didache (*The Teaching of the Twelve
    Apostles*)
    audience, intended, 41
    authorship theories, 13*s*, 40–41
    baptism instruction, 18–19
    canonical inclusion, 9*n*1, 44–45
    date of composition, 12, 42
    as extracanonical writing of, 12
    historical context methodology, 39
    historical setting, summary, 43*c*
    Latin translation of, 44
    literary genre of, 14*c*, 17, 46*s*
    literary integrity of, 43–44
    outline of, 39–40*c*
    place of composition, 42–43
    rediscovery of, 41–42*s*
    sayings and sources of, 34*s*
    theology and ethics, 18–19, 39*s*,
        46–51, 52*s*, 160
    word origins, 38

Diognetus, 79
Diotrephes, 94, 112–13s, 121–22
discipleship, 71, 82
discipline and self-control, 72–73, 108, 131s, 139s, 152, 161s, 203
disobedience, 139s, 141, 210
dispersion (term usage), 24, 25, 56
dissenters. *See also* false teachers and teachings
   church leadership conflicts, 94, 126–29, 129s
   denouncement of, 94, 96s, 104, 105–6, 106s, 112–13s, 114s
   dissention as immorality, 96s, 104, 105, 106s
   early Christian approaches to, comparisons, 131s
   embezzlers as, 130, 131s
   eschatological symbolism of, 120
   secessionists as, 118s, 121s, 131s
   slogans used by, 117–18s
divorce, 203
Docetism, 82, 83, 95
Doctrina apostolorum, 44
Domitian, emperor of Rome, 124n35, 183n15
Donusa (Sporades island), 183s
double-mindedness. *See* "two minds"
doxologies, 96s, 99s, 161s
dragons, 176–77s, 178s, 185, 185i, 187s, 190s, 201–2s
drunkenness, 196s

E

Ecclesiastes, book of, 23n5
ecclesiology
   of *First Clement*, 126–29
   of First Peter, 58s, 71
   of Ignatius, 82
   of Letter of Jude, 104, 105
   of Revelation of John, 192–93
   of *Shepherd of Hermas*, 200–201

Egypt
   composition location of extra-canonical texts, 103n13, 156–57, 163, 207
   composition location of New Testament books, 26, 27m, 103n13
elders
   church (*see* presbyters)
   as Johannine letter author, 111, 115, 118s, 119–22
   Revelation visions of twenty-four, 175s, 177s, 187s
election (the chosen), 56, 70, 71, 111s, 115, 157s, 187s
Elijah, 37, 206s, 209
elm tree and vine parable, 197s
embezzlement, 130, 131s
end times. *See also* Parousia
   aftermath for faithful, 175s, 178s, 187s, 189, 206s, 208
   aftermath for sinners, 189–90, 200, 203, 205–6s, 208, 209, 210s
   angels for, 210s
   anticipation and belief of, as obligation, 161s
   apocalyptic descriptions of, 185–86, 189–90, 200–201, 204–6s
   delay of, 99s, 107–8
   denial of, 99s, 104–5, 107–8, 107s, 164–65
   descriptions of, 40s, 42s, 47–48, 165
   for faith inspiration, 150–51
   preparation for, 22s, 26, 33–35, 42, 72, 154s, 160
   repentance as preparation for, 99s, 135, 164, 167, 191, 200
   salvation statistics, 176s, 177s, 187s, 188
   signs of impending, 40s, 47, 72, 120, 182s, 185–86, 194
   views on, comparisons, 108

Index **221**

endurance, faithful, 58s, 72–74, 108, 182s, 193
Ephesians, Letter to, 67, 68, 75s
Ephesus (Asia Minor)
   as composition location of Johannine texts, 110, 116
   as Revelation church and audience, 175s, 180, 180s, 181
"epistle" (term usage), 10
Epistle of Barnabas
   audience, intended, 155
   authorship, 13s, 155
   date of composition, 12, 155–56
   Didache contents in, 43
   as extracanonical writing, 12
   historical context methodology, 153
   historical setting, summary, 158c
   literary genre of, 15c, 135, 136
   outline and contents descriptions, 136, 153–54s, 155, 157s, 158–61
   place of composition, 156–57
   writing purpose, 135, 136–37, 158
Epistle to Diognetus
   audience, intended, 79
   authorship, 13s, 79
   contents descriptions and themes, 79, 87–89, 88s
   date of composition, 12, 57, 79–80
   destruction of, 79s
   as extracanonical writing, 12
   historical context, 55
   historical setting, summary, 80c
   literary genre of, 15c, 79, 87, 89
Epistle to the Philippians (Polycarp)
   audience, intended, 125
   authorship, 125
   contents descriptions and themes, 95, 129–30, 131–32
   date of composition, 12, 125–26
   as extracanonical writing, 12, 93
   form and function, 94
   historical context methodology, 123
   historical settings, summary, 126s
   letter-bearers for, 130
   literary genre of, 15c
   literary integrity debates, 125
   New Testament texts quoted in, 63, 110, 117
   resources for, 130–32
Erasmus, 31
eschatology. *See also* Parousia
   of *Apocalypse of Peter*, 204–6s, 208–10
   of *Didache*, 40s, 42s, 47–48
   of *Epistle of Barnabas*, 154s, 160
   of First Peter, 72
   of Hebrews, 150–51
   of Letter of James, 22s, 26, 33–35, 42
   of Pauline Letters, 108, 108s
   of Revelation of John, 182s, 185–86, 189–90
   of *Second Clement*, 161s, 164–65
   of Second Peter, 99s, 104–5, 107–8, 107s
   of *Shepherd of Hermas*, 200–201
Ethiopic Orthodox Church, 97cap, 173n3, 204n35
Eucharist, 19, 47s, 50
Eusebius of Caesarea
   Apology of Quadratus references, 78, 78–79n26, 86, 86s
   Catholic Letters, terminology usage, 9
   Didache references, 45
   extracanonical text copies owned by, 86
   Gospel of John composition location, 110
   Hebrews authorship theories, 140s

222 Index

James of Jerusalem references, 24*s*
Letter of James authenticity
  debates, 9–10
Second Peter authenticity
  debates, 103*s*
Eve, 23*n*5, 89
evil
  avoid returning evil for, 73
  commandments against, 196*s*, 197*s*
  condemnation of, 122
  eschatological battles and victory
    over, 176–78*s*, 184, 188, 189,
    190*s*
  as path of death, 48
  refrain from, 130, 196*s*
exhortations, 12, 13, 15*c*, 44*s*, 135.
  See also Christian conduct,
  exhortations on; *Epistle of
  Barnabas*; Hebrews, book of;
  Second Clement
Ezekiel, book of, 173, 179
Ezrael (angel), 210*s*

F

factiousness, 126–29, 129*s*
faith, defense of
  Christian superiority as, 87, 157*s*
  instructions for, 58*s*
  as letter writing purpose, 13
  as literary genre, 15*c*, 55, 57
  martyrdom as, 82, 84–85
  miracles as, 86–87, 86*s*
  social conformity as, 88
  texts as (see *Apology of Quadratus*; *Epistle to Diognetus*; First
  Peter; *Martyrdom of Polycarp*)
faith and faithfulness. *See also* faith,
  defense of; faith in action; "two
  minds"
  as believer's debt reciprocity,
    161*s*, 164, 167
  confession of, 135, 141
  endurance of, 58*s*, 72–74, 108,
    182*s*, 193
  laxity of, 144–45, 151–52, 181,
    182, 183
  Old Testament models of, 139*s*,
    151
  right conduct of, 193–94
  for salvation, 191
  testing, 25, 30*c*
faith in action
  debates on, 28–29, 35–36
  as ethical imperative, 21*s*, 23, 28,
    35, 44*s*, 210
  Old Testament models of, 21*s*,
    36, 36*s*, 129*s*
  for spiritual perfection, 32, 33
false teachers and teachings
  assessment and identification of,
    50–51, 51*i*, 196*s*
  as church opponents, 120*n*29,
    121*n*30, 179–80, 181, 183
  community members as, 106–7*s*
  criticism and denunciation of,
    98–99*s*, 114*s*, 121*s*
  episcopal control and unity for
    defense against, 82–83
  eschatological denial of, 99*s*,
    104–5, 107–8, 107*s*, 109,
    164–65
  as eschatological sign, 40*s*, 120
  former community members as,
    114*s*
  humanity of Jesus denial of, 83,
    119–20
  Jewish practices as, 82, 83–84
  as negative influences, 95, 165,
    181–82, 193, 203
  Revelation imagery for, 178*s*,
    187*s*
  textual sources for condemnation
    of, 98
  warning and avoidance of, 130,
    152

fasting, 19, 39s, 50, 158, 164
fear of God, 196s, 200
fig tree parables, 204–5s
first (numerology), 187s
First Clement
    audience, intended, 94, 124
    authorship, 13s, 94, 124
    contents descriptions and themes, 94, 126–29, 129s, 131s
    date of composition, 12, 124
    as extracanonical writing, 12, 93
    historical context methodology, 123
    literary genres of, 15c, 128n39
    place of composition, 124
First Corinthians
    baptism references, earliest, 50
    church leadership conflicts, 127
    Eucharist references, earliest, 47s
    extracanonical texts using, 163
    household codes, 75s
    James of Jerusalem references in, 24s
    Parousia, views on, 108s
First Enoch, 155, 173, 197n26, 210s
First John
    audience, intended, 115
    authorship, 11s, 115
    canonical inclusion, 93
    Christology of, 116s
    date of composition, 9, 116–17
    dissenters and false prophets, 94, 95, 117–18s, 119, 121s, 131s
    ethics of, 114s, 122
    form and function, 94
    Gospel of John relationship with, 110, 116s, 117
    historical context methodology, 109–10
    historical setting, summary, 118–19c
    Johannine letters and composition sequence, 117
    literary genre of, 15c
    opponents in, 120n29
    outline of, 113–14s
    place of composition, 116
    prolog and conclusion comparisons, 116s
    terminology used in, 110
    theology of, 119–20, 191s, 192s
First Peter
    audience, intended, 56, 57s, 62
    authorship, 11, 11s, 59–61, 61s, 103s
    Christian identity in, 56
    communication networks and delivery route of, 63m
    date of composition, 9, 12, 62–63
    historical context, 55
    historical context methodology, 57
    historical setting, summary, 64c
    Jewish Scriptures in, 72s
    literary genre of, 15c
    outline of, 57–59s
    Pauline Letters relationship to, 67–68, 75s
    place of composition, 64
    theology and ethics, 69–74, 73–74c, 75s, 88s
First Thessalonians, 61s, 108s
First Timothy, 75s, 108s
Flood, the, 69i, 72s, 98s
forgiveness of sins, 37s, 50, 51, 120, 131s
four (numerology), 187s
Four Ezra, 173

G

Gaius (church elder), 112s, 113s, 115, 121
Galatia (Asia Minor), 56, 57s, 62, 63m, 77m

Galatians, Letter to the
  faith and works, 28–29, 29, 35, 129s
  James brother of Jesus references, 26s
  James of Jerusalem references in, 24s
  two ways/paths, 49s
  virginal conception of Jesus, 83n29
Genesis, book of, 129s, 148i, 149s
Gentile Christians
  as audience, 41, 56, 141, 155, 162
  faith and works debates and, 28, 29
  Jewish character and omission of, 18
  Jews' relationship with, 26
Gentiles (non-believers), 58s, 72–74
gluttony, 196s
God
  apocalyptic perception and eschatological role of, 172, 177s, 184–86, 189–90, 209
  children of, 110, 111s, 114s, 115, 120
  descriptions and references of, 32–33, 32n13
  enemies of, 176–77s, 178s, 185, 185i
  Father and Son duality themes, 110, 114s, 120
  fear of, 196s, 200
  martyrdom as will of, 84
  reciprocity and obligation to, 161s, 164, 167
  slaves of, 197s
  thrones of, 185, 187s
  and world dualism, 110
Gospel of Peter, 66s
Gospel of the Egyptians, 163
Gospel of Thomas, 163

Gospels. *See also specific Gospels: John, Luke, Mark, Matthew*
  baptism references, 50
  canonical acceptance of, 163n27
  Christocentric theme of, 18
  date of composition, 9, 102
  eschatology in, 47–48
  Jude references, 97
  Passion of Christ, 84–85
  Son of Man references, 206
Greek Apocalypse of Peter, 66s
green (color symbolism), 187s
Gyarus (Sporades island), 183s

H

Hadrian, emperor of Rome, 78, 86, 156
half (numerology), 187s
harlots, 178s, 187s
hatefulness, 110, 114s, 122
healing miracles, 86–87, 86s
heaven, 89, 175s, 178s, 206s, 208, 209, 210s
Hebrew Bible. *See* Old Testament
Hebrews, book of
  audience, intended, 141
  authorship, 11s, 139–40, 140–41s, 151s
  canonical inclusion, 139, 140s
  Christian identification in, 136
  church circulation and text association history, 10
  date of composition, 9, 142–43
  historical context methodology, 137
  historical setting, summary, 143–44c
  Jewish and Platonic influences in, 145–46, 145s
  literary genres of, 15c, 135, 136
  Old Testament references in, 36s
  outline of, 137–39s

Pauline Letters comparisons, 151
place of composition, 143
theology and ethics, 138*s*,
  147–52, 149*s*
writing purpose, 136–37
Hegesippus, 24*s*
hell, 89, 189–90, 205, 208, 209, 209*i*,
  210*s*
Hermas, 197–98
Herod Agrippa I, 22, 85
high priest (title), 138*s*, 148–49
holiness, 73, 73*s*, 99*s*, 109
homilies, 79, 87, 89, 162, 166*s*
hospitality, 58*s*, 121*n*30
household codes, 48, 73, 75*s*, 130
humility, 21*s*, 35, 73, 128
hymns of praise, 96*s*, 99*s*, 161*s*
hypocrisy, 160, 203

I

idolatry, 87, 160, 162*ic*, 181, 192*s*,
  193, 194
Ignatius of Antioch, 13*s*, 76, 81–82,
  81*i*. See also Letters of Ignatius
immorality. See also sinners
  commandments against, 196*s*
  dissention as, 96*s*, 104, 105, 106*s*
  of false teachers, 104, 105, 106*s*,
    107, 136, 154*s*, 165
  sexual, 106*s*, 194, 196*s*, 203
imperial cults, 180*s*, 181–82, 190*s*,
  193
imposters and intruders. See false
  teachers and teachings
Irenaeus of Lyon
  as early apologist, 57
  First Clement authorship, 124
  First Peter authorship, 59
  Gospel of John composition
    location, 110
  Gospels and canonical acceptance, 163*n*27

Hebrews authorship, 140*s*
miracles, legitimacy of, 87*n*31
Isaac, 21*s*, 25, 29, 129*s*
Isaiah, 72*s*
Israel
  Christian ecclesiology and, 62,
    69, 71, 75*s*, 84
  Christian identity with, 56
  covenant of, 28, 136, 141, 146,
    149
  parable symbolism, 205*s*
  tribes of, 25, 176*s*, 187*s*

J

James (apostle), 22
James, Letter of
  audience, intended, 24, 25
  authorship, 9–10, 11*s*, 22–25,
    32*s*
  canonical acceptance and
    authenticity debates, 9–10,
    25, 30–31
  date of composition, 9, 25–26
  historical context for, summary,
    27*c*
  historical context methodology,
    19–20
  Jewish character of, 18, 32*s*
  literary genre of, 14, 14*c*, 17
  outline of, 20–22*c*
  Pauline Letters relationship to,
    28–29
  place of composition, 26–27,
    27*m*
  sayings and sources used in, 34*c*
  theology and ethics, 20*s*, 32–38,
    36*s*, 38*s*, 48
James of Jerusalem, 11*s*, 22–23, 24,
  24*s*, 26*s*
jealousy, 21*s*, 25, 34*c*, 35, 126–29
Jeremiah, 146
Jerome, 30, 79

Jerusalem
    composition location of New Testament books, 26–27, 27m
    new, 178s, 179, 187s, 188, 189
    Temple in, 23, 142–43, 142i, 156, 183, 189
Jesus Christ. See also Christology; Parousia
    ascension of, 150
    brothers of, 11s, 23, 26s
    church hierarchy and accessibility of, 193
    death of, 46, 84–85, 150
    as fulfillment of Jewish Scriptures, 145–46
    humanity of, 83–84, 95, 114s, 118s, 120
    Jewish-dominant texts and omission of, 18, 33–34
    as leadership model, 128
    miracles of, 86, 86s
    New Testament authorship and familial claim to, 11s
    Resurrection, 18, 46, 70
    Revelation visions of, 174–78s
    as salvation, 138s, 165, 166–67, 191s
    sayings of, 23, 30s, 34s, 46, 48
    as suffering model, 58–59s, 70, 82, 84–85, 138s
    superiority of, 138s, 147–48
    theological interest in family of, 26s
    Transfiguration, 206, 206s, 209
Jewish Christians, 82, 83–84, 141, 179
Jewish Scriptures. See Old Testament
Jews, 26, 50, 120n29, 142. See also Judaism
Jezebel (false prophet), 180, 181, 192s, 193

Jezebel, queen of Judea, 37n15
Johannine community, 111, 115
Johannine school, 110–11
John (apostle), 11s, 179
John, Gospel of
    Johannine letters relationship with, 110, 117
    opponents in, 120n29
    place of composition, 110
    prolog and conclusion comparisons, 116s
    soteriology of, 191s, 192s
Josephus, 23, 26s
Judaism. See also Old Testament
    Christian break from, 83–84
    Christian practice and inclusion of, 82, 83–84, 84s
    Christian self-identification with, 136
    covenant, 136, 138s, 141, 146, 149, 157s
    criticism of, 87, 157s
    New Testament texts predominately Jewish, 18, 32–34
Judaizers, 82, 83–84
Judas (apostle), 97
Judas Barsabbas, 97
Judas Iscariot, 97
Jude (brother of Jesus and James), 11s, 96–97
Jude (son of James), 97
Jude, Letter of
    audience, intended, 102
    authenticity debates, 9–10
    authorship, 11s, 96–98
    canonical inclusion, 93
    date of composition, 9, 101–2
    form and function, 94
    historical context methodology, 95
    historical setting, summary, 104c
    literary genre of, 15c

outline and contents descriptions, 94–95, 95–96*s*, 104, 105, 106*s*, 121*s*, 131*s*
place of composition, 103
Second Peter relationship to, 100–101*cs*
theology and ethics, 104–6
writing purpose, 96*s*
judgment, 20*s*, 21*s*
judgment day. *See* end times
Jupiter Capitolinus, 156
Justin Martyr, 57, 87

K

knowledge, 89, 110, 120, 121–22

L

Lady, 115, 195*s*, 199
Lamb of God, 175*s*, 177*s*, 184, 186*i*, 187*s*, 188–89
Laodicea (Asia Minor), 175*s*, 180, 180*s*, 181
later New Testament writings, overview, 9, 9*n*1
letters
  as communication method, 13
  epistles *versus*, terminology comparisons, 10
  genre styles used in, 13–14, 30*s*
  as literary genre, definition and description, 12, 15*c*, 29–30*c*
  multiple forms and functions of, 94
  New Testament and extracanonical books as, 15*c*, 93
  purpose of, 13
  as sermons, 136–37
Letters of Ignatius
  audience, intended, 76
  authorship, 76

contents descriptions and themes of, 81–84
date of composition, 12, 77–78
as *Epistle to the Philippians* attachments, 130
as extracanonical writing, 12
historical context, 55
historical context methodology, 76
historical setting, summary, 80*c*
language of composition, 77*s*
literary genre of, 15*c*
place of composition, 77*sm*, 78
life, path of, 39*s*, 48–49, 49*s*, 154*s*, 159–60
Life of Adam and Eve, The, 23*n*5
light *versus* darkness, 110, 113–14*s*, 122, 154*s*, 159–60
living church, 166–67
Lord (title), 32*n*13, 33, 47, 149
Lord's Prayer, 50
Lot, 98*s*
love
  for defense of faith, 58*s*
  exhortations for Christian conduct, 58*s*, 73, 73*s*, 98*s*, 108, 120, 152, 164
  hospitality as, 121
  as Johannine theme, 110, 114*s*, 121–22
  Mosaic Laws on, 20*s*
  as path of life/light, 48, 113–14*s*
  terminology usage, 110
  truth associations, 121–22
Luke (Gospel writer), 140*s*
Luke, Gospel of
  Jesus' arrest and seizure, 84
  Lord's Prayer, 50
  prolog comparisons, 87
  sayings of Jesus from, 34*c*, 48
  Second Clement references to, 163
  Son of Man references, 206
Luther, Martin, 31

M

magic, 49, 183
mandates (commandments), 195, 196s, 199–200, 202–4
Marcion, 78
marginalization, 56
Mark (associate of Paul), 59s, 67
Mark, Gospel of, 11s, 24s, 26s, 48n26, 50, 206
martyrdom
  apocalyptic visions honoring, 176s, 177s, 188, 201
  community members as models for, 181, 182s
  Jesus as suffering model for, 82, 84–85
  judgment and persecution of Babylon/Rome for, 178s, 189
  of Polycarp, 84–86, 85i
  preparation for, 81–82, 81i
Martyrdom of Polycarp
  audience, intended, 78
  authorship, 78
  contents descriptions and themes, 78, 84–86
  date of composition, 12, 78
  as extracanonical writing, 12
  historical context, 55
  historical setting, summary, 80c
  literary genre of, 15c
  place of composition, 78
Mary (Mother of Jesus), 83, 187s
Matthew, Gospel of
  baptism references, 40
  Didache historical context comparisons, 41, 42–43
  James references in, 11s, 24s, 26s
  Jesus' arrest and seizure, 84–85
  Jesus' sayings from Sermon on the Mount, 46, 48
  Lord's Prayer, 50
  Second Clement references to, 163
  Son of Man references, 206

Melchizedek, 138s, 148, 148i, 149s
mercy, 21s, 36, 96s, 106, 109s
Messiah, 41, 116s, 120
Methodius of Olympia, 207n42
Michael (archangel), 177s
miracles of Jesus, 86–87, 86s
monotheism, 87n32, 162, 196s, 202
monsters, 201–2s. *See also* beasts; dragons
Mosaic Law ("royal law")
  authorship theories and references to, 23, 155
  Christian interpretations of, 154s
  faith and works debates, 28, 29, 35
  wealth and preferential treatment, 20s
Moses, 23n5, 138s, 146, 206s, 209
Muratorian Canon, 30, 198, 207
murder, 160, 181, 194, 209, 210. *See also* abortion

N

Nero, emperor of Rome, 65, 142, 183n15, 187s
Nicolaitans, 179–80, 181, 193
Noah's ark, 69i, 72s, 98s
non-believers. *See* outsiders
numerology, 187s

O

oath swearing, 34
obedience, 58s, 73, 74, 129, 138s, 149s, 152
Old Testament (Hebrew Bible, Jewish Scriptures)
  apocalypses in, 173
  audience theories due to references from, 25
  belief without seeing models in, 139s, 151

Christian interpretations of,
  154*s*, 158–59
factiousness examples, 127
faith and works in, 21*s*, 36, 36*s*
for false prophet confrontation,
  96*s*, 97–98
in First Peter, 72*s*, 84*s*
high priests in, 148*i*, 149*s*
Jesus as fulfillment of, 145–46
for Jewish heritage and church
  legitimacy, 84*s*
leadership models from, 128
Noah's Ark references, 69*i*, 72*s*
prayer instruction models in, 37
two paths theology, 49*s*
wisdom traditions from, 18
wisdom writings and authorship
  attributions, 23*n*5
one (numerology), 187*s*
144,000 saved, 176*s*, 177*s*, 187*s*
oracles, prophetic, 175*s*, 180–82, 180*s*
Origen of Alexandria
  Catholic Epistles, term usage,
    10*n*2
  Didache canonical acceptance, 45
  Hebrews authorship theories,
    140*s*
  Letter of James canonical
    acceptance, 30
  miracles, legitimacy of, 87*n*31
  Peter-associated texts as
    quotations, 67*s*
  Second Peter authenticity
    debates, 103*s*
  Shepherd of Hermas authorship
    theories, 199*n*31
outsiders (non-believers)
  apocalyptic visions and fate of,
    177*s*, 186, 189–90
  Christian conduct for relations
    with, 58s, 72–74, 88, 88*s*
  dissenters/intruders as, 96*s*, 104,
    105–6, 106–7*s*

Jewish, 50, 120*n*29
pagan cult influences and
  over-assimilation, 180*s*,
  181–82
path of darkness and descriptions of, 154*s*
persecution from (*see* persecution)

P

paganism, 87, 95, 180*s*, 181–82,
  190*s*, 193
Papias of Hierapolis, 13*s*, 59
parables, 195, 196–97*s*, 199–201,
  204–5*s*
Parousia (second coming of Christ).
  See also end times
  apocalyptic visions of, 175–77*s*,
    188–89, 208–9
  expectations and descriptions of,
    72, 105
  expectations and timeline
    variations, 108*s*
  false teachings on denial of, 99*s*,
    105
  preparation for, 33–34, 72
Passion of Christ, 46, 84–85, 150
patience, 34, 38*s*, 99*s*, 196*s*
Patmos (Greece), 171, 174*s*, 180,
  182, 183*s*
Paul (apostle). *See also* Pauline Letters
  associates of, 59*s*, 61*s*, 67, 139,
    140–41*s*, 155
  church leadership influence, 51
  extracanonical texts associated
    with, 67*s*
  extracanonical texts with
    references to, 124
  Hebrews authorship theories,
    11s, 139, 140*s*, 151*s*
Pauline Letters
  baptism, 50
  Christocentric themes of, 18

church leadership conflicts, 127
date of composition, 9
eschatological misinterpretations of, 108
eschatological views in, 108s
Eucharistic instruction, 47s
faith and works debates, 28–29, 35–36
First Peter relationship to, 67–68, 75s
Hebrews comparisons, 151s
household codes in, 75s
James of Jerusalem references in, 24s
later New Testament writings associated with, 10, 11s
letters *versus* epistles, terminology usage and definition, 10
Second Clement use of, 163
Shepherd of Hermas comparisons, 198
virginal conception of Jesus, 83n29
penal colonies, 183s
perfection, 32, 33, 38s, 49
Pergamon [Pergamum] (Asia Minor)
  Christian persecution in, 181, 182s
  false prophets identified in, 179–80
  as Revelation church and audience, 175s, 180, 180s, 181
  Satanic presence in, 190s
persecution. *See also* martyrdom
  Christian identity and, 56, 58s
  Christology for, 58–59s, 70, 74s, 82
  counsel and instruction for, 58–59s, 65–66, 193
  as discipleship component, 71
  endurance models for, 181, 182s
  as historical context, 55, 62, 142
  as sign of end times, 72, 182s, 185–86
  sources of, 65, 184, 186
perseverance, 34
Peter (apostle)
  biographical information and authorship theories, 60
  early Christian writings connected to, 11s, 59–60, 66–67s, 96, 99, 103s, 206
  extracanonical texts with references to, 124
Petrine community, 61
Pharisaic Jews, 50
Philadelphia (Asia Minor), 175s, 180, 180s, 181, 190s
Philip (apostle), 67s
Philippi (Macedonia), 125
Philo, 156–57
Philomelium (Phrygia), 78, 84
Pius I, pope, 198n28
Plato, 145s, 146
Pliny, 183s
Polycarp of Smyrna
  as apostolic father, 13s
  epistles authored by (see *Epistle to the Philippians*)
  Ignatius's letters to, 12, 55, 76, 77–78, 77sm, 125
  letters on martyrdom of (see *Martyrdom of Polycarp*)
  martyrdom descriptions, 84–86, 85i
polytheism, 87, 162, 162c, 181
Pontus (Asia Minor), 56, 57s, 62, 63m
poor (poverty)
  exploitation of, 25, 36
  preferential treatment of, 20s, 32, 33, 36, 160
prayer
  exhortations on, 164
  instructions on, 19, 22s, 37, 50
  for sinners, 114s, 122

Preaching of Peter, 67*s*
presbyters (church elders)
    church leadership roles, 59*s*, 62, 82
    conduct codes for, 130
    as Johannine letter author, 111, 115, 118*s*, 119–22
pride, 35, 196*s*
Prisca (Priscilla), 140–41*s*, 140*n*5
prophets. *See* false teachers and teachings; teachers
Protestant Reformation, 31, 140*s*
Proverbs, 18, 23*n*5
pseudepigrapha (pseudonymity)
    apocalypse traditions of, 197*n*26
    for authority, 105
    definition, 11*s*
    extracanonical texts as, 206
    fictive practices of, 64
    New Testament books as, 23, 24–25, 60, 97, 99–100
    Old Testament texts as, 23*n*5
purification rituals, 47*s*, 50
purple (color symbolism), 187*s*

Q

Q (Sayings Source), 34*c*, 46, 48, 50
Quadratus. See *Apology of Quadratus*
quarreling, 25, 126–29, 160

R

Rahab, 21*s*, 36, 36*s*
reality, 145, 145*s*, 146
reciprocity of believer's debt, 161*s*, 164, 167
recycling, literary, 101*s*
red (color symbolism), 187*s*
repentance
    as apocalyptic message, 195
    baptism and, 50, 203
    for salvation, 99*s*, 135, 161*s*, 164, 167, 191, 200, 201, 203, 210

Resurrection, 18, 46, 70
resurrection of dead, 128, 143, 161*s*, 210*s*
retribution, divine, 96*s*, 98*s*
Revelation of John
    audience, intended, 174*s*, 175*s*, 180
    authorship, 10, 11*s*, 179
    canonical inclusion, 31
    date of composition, 9, 173, 182–83
    ethics of, 193–94
    historical context methodology, 174
    historical setting, summary, 184*c*
    illuminated manuscripts illustrating, 186*i*
    literary genre of, 171
    Old Testament resources for, 173
    outline and contents descriptions, 174–78*s*, 180–82, 180*s*
    Pauline Letters associations, 10
    revelatory methodology of, 173
    symbolism and decoding, 186–87*s*
    theology of, 177*s*, 184–86, 188–90, 191–93
rhetoric (literary genre), 128*n*39
righteousness
    as believer's debt payment, 161*s*
    characteristics of, 37
    commandments and parables for, 196 97*s*
    eschatological reward for, 105, 189–90, 205–6*s*, 208, 209
    faith in action as, 39
    First Peter and Pauline Letters use of, 67
    Johannine moral instruction, 122
rivalry, 126–29
Roman Empire
    Christian persecution, 65, 184, 186

eschatological destruction of, 190
paganism and cults of, 180s, 181–82, 190s, 193
penal colonies of, 183s
social conformity within, 74, 88s
symbolic imagery in visions of, 187s
Romans, Letter to
baptism associations, 50
Christian persecution, 65
faith in action themes, 26, 28, 35, 129s
First Peter relationship to, 67, 68
Second Clement use of, 163
Rome
Christian persecution in, 65
composition location of extracanonical texts, 124, 198
composition location of New Testament books, 59s, 63, 64, 103n13, 143
congregation of, as intended audience, 198
expulsion of Jews from, 142
Petrine community and authorship theories, 61
Revelation visions and symbolism of, 177s, 178s, 187s
royal law, 20s, 25
Rufinus, 30

S

Sabbath, 83, 87
salvation
believer's debt and reciprocity for, 161s, 164, 167
Christ as, 138s, 165, 166–67, 191s
church leadership conflicts impacting, 127
as conditional *versus* unconditional, 191–92s

cross of Jesus Christ symbolizing, 70, 146, 149s, 150, 153s, 188
faith for, 191
new covenant for, 138s, 150
repentance for, 99s, 135, 164, 167, 191, 200, 201
saved statistics, 176s, 177s, 187s
San Callisto catacomb paintings, 19i
Sardis (Asia Minor), 175s, 180, 180s, 181
Satan
apocalyptic imagery symbolizing, 176–77s, 178s, 185, 185i, 187s, 190s, 201s
apocalyptic roles of, 190s
false teachers as first born of, 130
path of darkness and angels of, 154s
throne of, 190s
sayings of Jesus, 23, 30s, 34s, 46, 48
scarlet (color symbolism), 187s
scrolls, 175s, 176s, 187s, 188
seals, seven, 175–76s, 188
Second Baruch, 173
Second Clement
audience, intended, 162
authorship, 13s, 162
Christian identity in, 136
date of composition, 12, 163
as extracanonical writing, 12
historical assessment of, 165–66s
historical context methodology, 161
historical setting, summary, 163c
literary genres of, 15c, 135, 162, 166s
outline and contents descriptions, 161s, 164–67
place of composition, 163
writing purpose, 135, 136–37, 167
Second Corinthians, 61s, 67

Second Enoch, 72*s*
Second John
  audience, intended, 111, 115
  authorship, 11*s*, 111
  canonical inclusion, 93
  date of composition, 9, 116–17
  form and function, 94
  Gospel of John relationship with, 110, 117
  historical context methodology, 109–10
  historical setting, summary, 118–19*c*
  Johannine texts and composition sequence, 117
  literary genre of, 15*c*
  opponents in, 120*n*29, 121*n*30, 121*s*
  outline and contents descriptions, 95, 111–12*s*, 119–20, 122
  place of composition, 116
  terminology used in, 110
Second Peter
  audience/recipients, intended, 102
  authenticity debates, 103*s*
  authorship, 11*s*, 96–98, 99–100
  canonical inclusion, 93
  contents descriptions and themes, 94, 95, 98*s*, 104, 106–7*s*, 107–8, 121*s*, 131*s*
  date of composition, 9, 12, 63, 102
  form and function, 94
  historical context methodology, 95
  historical setting, summary, 104*c*
  Letter of Jude relationship to (literary dependency), 100–101*cs*
  literary genre of (letter), 15*c*
  outline of, 98–99*s*
  place of composition, 103
  theology and ethics, 98*s*, 107–9, 108*s*, 109*s*
  writing purpose, 107
Second Thessalonians, 61*s*, 102
self-control
  as Christian conduct for believer's debt, 161*s*
  and discipline, 131*s*, 139*s*, 152
  as faith supplement, 108
  sexual morality and, 106*s*, 194, 196*s*, 203
  of tongue/speech, 20*s*, 21*s*, 33, 35, 38*s*, 44*s*
selfishness, 33, 34*c*, 35
Sermon on the Mount, 46, 48
Sermon on the Plain, 48
seven (numerology), 187*s*
sexual morality, 106*s*, 194, 196*s*, 203
Shepherd of Hermas
  audience, intended, 198
  authorship, 13*s*, 197–98
  date of composition, 12, 198–99
  as extracanonical writing, 12
  historical context methodology, 195
  historical setting, summary, 199*c*
  literary genre of (apocalypse), 16*c*, 171, 200
  outline and contents descriptions, 195–97*s*, 199–204
  place of composition, 198
  revelatory methodology in, 195, 199
  theology and ethics of, 200–204
Silvanus (Silas), 59*s*, 60, 61*s*, 67
similitudes, 195, 196–97*s*, 199–201
Simon Magnus, 66*s*
sinners. *See also* repentance
  conversion of, 37
  eschatology on, 200, 203, 205–6*s*, 208, 209, 210*s*
  praying for, 18, 114*s*, 122

Index **233**

sins. *See also* repentance
   atonement of, 143, 146, 148, 150, 151*s*, 191, 210
   avoidance of evil and, 73, 122, 130, 196*s*, 197*s*, 205*s*, 210
   confession of, 22*s*, 37, 148, 160, 164, 205*s*
   forgiveness of, 37*s*, 50, 51, 120, 131*s*
   root of, 33
Sirach, book of, 18
six (numerology), 187*s*
666 (beast), 183*n*15
slander, 65, 73*s*, 196*s*
slaves, 73, 75*s*
slaves of God, 197*s*
Smyrna (Asia Minor)
   as Revelation church and audience, 175*s*, 180, 180*s*, 181
   Satanic presence in, 190*s*
social conformity, 58*s*, 74, 88, 88*s*
Sodom and Gomorrah, 96*s*, 98*s*
sojourners (term usage), 56, 57*s*, 62, 69
Solomon, king of Israel, 23*n*5
Son (title), 149
Son and Father unity (theme), 110, 114*s*
Son of God (title), 88–89, 114*s*, 116*s*, 149, 201
Son of Man (title), 188, 206
soteriology. *See also* salvation
   of First John, 191*s*
   of Gospel of John, 191*s*
   of Hebrews, 150
   of Revelation of John, 191–92*s*
   of *Shepherd of Hermas*, 200–201
Sporades islands, 183*s*
spouses, 58*s*, 73, 75*s*, 130
stones, 200–201, 203
suffering
   Christ as model of, 58–59*s*, 70, 74*s*, 82

   counsel and instruction on, 58–59*s*, 65–66, 193
   as discipleship component, 71
   due to marginalization, 56, 58*s*
   household codes to alleviate, 75*s*
   non-believers and eschatological, 177*s*
   sources of, 65
symbouleutikon, 128*n*39
Syria, 41, 42–43, 76

T

Tacitus, 183*s*
Tatirokos (angel), 210*s*
teachers (prophets). *See also* false teachers and teachings
   authenticity determinations, 19, 40*s*, 50–51, 51*i*
   support and welcome of visiting, 19, 40*s*, 111, 112*s*, 121, 123
Temlakos (angel), 210*s*
Temple in Jerusalem, 23, 142–43, 142*i*, 156, 183, 189
temptation, 25, 33, 37, 186, 203
Ten Commandments, 48, 160
Tertullian, 87*n*31, 140*s*
Testament of Abraham, 72*s*
Theophilus of Antioch, 87*n*31, 207*n*42
Third John
   audience, intended, 111, 115
   authorship, 11*s*, 111
   canonical inclusion, 93
   date of composition, 9, 116–17
   ethics of, 121*n*30, 122
   form and function, 94
   Gospel of John relationship with, 110, 117
   historical context methodology, 109–10
   historical setting, summary, 118–19*c*

Johannine letters and composition sequence, 117
literary genre of, 15*c*
opponents in, 94, 112–13*s*, 120*n*29
outline of, 112–13*s*
place of composition, 116
terminology used in, 110
theology of, 120, 121
Third Synod of Carthage, 30
thousand (numerology), 187*s*
thrones, 185, 187*s*, 190*s*
Thyatira (Asia Minor), 175*s*, 180, 180*s*, 181
Timothy (associate of Paul), 139
Titus, emperor of Rome, 65
Tobit, book of, 18
tongue, control of, 20*s*, 21*s*, 33, 35, 38*s*, 44*s*
To Polycarp (Ignatius), 12, 55, 76, 77–78, 77*sm*, 125
Torah, 40, 41, 48, 62
To the Ephesians (Ignatius), 12, 55, 76, 77–78, 77*sm*
To the Magnesians (Ignatius), 12, 55, 76, 77–78, 77*sm*
To the Philadelphians (Ignatius), 12, 55, 76, 77–78, 77*sm*
To the Romans (Ignatius), 12, 55, 76, 77–78, 77*sm*, 81
To the Smyrnaeans (Ignatius), 12, 55, 76, 77–78, 77*sm*
To the Trallians (Ignatius), 55, 76, 77–78, 77*sm*
Transfiguration, 206, 206*s*, 209
tree of knowledge, 89
Trinity, 46–47
Troas (Asia Minor), 76, 77*sm*, 78
trumpets, seven, 176*s*
truth, 47, 110, 120, 121–22, 164
twelve (numerology), 187*s*
"two minds" (double-mindedness)
characteristics of, 33, 203
extracanonical exhortations against, 44*s*, 160, 196*s*, 202, 203
factors contributing to, 35
salvific solutions to, 20*s*, 167, 201
two ways/paths, 39*s*, 43, 48–49, 49*s*, 154*s*, 159–60

U

Uriel (angel), 210*s*

V

Valens, 130
Vespasian, emperor of Rome, 65, 156
vices, 48–49, 196*s*, 202–3
virginal conception, 83
virtues
  commandments on, 164, 196*s*, 202–3
  for path of light, 154*s*
  to supplement one's faith, 98*s*, 108–9
visions, as revelatory methodology
  of Revelation of John, 173, 174–78*s*, 186–87*s*
  of *Shepherd of Hermas*, 195, 195*s*, 199–200

W

Watchers, 210*s*
wealth
  ancient associations, 33
  of church communities, condemnation of, 181
  as date indication theme, 26
  extracanonical warnings against, 130, 196*s*
  New Testament warnings against, 20*s*, 21*s*, 32–33, 36, 152, 193

preferential treatment of, 25, 44*s*
white (color symbolism), 187*s*
white horse riders, 178*s*
wisdom literature, 12, 13, 14*c*, 17*n*1. *See also Didache*; James, Letter of
witnesses, 187*s*
woman (vision), 177*s*, 178*s*, 187*s*
Word/Word of life (title), 113*s*, 116*s*, 119
worker exploitation, 25
works (action), 114*s*. *See also* faith in action
world and God dualism, 110
world-deceivers, 40*s*, 47
worldly abstinence, 20*s*, 33, 35, 38*s*, 73, 114*s*, 161*s*

Z

Zechariah, book of, 173, 179